WELCOME

Operation Market Garden might have been the crowning achievement of Allied arms in 1944... might have been. Welcome to this chronicle of the men, prominent and ordinary, who fought in the autumn of 1944 to take the proverbial "bridge too far."

The summer of that pivotal year was a heady time for the Allies. After weeks of fighting, the D-Day lodgement had been expanded in Normandy. The fighting in the hedgerows and the grinding battle for the communications and transport centre of Caen had been won. At Falaise, roughly 50,000 Germans had been killed, wounded or captured. Although the sluggishness of the Allied advance that finally slammed the door at Falaise had been vexing, the escape route of the retreating Nazi Fifth Panzer and Seventh Armies was finally cut off and much of Army Group B destroyed.

The defeat at Falaise was catastrophic for the Germans, and General Dwight D. Eisenhower, Supreme Commander Allied Expeditionary Force, toured the torn landscape in late August. He remarked, "The battlefield at Falaise was unquestionably one of the greatest 'killing fields' of any of the war areas. Forty-eight hours after the closing of the gap I was conducted through it on foot, to encounter scenes that could be described only by Dante. It was literally possible to walk for hundreds of yards at a time, stepping on nothing but dead and decaying flesh."

Further south, the Allied armies were pressing toward the frontier of Germany on a broad front. On August 25, the French 2nd Armoured Division rolled into Paris, the vanguard of the Allied forces that streamed through the City of Light. Free French leader General Charles de Gaulle proclaimed the triumph of the French people, ignoring sniper fire at Notre Dame Cathedral as he strode forward to address a delirious crowd.

In August, the US Third Army, under Lieutenant General George S. Patton, Jr., fought hard in Normandy and Brittany, then sprinted across France in an epic onslaught, crossing the River Moselle in early September.

General Bernard L. Montgomery, commander of Allied ground forces for the D-Day invasion, had faced a difficult task in capturing Caen. A D-Day objective, the city did not fall to the Allies for a month as German panzer divisions, including the fanatical 12th SS Hitler Jugend and 1st SS Leibstandarte Adolf Hitler, made Montgomery pay for every yard. Although Caen proved a tough nut to crack, Montgomery, subsequently in command of the 21st Army Group, had drawn the bulk of the enemy armoured strength to his own forces, assisting the US armies fighting to the south in executing Operation Cobra, the breakout from the Normandy beachhead, in late July.

British forces captured the deepwater port of Antwerp, Belgium, in early September, and it was hoped that utilisation of its facilities would alleviate persistent Allied supply challenges. However, weeks of fighting remained before Canadian and British troops cleared the Germans from the estuary of the River Scheldt. In the meantime, amid frustrating supply shortages, Montgomery still saw opportunity.

The hero of El Alamein, Montgomery was known for his penchant for planning and executing the setpiece battle. His preparations for major offensive action had always been meticulous, and he was stingy with the lives of his men and aware how precious the war materiel available to them actually was. However, the time had come, he believed, for a departure from standard operating procedure.

Contrary to the broad front strategy that General Eisenhower had pursued, Montgomery proposed a lightning stroke, a combined airborne and ground offensive into The Netherlands to seize key bridges along the Rivers Maas and Waal and the lower Rhine, opening a highway toward the German border and the Nazis' industrial heartland, the Ruhr. The Allied occupation of the Ruhr might so cripple the German war effort that the Third Reich would have no alternative but to surrender, ending World War Two by Christmas 1944.

At first, Montgomery conceived Operation Comet, utilising the unblooded 1st Airborne Division. Set for early September, Comet was cancelled after weather conditions proved uncooperative. The idea, however, did not fade into obscurity. Montgomery then proposed a larger offensive involving three Allied airborne divisions and the tanks and troops of his veteran XXX Corps ground force. Operation Market Garden was risky, but the potential return on investment captivated Montgomery, who persuaded Eisenhower to approve.

Welcome to Operation Market Garden. On this, the 80th anniversary, we explore the great offensive that began with promise but ended in controversy and with the lasting memory of unsurpassed heroism and sacrifice. ■

Allied paratroopers descend on The Netherlands during the opening hours of Operation Market Garden, September 1944. *(Public Domain US Army via Wikimedia Commons)*

Main cover image: Cromwell tanks of 2nd Welsh Guards crossing the bridge at Nijmegen, September 21, 1944. *(Sergeant Midgley/Imperial War Museums via Getty Images) Colourisation by colourbyrjm)*

CONTENTS

6 WAR ON THREE FRONTS
In the autumn of 1944, the walls were closing in on the Third Reich. The Red Army rolled inexorably from the east while the Western Allies gained momentum in France and the Low Countries and thousands of Nazi troops defended to the south in Italy.

8 BROAD FRONT STRATEGY
General Dwight Eisenhower's strategy of offensive action on a broad front in western Europe was challenged by General Bernard Montgomery with Operation Market Garden.

10 AIRBORNE BEGINNINGS
Between the world wars, military establishments in many countries began to develop airborne fighting forces.

12 XXX CORPS
Executing the Garden, or ground, phase of Operation Market Garden, XXX Corps fought tough German resistance and difficult terrain on a narrow route of advance.

14 DARING AIRBORNE AND GROUND STROKE
Operation Market Garden depended on the cooperation of both airborne and ground offensive action, and speed was the key to success in seizing bridges across the southern Netherlands.

17 OMINOUS SIGNS
Even as Operation Market Garden took shape, there were unknown threats to its success as well as warnings that were unheeded.

20 1ST AIRBORNE DIVISION
Tasked with seizing the bridges at Arnhem, the Red Devils took on the most difficult assignment of Operation Market Garden.

23 BRITISH AIRBORNE EVOLUTION
Although British development of airborne units began in earnest after the outbreak of World War Two, training and organisation came together rapidly.

Paratroopers of the 1st Airborne Division prepare to board gliders during training at RAF Netheravon in October 1942. *(Public Domain collections of the Imperial War Museums via Wikimedia Commons)*

25 82ND AIRBORNE DIVISION
The first airborne division in the US Army, the 82nd had been an infantry division that fought with distinction during World War One.

28 101ST AIRBORNE DIVISION
The 101st Airborne Division was activated in 1942 and served in major operations during World War Two in Europe.

31 US AIRBORNE PROGRESS
The US airborne trooper was outfitted to accomplish his assigned task, often isolated and holding key objectives until heavier units came forward.

33 1ST INDEPENDENT PARACHUTE BRIGADE (POLAND)
Constituted under the authority of the Free Polish Forces, the brigade was later transferred to First Allied Airborne Army for operations in Western Europe rather than participating in the liberation of its home country.

35 FIELD MARSHAL BERNARD L. MONTGOMERY
Operation Market Garden was the brainchild of Great Britain's best known and most controversial soldier of World War Two.

38 GENERAL FREDERICK 'BOY' BROWNING
Deputy commander of the Allied First Airborne Army, Browning has often been criticised for his role in discounting intelligence reports of strong German panzer divisions in the vicinity of Arnhem prior to Operation Market Garden.

41 GENERAL ROY URQUHART
General Urquhart led the Red Devils of the 1st Airborne Division in their heroic attempt to seize the crucial bridge at Arnhem during Operation Market Garden.

43 GENERAL BRIAN HORROCKS
General Brian Horrocks commanded XXX Corps during the ground, or 'Garden' phase of Operation Market Garden.

45 LIEUTENANT COLONEL JOHN FROST
A true inspirational leader, Frost commanded the 2nd Battalion, Parachute Regiment during the arduous struggle at Arnhem bridge.

47 LIEUTENANT COLONEL J.O.E. VANDELEUR
Commanding the 3rd Battalion, Irish Guards and the Irish Guards Battle Group, spearheading the Garden, or ground, phase of Operation Market Garden, Vandeleur exhibited strong tactical leadership.

49 GENERAL MAXWELL D. TAYLOR
General Taylor led the 101st Airborne Division during Operation Market Garden, holding open a vital sector of 'Hell's Highway.'

51 GENERAL JAMES M. GAVIN
The youngest general in the US Army since the Civil War, General Gavin commanded the 82nd Airborne Division during the pivotal fight for the Waal bridges at Nijmegen.

53 GENERAL STANISLAW SOSABOWSKI
The fiery commander of the Polish 1st Independent Parachute Brigade questioned the risks of Operation Market Garden but led his command during its late deployment.

54 9TH SS PANZER DIVISION HOHENSTAUFEN
One of two SS panzer divisions sent to the Arnhem area to rest and refit, the 9th fought the British 1st Airborne Division and drove them away from the crucial highway bridge.

56 10TH SS PANZER DIVISION FRUNDSBERG
The 10th SS Panzer Division contributed to the defence of Arnhem and deployed to Nijmegen to cover the road and rail bridges across the River Waal.

A parachute trainee gathers his chute in after plummeting to earth at RAF Ringway. *(Public Domain collections of the Imperial War Museums via Wikimedia Commons)*

Two paras of the British 1st Airborne Division are dug in at the fragile Oosterbeek perimeter during fighting in and around Arnhem. *(Public Domain United Kingdom Government via Wikimedia Commons)*

A German 88mm flak cannon lies destroyed after the bitter fight for control of Nijmegen by the 82nd Airborne Division and elements of XXX Corps. *(Creative Commons Regional Archives Nijmegen via Wikimedia Commons)*

58 GENERAL WILHELM BITTRICH
Commander of the II SS Panzer Korps in The Netherlands, General Bittrich quickly recognised the Allied threat to critical bridges in the region and coordinated an effective response.

60 FIELD MARSHAL WALTER MODEL
Model commanded German Army Group B and played a key tactical role in thwarting Operation Market Garden.

62 DUTCH RESISTANCE AND COVERT OPERATIONS
The Dutch Resistance supplied intelligence to the Allies although concerns as to its credibility had arisen.

65 AIR TRANSPORT
Allied airlift capability played a critical role in the insertion, reinforcement, and resupply of airborne forces during Operation Market Garden, though hampered by adverse weather conditions and numbers of available aircraft.

68 101ST AIRBORNE IN ACTION
The Screaming Eagles of the US 101st Airborne Division fought for control of the southernmost bridges in The Netherlands and liberated to town of Eindhoven during Operation Market Garden.

73 FIGHT AT SON BRIDGE
The 506th Parachute Infantry Regiment, 101st Airborne Division, reached the bridge across the Wilhelmina Canal at Son and fought a bitter battle with the Germans only to see the span blown up.

75 THE ISLAND
Rather than pulling out of The Netherlands after their brisk combat during Market Garden, the 101st Airborne Division and elements of the 82nd Airborne defended a narrow section of land between the Lower Rhine and River Waal that was known as The Island.

77 82ND AIRBORNE IN ACTION
The veteran 82nd Airborne Division fought heavy German resistance and worked with elements of XXDX Corps to capture the vital bridges across the River Maas at Grave and spanning the River Waal at Nijmegen.

82 MAJOR COOK'S CROSSING
Leading the 3rd Battalion, 504th PIR, 82nd Airborne Division across the wide River Waal during the bridge assault at Nijmegen, Major Julian Cook and his command executed a stirring operation.

85 1ST AIRBORNE IN ACTION
The Red Devils, under General Roy Urquhart, fought bravely to reach the bridges at Arnhem, but stiff German resistance and difficult circumstances prevented the movement, effectively rendering Market Garden a failure.

92 2ND BATTALION AT ARNHEM
Under Lieutenant Colonel John Frost, the 2nd Battalion, Parachute Regiment fought doggedly at the north end of Arnhem Bridge before succumbing to overwhelming enemy forces.

The city of Arnhem was a shambles after heavy fighting during Operation Market Garden. *(Creative Commons Dutch National Archives via Wikimedia Commons)*

A British para stands ready for action with full equipment and Sten gun strapped to his chest. *(Public Domain collections of the Imperial War Museums via Wikimedia Commons)*

97 CAPTAIN GRÄBNER'S ATTACK
Elements of the 9th SS Panzer Division attempted to drive the 2nd Battalion, Parachute Regiment from the north end of Arnhem bridge and met with utter defeat.

99 OPERATION BERLIN – ARNHEM EVACUATION
The battered remnant of the heroic 1st Airborne Division withdrew from the Arnhem area on the rainy night of September 25-26, 1944. The Operation was sardonically labelled Operation Berlin.

101 VICTORIA CROSS IN MARKET GARDEN
Five men of the British armed forces received the Victoria Cross during Operation Market Garden, four of the posthumously.

104 MEDAL OF HONOR IN MARKET GARDEN
A pair of American paratroopers received the Medal of Honor posthumously for gallantry during Operation Market Garden.

107 MARKET GARDEN IN FILM AND TELEVISION
The story of Operation Market Garden has been told in feature films, documentaries, and television programming, each demonstrating its own perspective on the epic war saga.

110 MARKET GARDEN ASSESSMENT
In the end, Operation Market Garden failed to achieve a bridgehead across the Lower Rhine. Was it worth the risk? Who was responsible? Decades later the debate continues.

113 REMEMBERING MARKET GARDEN
Memorials, monuments, cemeteries, and the hallowed ground on which brave men fought keep the remembrance of Operation Market Garden alive after 80 years.

ISBN: 978 1 80282 990 7
Editor: Mike Haskew
Senior editor, specials: Roger Mortimer
Email: roger.mortimer@keypublishing.com
Cover Design: Steve Donovan
Design: SJmagic DESIGN SERVICES, India
Advertising Sales Manager: Sam Clark
Email: sam.clark@keypublishing.com
Tel: 01780 755131
Advertising Production: Becky Antoniades
Email: Rebecca.antoniades@keypublishing.com

SUBSCRIPTION/MAIL ORDER
Key Publishing Ltd, PO Box 300,
Stamford, Lincs, PE9 1NA
Tel: 01780 480404
Subscriptions email: subs@keypublishing.com
Mail Order email: orders@keypublishing.com
Website: www.keypublishing.com/shop

PUBLISHING
Group CEO and Publisher: Adrian Cox

Published by
Key Publishing Ltd, PO Box 100,
Stamford, Lincs, PE9 1XQ
Tel: 01780 755131
Website: www.keypublishing.com

PRINTING
Precision Colour Printing Ltd, Haldane,
Halesfield 1, Telford, Shropshire.
TF7 4QQ

DISTRIBUTION
Seymour Distribution Ltd, 2 Poultry
Avenue, London, EC1A 9PU
Enquiries Line: 02074 294000.

WAR ON THREE FRONTS

The scene at Falaise was indeed bleak as Nazi resistance had been broken and the Normandy campaign was won in the summer of 1944. The losses suffered by the Germans were irreplaceable, indicative that the days of the Third Reich were numbered. But months of fighting remained.

The German armed forces had been wounded but had not yet succumbed, remaining a potent adversary even as Allied forces pressed toward the frontiers of the Reich on three fronts. In the East, the vengeful Red Army juggernaut was on the offensive. In the south, Axis forces had been defeated in North Africa and Sicily, and the Germans continued to expend vast resources to hold British and American forces in check as they pushed up the boot of Italy.

In the West, the Allies landed in Normandy on June 6, 1944, and then fought for weeks around the city of Caen and through the hedgerow country before breaking out and putting the Germans to temporary flight. When General Dwight Eisenhower, Supreme Commander of Allied Forces in Europe, inspected the grim battlefield at Falaise weeks later, optimism among American and British senior officers ran high. Many believed the German Army was disintegrating. Among those who saw an opportunity to administer the coup de grace in the West was General Bernard Montgomery, the architect of Operation Market Garden, the ill-fated offensive that he had hoped would open pry the door to the Ruhr and win World War Two in the West by Christmas 1944.

Meanwhile, Adolf Hitler and the German high command were confronted with a myriad of difficulties. While their forces were spread

Allied troops wade ashore in Normandy, opening a third front against Nazi Germany, June 6, 1944. *(Public Domain Unites States Coast Guard via Wikimedia Commons)*

thinly in France and the Low Countries, the Eastern Front posed difficulties that would at length prove insurmountable. On June 23, 1944, the Red Army unleashed Operation Bagration, a major Eastern Front offensive into Belorussia in support of the D-Day landings in French Normandy. The Soviets assembled 166 infantry and armoured divisions on a 450-mile front and in five days of epic combat captured or killed thousands of German soldiers.

Bagration is remembered historically as one of Soviet Premier Josef Stalin's "Ten Blows" against the Nazis during the pivotal year of 1944. The Soviet armed forces amassed more than six million troops, 5,600 tanks, 90,000 pieces of artillery, and 8,800 various aircraft to drive the Germans from their conquered territory in the Motherland and exact retribution for the devastation of lands occupied by the enemy during Operation Barbarossa in 1941.

Amid the progress of Bagration, German Army Group Centre was virtually annihilated. The sprawling Red Army formations drove westward to eject the Germans from the city of Vitebsk and then swept southward toward Minsk, the capital city of Belarus. The left flank of Operation Bagration, under the command of Marshal Konstantin Rokossovsky, breached the Wehrmacht defensive line at the Pripet Marshes and rolled ahead an astonishing 150 miles in a week. Minsk was captured on July 3.

Elsewhere, as the Germans fought desperately to avoid encirclement, Red Army mechanised forces advanced into Lithuania and crossed the Polish frontier. As the Germans met the threat in the north, Rokossovsky renewed his onslaught, reaching the River Vistula. Soviet forces advanced up to 15 miles per day and approached the Polish capital of Warsaw, where they paused to allow the Nazi SS occupiers to suppress the famous uprising in the capital city. The Poles had expected the Soviets to join them in fighting the Nazis, but the pragmatic Stalin ordered a halt for six months, permitting the Germans to destroy any potential Polish nationalist postwar opposition to Soviet policies in Eastern Europe.

Still, the lightning advance of the Red Army had covered 450 miles in five weeks. Estimates of German casualties are as high as 670,000, vast

A soldier of the Red Army climbs atop the hulk of a destroyed German tank on the Eastern Front, June 1944. *(Public Domain via Wikimedia Commons)*

Soviet soldiers march through a village during the rapid advance of Operation Bagration in the summer of 1944. (Public Domain via Wikimedia Commons)

General Mark Clark, commander of the Allied Fifth Army, arrives in Rome on June 5, 1944. (Public Domain US Army via Wikimedia Commons)

numbers of them paraded through the streets of Moscow in grand humiliation. Operation Bagration ended on August 19 with Soviet troops poised on the doorstep of East Prussia. Renewing its offensive in Romania the next day, the Red Army compelled the government of that country to surrender three days later and entered Bucharest in triumph on August 31.

Two weeks later, the Soviets launched their Baltic Offensive, which led to the encirclement of German Army Group North in the Courland Pocket. These

Thousands of German prisoners are paraded through the streets of Moscow on July 14, 1944. (Creative Commons RIA Novosti via Wikimedia Commons)

German forces remained cut off from the rest of the Wehrmacht and surrendered to the Red Army at the end of the war. By late September 1944, the Red Army had thrust deep into Poland, and when this ground offensive concluded in November, the Soviets were in possession of the Baltic States of Lithuania, Estonia, and Latvia.

In the Mediterranean, the Allies completed the liberation of Sicily and invaded the Italian mainland in early September 1943. Months of bitter fighting followed as the Fifth and Eighth Armies advanced northward, and the formidable German Gustav Line was finally cracked south of Rome in May 1944. Allied forces entered the Eternal City, the first Axis capital city to fall in World War Two, on June 4, 1944. The great city of Florence on the River Arno was captured in mid-August, and as the Allies reached Hitler's Gothic Line of prepared defences, the last such obstacle in Italy, they launched Operation Anvil-Dragoon, the invasion of southern France, on August 15.

The end of the Third Reich was eagerly anticipated, and General Montgomery envisioned his rapid offensive stroke into The Netherlands to exploit the incredible gains already realised in 1944. His plan for Operation Comet and then the larger Market Garden was taking shape even as Eisenhower followed through on the plan to assume personal command of Allied ground forces in the West, taking over for Montgomery who would retain command of 21st Army Group.

Monty believed a grave mistake was being made in Eisenhower's edict. The American general had never commanded troops in battle, and there were already rumblings against his broad front strategy. Promotion

to field marshal did little to assuage Monty's personal resentment, but it was clear that American military leadership would eclipse that of Great Britain as the drama of the conflict played out, just as American war production and its manpower contribution to the Allied military effort had already done.

While many senior Allied officers had become infected with the so-called "Victory Disease," Montgomery was convinced that the Germans on the run, and he intended to act. On September 3, 1944, he issued orders to subordinate Canadian and British officers of 21st Army Group that he anticipated an offensive that would "occupy the Ruhr." A day later, he sent Eisenhower a pointed assessment of the current situation, a rationale for Operation Market Garden.

The message began, "I consider we have now reached a stage where one really powerful and full-blooded thrust towards Berlin is likely to get there and thus end the German war... The selected thrust must have all the maintenance resources it needs without any qualification, and any other operation must do the best it can with what is left over..."

Montgomery's thrust was to be across the bridges of the southern Netherlands, a swift inexorable drive to the Ruhr, its outcome a crowning achievement in his illustrious career. ■

An American mortar team fires at German positions along the Gothic Line north of Rome in late 1944. (Public Domain US National Archives and Records Administration via Wikimedia Commons)

This photo of senior SHAEF commanders was taken in February 1944. General Dwight Eisenhower is at centre. Clockwise from left are General Omar Bradley, Admiral Bertram Ramsay, Air Chief Marshal Sir Arthur Tedder, Eisenhower, General Bernard Montgomery, Air Chief Marshal Sir Trafford Leigh-Mallory, and General Walter Bedell Smith. *(Public Domain collections of the Imperial War Museums via Wikimedia Commons)*

BROAD FRONT
STRATEGY

For weeks prior to and after the Allies established their beachhead in Normandy on June 6, 1944, military planners at SHAEF (Supreme Headquarters Allied Expeditionary Force) had been considering options for the prosecution of World War Two on the Western Front. Of course, a strong foothold, expanded beachhead, and successful campaign in Normandy were given elements of overall strategy, but what then?

General Dwight Eisenhower, Supreme Allied Commander in Europe, announced in August 1944 that he intended to take control of Allied land forces in western Europe on September 1, with his subordinates, British General Bernard Montgomery and US General Omar Bradley, commanding the 21st and 12th Army Groups respectively. Montgomery had been in charge of Allied ground forces since D-Day and resisted the change of command, but it had been planned, and he received promotion to field marshal to salve the wound to his ego and in recognition of his wartime achievements. However, he was convinced that Eisenhower was in over his head and freely expressed that opinion.

Regardless, Eisenhower had been presented with options for the prosecution of the war in the West and began to consider these as early as May 3, a month before D-Day. Several of them involved the occupation of the Ruhr, Germany's heavily industrialised region that sustained its war effort, and then the capture of the Nazi capital of Berlin.

While the occupation of the Ruhr was considered a primary objective, Eisenhower quickly ruled out Berlin. He was correct in his belief that there was no military reason to drive for the Nazi capital, and such an endeavour was tangential at best to his stated mission for the Allied forces under his command "...to undertake operations aimed at the heart of Germany and the destruction of her armed forces."

In pursuit of the capture of the Ruhr, Eisenhower recognised the difficulty of the terrain. A direct thrust would be obliged to proceed through the rugged, heavily wooded Ardennes Forest. Therefore, he envisioned a classic double envelopment of the industrial heart of Germany involving pincer thrusts north and south on a broad front. These pincers would meet to the east of the Ruhr, closing the encirclement.

By August 1944, the Allied armies had won the battle in Normandy, and the German forces confronting them had fallen back, at times in disarray. Some Allied commanders believed the German Army was beaten, but in the succeeding weeks their assumption was proven erroneous.

General Eisenhower was convinced that prosecution of the war on a broad front, pressing the Germans at multiple points continually and denying the enemy the opportunity to mass its forces to repel a single, more direct thrust and possibly deal the Allies a significant setback, was the proper course of action. At the same time, Montgomery and several high-ranking British officers, including Field Marshal Sir Alan Brooke, Chief of the Imperial General Staff, were critical of Eisenhower's strategy, at times openly. One British officer proclaimed, "The American conception of always attacking all along the front, irrespective of strength available, is sheer madness." On several occasions in the post-war era, senior British officers caustically criticised Eisenhower, and Montgomery once tersely characterised his superior officer as "Nice chap. No general."

German soldiers surrender in France in August 1944. The retreat of the German Army in northern France caused some Allied commanders to believe it was a beaten force. *(Public Domain Library and Archives Canada via Wikimedia Commons)*

General Omar Bradley wanted a major role for XII Army Group in the liberation of Western Europe. *(Public Domain Library of Congress via Wikimedia Commons)*

Ships are unloaded at Antwerp, Belgium. Eisenhower stressed the importance of a deep-water port to Montgomery and considered the capture of a Rhine bridgehead an extension of the broad front strategy. *(Public Domain US Army via Wikimedia Commons)*

Montgomery made a strong case for the single thrust, and his message to Eisenhower on September 4, just days before Operation Market Garden, sums it up: "If we attempt a compromise solution and split our maintenance resources so that neither thrust is full-blooded, we will prolong the war."

In context, it is necessary to understand that Eisenhower was charged not only with defeating the Germans, but also with holding together a sometimes fractious coalition. American and British officers were regularly at odds with one another over some issue, and it was the supreme commander's job to maintain focus on winning the war. Some historians do acknowledge that few men, if any other at the time, might have succeeded as fully as Eisenhower did in this respect. Truly, the military argument for the broad front strategy had to consider the movement of Bradley's 12th Army Group. Bradley was advocating an offensive of his own to take priority with the First and Third US Armies slashing through Lorraine, breaching the Siegfried Line and rolling into the Saar. To complicate matters, General George S. Patton, Jr., commanding Third Army was loathe that the majority of available supplies might be diverted to his rival Montgomery.

General Dwight Eisenhower surveys the wreck of a German Tiger II tank destroyed in France, August 1944. *(Public Domain US Government Acme News Service via Wikimedia Commons)*

In the autumn of 1944, the Allied armies had made progress, broadly speaking, but supply and logistics issues had led to shortages of every necessary commodity for continued offensive operations, including replacement troops. Eisenhower was keenly aware of the necessity of an operational deep-water port, and although Antwerp, Belgium, was liberated on September 4, the Germans controlled the estuary of the River Scheldt and had to be cleared for Allied shipping to reach Antwerp. While Antwerp was an obvious priority, Eisenhower also considered a bridgehead across the great River Rhine a primary objective.

When Eisenhower and Montgomery met on September 10, 1944, the latter lobbied strongly for his airborne/ground thrust into The Netherlands to seize bridges and breach the Lower Rhine, positioning his 21st Army Group for a potentially war-winning thrust into the Ruhr. Eisenhower listened and then approved the Market Garden plan, postponing for time the effort to make Antwerp operational. For Eisenhower, the objective of the airborne/ground offensive was the bridgehead over the Lower Rhine. Other aspirations would be too difficult to achieve as rapidly as Montgomery envisioned with his boast that the occupation of the Ruhr would potentially be followed by a drive to Berlin and that the war would be over by Christmas 1944.

"I explained to Montgomery the condition of our supply system and our need for early use of Antwerp," Eisenhower wrote in his post-war memoir *Crusade in Europe*. "I pointed out that, without railroad bridges over the Rhine and ample stockages of supplies on hand, there was no possibility of maintaining a force in Germany capable of penetrating to its capital. There was still a considerable reserve in the middle of the enemy country and I knew that any pencillike thrust into the heart of Germany such as he proposed would meet nothing but certain destruction. This was true, no matter on what part of the front it might be attempted. I would not consider it."

Eisenhower described the upcoming operation clearly in the context of the broad front strategy. "I instructed him (Montgomery) that what I did

Promoted field marshal on September 1, 1944, Bernard Montgomery opposed Eisenhower's broad front strategy, advocating a strong single thrust into the Ruhr. *(Public Domain collections of the Imperial War Museums via Wikimedia Commons)*

want in the north was Antwerp working, and I also wanted a line covering that port. Beyond this I believed it possible that we might with airborne assistance seize a bridgehead over the Rhine in the Arnhem region, flanking the defences of the Siegfried Line. The operation to gain such a bridgehead – it was assigned the code name Market-Garden – would be merely an incident and extension of our eastward rush to the line we needed for temporary security."

In practice, the broad front was successful in defeating the enemy in Europe for several reasons. Among them are the simple facts that it was logistically sustainable; it did effectively wear down the Germans and deplete their capacity to continue to wage war; and it prevented the enemy from massing their forces against a single dagger thrust, possibly inflicting a serious defeat.

The debate regarding Eisenhower and the broad front versus the mass of power and logistics for a single thrust against the Nazis has continued for decades. Both military and political factors weighed on the conduct of the war, and historians are left to speculate. ■

Soviet airborne soldiers rush across an open field while others come down in their parachutes during a 1935 exercise. *(Creative Commons Ministry of Defence of Russia via Wikimedia Commons)*

AIRBORNE BEGINNINGS

An early French parachute demonstration is featured in this colourful artist's rendering. *(Public Domain unknown artist via Wikimedia Commons)*

DESCENTE DE JACQUES GARNERIN EN PARACHUTE (1797)

It is widely accepted that US Army Captain Albert Berry successfully completed the first parachute jump from an airplane over Jefferson Barracks, Missouri, on March 1, 1912.

Prior to that historic event, the parachute had been an item of curiosity, novelty, and even daring. Englishman John Hampton made the first successful British jump from a balloon near Cheltenham, Gloucester, in 1838, from an impressive altitude of 9,000 feet. Sporting demonstrations drew crowds, for sure, and the prospect of military application was ever present. In fact, American inventor and diplomat Benjamin Franklin is credited with a visionary perspective on airborne warfare in the 18th century. While observing a demonstration of hot air balloons in Paris, he is said to have remarked, "Where is the prince who can afford to cover his country with troops for its defence as that 10,000 men descending from the clouds might not in many places do an infinite deal of mischief before a force could be brought together to repel them?"

Franklin had uttered the essence of airborne warfare. However, such application of the parachute would not occur until roughly 150 years later, between the two world wars of the 20th century.

The military employment of the parachute was minimal during the Great War. Stout hearted men who hung in baskets beneath hydrogen-filled observation balloons wore them in the event of a fighter attack. But they were expected to stay where they were until the last moment when the destruction of their balloon was imminent. As the conflict wore on, the use of parachutes as lifesaving devices increased. Airmen wore the parachute more extensively by 1916, and there are records indicating the French and Italians deployed demolition teams and intelligence agents into enemy territory by parachuting them from planes.

By 1918, American General Billy Mitchell, famed for his advocacy of the airplane itself in war and remembered for the defiant stance that brought on a 1925 court martial, had considered the use of parachute troops on a larger scale. In a practical sense, the airborne

developed along with technological advances in air and ground warfare, each of them at least somewhat born out of the horrific experience of stagnant trench warfare on the Western Front during World War One.

Mitchell proposed the idea of the "vertical envelopment," parachuting soldiers behind enemy lines in great numbers to seize objectives, even before the end of the Great War. In

Captain Albert Perry's parachute billows as he comes to earth during his 1912 parachute jump. (Public Domain unattributed via Wikimedia Commons)

A recruit jumps from a parachute training tower in Britain in the autumn of 1942. (Public Domain collections of the Imperial War Museums via Wikimedia Commons)

the autumn of 1918, he presented a plan to parachute troops from British Handley Page and Italian Caproni bombers against enemy fortifications around the city of Metz to attack and hold the positions until relieved by ground forces. The plan was shelved by the armistice.

During the interwar years, the British Army expressed little interest in airborne warfare, and in fact some quarters of the military establishment considered such endeavours foolish. Elsewhere, though, concerted efforts to develop airborne troop formations proceeded. In the United States, there was some experimentation with parachute and glider formations, but no substantial progress was made until the late 1930s.

Meanwhile, the Soviet Union led the way in the development of airborne military forces, establishing the first parachute unit of the Red Army, the Parashutno Desantniy Otriad (PDO), under the command of Marshal Mikhail Tukhachevsky, a strategic visionary remembered for his development of the concept of "deep battle." By the mid-1930s, the Soviets had conducted exercises involving as many as 2,500 parachute and glider-borne troops.

Among those taking note of the Soviet airborne initiative was Hermann Goring, chief of the German Luftwaffe. Energised by the prospect of a Nazi airborne force, he authorised the conversion

of a military police unit into the first German airborne formation. By 1936, the Fallschirmjager were organised under General Kurt Student.

In the summer of 1940, Soviet airborne troops jumped into action, occupying objectives during the seizure of Bessarabia.

On April 9 of that year, the Germans executed the first mass wartime airborne operation in history with the conquest of Norway. A month later, German glider forces rapidly seized the Belgian fort of Eben Emael in a dazzling stroke that electrified the world. Further German airborne operations were conducted in Greece, and then Operation Mercury, the insertion of Fallschirmjager to seize airfields and other objectives on the island of Crete, brought a reckoning. The heavy losses sustained in airborne troops and Junkers Ju-52 transport aircraft during Operation Mercury stunned Hitler, who suspended further large-scale airborne operations for the duration of World War Two.

Nevertheless, British Prime Minister Winston Churchill was enthusiastic in his support for the development of airborne forces in the British Army. "We ought to have a corps of at least 5,000 troops," he commented. Further, Churchill wanted these paras operational by the winter of 1940. The Parachute Regiment was established on June 22, 1940, and a training program was commenced at RAF Ringway, Manchester. By late November, No. 2 Commando was redesignated the 11th Special Air Service Battalion, and this unit conducted the first offensive airborne action in British military history with Operation Colossus to destroy an aqueduct in Italy on February 10, 1941. Operation Biting, the successful Bruneval Raid a year later, validated the potential of the airborne forces.

In September 1941, the 11th SAS Battalion was redesignated the 1st Parachute Battalion, and together with the 2nd and 3rd Battalions, raised from volunteers, formed the 1st Parachute Brigade. During the course of World War Two, 17 British airborne battalions were activated. The British Airborne was then organised in two divisions, the 1st and 6th, each consisting of two parachute brigades of three battalions each, an airlanding brigade with three glider-borne infantry battalions, and the required supporting units, such as headquarters, reconnaissance, artillery, and

Airborne troops of the 6th Royal Welch Parachute Battalion undergo physical training at RAF Ringway in 1942. (Public Domain collections of the Imperial War Museums via Wikimedia Commons)

German Fallschirmjäger prepare to board a Ju-52 transport aircraft in Greece. (Creative Commons Bundesarchiv Bild via Wikimedia Commons)

others. The 1st Airborne Division served in North Africa, the Mediterranean, and later in Operation Market Garden. The 6th Airborne Division, meanwhile, etched its name in glory during Operation Overlord, the D-Day invasion, Operation Varsity, the airborne crossing of the River Rhine in the spring of 1945, and elsewhere.

The I Airborne Corps was formed in 1943 under the command of General Frederick "Boy" Browning, rightly credited as the father of the British airborne forces. The I Corps was then incorporated into the First Allied Airborne Army along with the US XVIII Airborne Corps, under US General Lewis Brereton, and Browning became its deputy commander.

Meanwhile, in the United States, General George C. Marshall, Army Chief of Staff, authorised the formal study of an airborne command. On September 16, 1940, the first operational airborne unit in the US Army, the 501st Parachute Battalion, was activated at Fort Benning, Georgia, with 446 volunteer officers and enlisted men. By the end of 1941, three more battalions had formed, and the Provisional Parachute Group was established under Lieutenant Colonel William C. Lee, who is considered the father of the US airborne. Lee had overcome considerable opposition to the airborne initiative, and steady growth and organisational restructure followed during the war years.

On March 25, 1942, the 82nd Infantry Division was reactivated, and four months later the 82nd became the first of five US Army airborne divisions fielded during World War Two, along with the 101st, 11th, 13th, and 17th. The XVIII Airborne Corps, under General Matthew Ridgway, was established in August 1944.

After the 509th Parachute Infantry Regiment conducted the first US airborne operation of World War Two during the North African campaign, the 82nd Airborne Division was active in Sicily, Italy, and along with the 101st, in the D-Day invasion, Operation Market Garden, the Battle of the Bulge, and Operation Varsity. The 17th Airborne Division also deployed during the Battle of the Bulge and the Rhine crossing. ■

XXX CORPS

Troops of the 7th Somerset Light Infantry, 43rd Wessex Division rest in The Netherlands in autumn 1944. *(Public Domain collections of the Imperial War Museums via Wikimedia Commons)*

Lieutenant General Brian Horrocks led XXX Corps during Operation Market Garden. *(Public Domain collections of the Imperial War Museums via Wikimedia Commons)*

The road was narrow, often quite exposed to ambush, and more than 60 miles from the Belgian frontier with The Netherlands to the proposed bridgehead across the Lower Rhine at Arnhem. General Bernard Montgomery had confidence in XXX Corps and its leadership. Commanding officer General Brian Horrocks was one of the most respected officers of the British Army, and the Irish Guards, the vanguard of the ground thrust of Operation Market Garden, were capably led as well.

There were issues, however, and these became apparent from the outset. The 3rd Battalion Irish Guards and the 2nd Guards Armoured Battalion, together the Irish Guards Battle Group, were led by Lieutenant Colonel J.O.E. "Joe" Vandeleur, tasked with punching through the enemy defensive line and racing across the bridges secured by the American 101st and 82nd Airborne Divisions to reach the British 1st Airborne Division at Arnhem, where the most distant of the spans was located.

When the lead tanks of XXX Corps moved out, everything seemed to be proceeding as planned for a few moments, but then as Vandeleur remembered, "The Germans really began to paste us."

Lieutenant Cyril Russell, in one of the leading vehicles, recalled, "We had just crossed the border when we were ambushed. Suddenly the tanks in front either slewed across the road or burned where they stood. The awful realisation dawned on me that the next one to go was the

one I was sitting on. We jumped into the ditches by the roadside." Russell moved forward to assess the situation and was seriously wounded in the arm. He was evacuated to a hospital.

Along the XXX Corps route, the scene was repeated several times. German anti-tank weapons and machine guns ensconced in wooded areas along the line of advance would open concentrated fire on the British armoured column, requiring a disposition of infantry to clear the way forward and then the removal of any destroyed or damaged vehicles from the highway. Compounding the issue was the stark reality that the single road was narrow and often elevated above the surrounding polder country, which was too marshy to support armoured vehicles. As they advanced, British tanks were sometimes silhouetted against the sun, which made them perfect targets for sharp-eyed German anti-tank gunners.

The veterans of XXX Corps, including the Guards Armoured Division, 43rd Wessex, and 50th Northumbrian Infantry Divisions, were well-trained and well-equipped for the fight up the narrow road, but virtually every advantage lay with the defenders, particularly as weather conditions restricted the involvement of Hawker Typhoon fighter bombers in providing tactical air support.

By the time XXX Corps had jumped off in the ground, or Garden, phase of Operation Market Garden, the unit had spent many weeks in combat.

Constituted in the Western Desert in September 1941, its first commanding officer, General Vyvyan Pope, was killed in a plane crash in October before he could take the force into battle as a component of the newly-formed Eighth Army. General Willoughby Norrie took command of XXX Corps, which suffered mightily during Operation Crusader, and then played a key role in the pivotal Second Battle of El Alamein in October 1942. During the resounding victory at El Alamein, the Eighth Army, under command of General Montgomery, including XXX Corps led by General Oliver Leese, participated in heavy fighting and subsequently drove the Axis forces of Panzerarmee Afrika westward across hundreds of miles of trackless desert.

After Allied forces trapped German and Italian troops in Tunisia, prompting the surrender of roughly 275,000 enemy soldiers, General Leese led XXX Corps in Operation Husky, the invasion of Sicily. After coming ashore on the left flank of Eighth Army at Pachino on July 10, 1943, XXX Corps fought through difficult mountain

The shoulder flash of XXX Corps depicts a wild board. *(Public Domain collections of the Imperial War Museums)*

terrain toward the port of Messina. Axis forces began withdrawing to the Italian mainland, and by mid-August Sicily was in Allied hands.

Withdrawn from the Mediterranean theatre to rest and refit for Operation Overlord, the Allied invasion of Normandy on June 6, 1944, XXX Corps was assigned to come ashore on Gold Beach, the westernmost of the British and Commonwealth landing beaches. With the 50th Division spearheading the landings, XXX Corps then streamed inland, subsequently linking up with US forces advancing from Omaha Beach and engaging in heavy combat in Normandy. The progress of XXX Corps was questioned, and General Montgomery relieved its commander, General Gerard Bucknall in favour of Horrocks.

Under this new command, the performance of XXX Corps was reinvigorated, and the formation advanced at pace with the rest of Montgomery's 21st Army Group, turning northeast to assist in the post-Falaise gains. In early September elements of XXX Corps had liberated both the Belgian capital of Brussels and the vital deep water seaport of Antwerp. On the eve of Operation Market Garden, the Guards Armoured Division and other units had coordinated an effort to seize a bridge across the Meuse-Escaut Canal into The Netherlands.

As General Montgomery finalised his plans for Operation Market Garden, XXX Corps, 50,000 strong, stood poised to execute the ground phase of the ambitious plan. Although there were concerns, its officers expressed optimism when the orders came down for the Irish Guards to lead the offensive.

Lieutenant Colonel Giles Vandeleur, cousin of Joe Vandeleur and commander of the 2nd Guards Armoured Battalion, informed his subordinates of their key role, and Major Edward Tyler recalled a "half moan" rippling among the gathered officers. "We figured that we deserved a bit of a break after taking the bridge over the Escaut Canal," he said later, "...but our commanding officer told us that it was a great honor for us to be chosen. We were used to one-tank fronts, and in this case we were trusting to speed and support. No one seemed worried."

In the event, XXX Corps advanced and fought, slowed by unexpectedly heavy German resistance, and the inevitable delays that

A XXX Corps tank rolls up the single road toward Nijmegen during Operation Market Garden. *(Creative Commons Willem van de Poll via Wikimedia Commons)*

accompanied a resourceful enemy blowing up and defending bridges on the contested northward route. At Son, the 101st Airborne Division had seen the bridge over the Wilhelmina Canal blown up. As engineers brought a Bailey bridge forward, XXX Corps was powerless to move in large numbers until it was completed. At Nijmegen, the large road bridge over the River Waal had been staunchly defended by the Germans, and it was necessary for XXX Corps to deploy tanks and infantry to clear the town and assist the 8n2 Airborne Division in securing the bridge.

After the fighting in Nijmegen was over, the road to Arnhem was still contested by the Germans. Giles Vandeleur told a group of officers, "I can just imagine the Germans sitting there, rubbing their hands with glee, as they see us coming." Joe Vandeleur looked up the road and acknowledged that it was impossible for tanks to operate in the marshy surrounding terrain. They would have to use the roadway along the top of a steep dike. He said grimly, "Nevertheless, we've got to try."

Three tankers of the Irish Guards pose in front of their Covenanter tank in this 1942 photo. *(Public Domain collections of the Imperial War Museums via Wikimedia Commons)*

After a few minutes the XXX Corps column, which by September 21 had been fighting for five straight days, lurched ahead. Initially, good progress was made. But then a German self-propelled gun barked from a wooded area and set all four lead tanks of the Irish Guards ablaze. "It was a mess up there," Joe Vandeleur remembered. There was little available artillery support. RAF Typhoons flew overhead, but communications with them had been severed.

The way forward was blocked with the beleaguered remnants of the 1st Airborne Division trapped just west of Arnhem in the suburb of Oosterbeek, roughly six miles away. The 43rd Division was brought forward on September 22 to link up with the Polish 1st Independent Parachute Brigade at the Lower Rhine across the river from Oosterbeek, but evacuation of the survivors had become the only option left for the airborne.

After Operation Market Garden, XXX Corps, which lost approximately 70 tanks during the offensive, battled elements of the German 2nd Panzer Division during the Battle of the Bulge and participated in the fighting in the Reichswald before linking up with the US Ninth Army and concluding its wartime action in Germany. ■

An ammunition carrier explodes after taking a direct hit from German guns during the XXX Corps advance near Eindhoven, Operation Market Garden. *(Public Domain collections of the Imperial War Museums via Wikimedia Commons)*

DARING AIRBORNE AND GROUND STROKE

A German soldier readies machine-gun ammunition near Arnhem. Enemy resistance during Operation Market Garden was much stiffer than the Allies anticipated. *(Creative Commons Bundesarchiv Bild via Wikimedia Commons)*

No one was more surprised by the disclosure of the daring airborne and ground thrust than General Omar Bradley, commander of the US 12th Army Group. He knew General Bernard Montgomery as a meticulous planner, and this offensive fraught with risk was out of character.

"Had the pious teetotaling Montgomery wobbled into SHAEF with a hangover," Bradley thought, "I could not have been more astonished than I was by the daring adventure he proposed."

Montgomery, the hero of the Battle of El Alamein in North Africa, commander of Allied ground forces during the D-Day invasion, and then leader of the 21st Army Group, was known to favour complete preparation before launching an offensive. However, his perspective had been altered in the late summer of 1944. His distaste for the broad front strategy employed by General Dwight D. Eisenhower, supreme commander of the Allied forces in Europe, was well known, and Monty now favoured a single, rapier thrust into the Ruhr, the industrial heart of Germany. If the

Allies occupied the Ruhr, the Nazis would no longer be able to support their armed forces sufficiently, and World War Two would be over.

After their defeat in Normandy and the debacle at Falaise in August, the Germans had pulled back in disarray. Many Allied military commanders believed that the German Army was beaten, no longer an effective fighting force, and that it was largely comprised of "old men and boys." Still, Allied supply lines were stretched thin. The available ports along the French coastline were too distant to support a drive into The Netherlands as Montgomery envisioned, and even with the capture of the deepwater port of Antwerp, Belgium, on September 4, the Germans still controlled the estuary of the River Scheldt and access to the open sea.

Montgomery's proposed single thrust would outflank the stout German fixed fortifications of the Siegfried Line or West Wall, clear the French ports for full operation, and overrun the launching sites of Hitler's V-1 buzz bombs and V-2 rockets, the so-called "Vengeance Weapons" that were terrorising London and

other British cities. His ground forces would defeat the supposedly disorganised Germans in front of them, and 21st Army Group would be positioned to deliver the decisive blow into the Ruhr and then even on to the German capital.

Brimming with confidence, Montgomery declared to his staff during a meeting at Laaken, Belgium, "One bold thrust will take us to Berlin, and the war can be finished by Christmas."

To accomplish his lofty goal, Montgomery prevailed upon Eisenhower that the preponderance of available supplies should be allocated to his own 21st Army Group, while the 12th Army Group should be halted where it was and assume a temporarily defensive posture. This reorientation would provide the necessary support needed for the movement into The Netherlands and the war-winning offensive.

King George VI reviews soldiers of the South Staffordshire Regiment in the spring of 1943. *(Public Domain United Kingdom Government via Wikimedia Commons)*

General Bernard Montgomery, chief proponent of Operation Market Garden, talks to war correspondents in 1944. *(Public Domain collections of the Imperial War Museums via Wikimedia Commons)*

General Bernard Montgomery stands at right in Normandy with American Generals George S. Patton, Jr., and Omar Bradley, who was stunned by the proposed Operation Market Garden. *(Public Domain collections of the Imperial War Museums via Wikimedia Commons)*

There was, however, a necessary prerequisite. The "thunderclap" stroke that would initiate the final defeat of the Third Reich would involve both airborne and ground troops, moving swiftly and in cooperation to take and hold several bridges across the rivers and canals of the southern Netherlands. On September 10, 1944, Montgomery met with Eisenhower to outline his strategic and tactical blueprint.

One of the pieces on the SHAEF (Supreme Headquarters Allied Expeditionary Force) chessboard was the First Allied Airborne Army, activated just a month earlier, under the command of American General Lewis H. Brereton. Comprised of the US XVIII Airborne Corps, including the 17th, 82nd, and 101st Airborne Divisions, IX Troop Carrier Command, and independent units, along with the British I Airborne Corps and its 1st and 6th Airborne Divisions, 1st Polish Independent Parachute Brigade, SAS Brigade, No. 38 Group and No. 46 Group of RAF Transport Command, the airborne army consisted of superbly trained shock troops. The XVIII Airborne Corps was under the command of General Matthew B. Ridgway, while I Airborne Corps was led by General Frederick "Boy" Browning, who was also deputy commander of the airborne army. The American 82nd and 101st divisions and the British 6th had participated in Operation Overlord, the D-Day invasion in June.

Since its inception, Eisenhower had been looking for an opportunity to employ the airborne army, and from D-Day through the first week of September no fewer than 14 airborne operations had been considered and cancelled.

Montgomery was actually thinking along parallel lines, utilising the airborne to facilitate his major offensive. In August he had put together a plan called Operation Comet. He

Troops of the British 1st Airborne Division board a transport plane as Operation Market Garden begins. *(Public Domain United Kingdom Government via Wikimedia Commons)*

conceived an insertion, first across the border between The Netherlands and Germany to seize a crossing over the Lower Rhine near Wesel. The discovery of a heavy concentration of antiaircraft guns, though, caused a shift in the target to the Lower Rhine bridges at Arnhem, then 75 miles from his lines. Operation Comet was ready to go by September 7, but stiffening ground resistance from the Germans, foul weather, and the objections of some officers caused postponement and then cancellation on September 7.

Nevertheless, the idea of an air/ground offensive remained viable as far as Montgomery was concerned. In the meeting with Eisenhower on September 10, Montgomery found the supreme commander unwilling to bend on the broad front strategy. Eisenhower further was reluctant to rankle Third Army commander General George S. Patton, Jr., Montgomery's bitter rival, by taking away the bulk of Patton's fuel and ammunition in handing them over to the 21st Army Group.

Eisenhower recalled the meeting years later in an interview with author Cornelius Ryan. He had told Montgomery, "What you're proposing is this – if I give you all of the supplies you want, you could go straight to Berlin – right straight to Berlin? Monty, you're nuts. You can't do it. What the hell! If you try a long column like that in a single thrust you'd have to throw off division after division to protect your flanks from attack. Now suppose you did get a bridge across the Rhine. You couldn't depend on that one bridge for long to supply your drive. Monty, you can't do it."

Montgomery, though, was not finished. He knew that ending the V-1 and V-2 attacks on British cities was a priority, and a swift strike into The Netherlands was necessary to accomplish that. He had already gone back to the drawing board, doubled down, and come up with Market Garden, an expanded version of Operation Comet. The earlier plan had been limited in scope with the intended use of only the 1st Airborne Division and the 1st Polish Independent Parachute Brigade. Market Garden was to be a much larger affair involving three airborne divisions, the 1st, 82nd, and 101st, along with the veteran XXX Corps as the ground component, its tanks and infantry proceeding from their jump-off point on the Belgian-Dutch border across the "airborne carpet" of captured bridges over canals and the rivers Maas and Waal, and then the Lower Rhine at Arnhem, 64 miles distant.

Eisenhower was struck by the audacity of the revised plan. He gave his support with two caveats. It should be understood that Market Garden was an extension of existing strategy, limited to an extension of the northern campaign aimed at the Rhine and the Ruhr. Also, the ambitious plan should be undertaken as soon as possible. Market Garden was set for Sunday, September 17.

General Browning was given tactical command of the airborne "Market" portion of the plan, while the "Garden" ground component was handed to General Brian Horrocks of XXX Corps. Since time was of the essence, the word was passed quickly. When General James Gavin, commander of the 82nd Airborne Division, was notified, he expressed concern that there were only seven days to adequately prepare for the fight against the Germans. Rather nonchalantly, Browning replied, "Why not? We've got them on the run."

Even though Browning had previously committed the airborne under his command to Operation

General Bernard Montgomery, architect of Operation Market Garden, confers with Admiral Bertram Ramsay of the Royal Navy in Britain. *(Public Domain United Kingdom Government via Wikimedia Commons)*

General Dwight Eisenhower stands at left with General Bernard Montgomery after a meeting in 1944. Also visible are General Omar Bradley and Air Chief Marshal Arthur Tedder. *(Public Domain Imperial War Museum, London via Wikimedia Commons)*

Standing atop a Jeep, General Bernard Montgomery addresses troops. Montgomery presented an optimistic and motivational figure to the ranks of the British armies in Europe. *(Public Domain collections of the Imperial War Museums via Wikimedia Commons)*

Comet, he expressed some concern with the scope of Market Garden. When Montgomery informed him that the airborne would be expected to hold the vital bridges for two days, he remarked, "We can hold it for four. But sir, I think we might be going a bridge too far." Browning managed to suppress his own misgivings and even later noted that the offensive would be a "party." He further discounted later intelligence reports that indicated German armoured forces in the vicinity of Arnhem.

As preparations moved ahead, the 101st Airborne Division, under General Maxwell Taylor, was to capture the southernmost bridges over canals and the River Aa north of Eindhoven at Son and Veghel. The division was ordered to hold open a 15-mile stretch of road for XXX Corps. The 82nd Airborne Division, under General Gavin, was to drop south of Nijmegen near Grave and take the bridges across the Maas and Waal. The 1st Airborne Division, under General Roy Urquhart, was given the toughest assignment: seizing the railroad, pontoon, and highway bridges across the Lower Rhine at Arnhem. Urquhart's division was to be reinforced by the follow-on insertion of the Polish airborne brigade. Furthest north, the Red Devils would be the last relieved by XXX Corps, supposedly rolling forward hell-for-leather to affect the link-up.

General Gavin was troubled as he considered the role of the 82nd Airborne. "The big Nijmegen bridge posed a serious problem," he commented. "Seizing it with overwhelming strength at the outset would have been meaningless if I did not get at least two other bridges: the big bridge at Grave and at least one of the four over the (Maas-Waal) Canal. Further, even if I captured it, if I had lost all of the high ground that controlled the entire sector, as well as the resupply and glider landing zones, I would be in a serious predicament. Everything depended on the weight and direction of the enemy reaction, and this could not be determined until we were on the ground. The problem was how much could be spared how soon for employment on the bridge."

In his assessment, Gavin highlighted one of the primary Allied concerns. Approximately 35,000 airborne troops were to be inserted into The Netherlands by parachute and glider along with 1,736 vehicles, 3,342 tons of ammunition,

and 263 artillery pieces and anti-tank guns. Airlift capability was at a premium, and the entire movement would require more than one wave. Recalling the scattered nocturnal D-Day airdrops, it was decided that "Market" would be a precision daylight insertion. Allied air superiority meant support from bombers against enemy targets as well as an umbrella of protective fighters, while the higher risk of enemy flak was worth the benefit of an efficient parachute and glider landing.

Although some officers were ebullient in the run-up to Market Garden, others, including General Stanislaw Sosabowski of the Polish Brigade, were quite worried about the strength of German resistance. He voiced his opinion loudly but was virtually ignored. Still, the ambitious operation faced some notable constraints, including the fact that XXX Corps would proceed along a single road at times having to fight its way forward, cross bridges that were captured intact mostly on the first day of the offensive and that had not been blown up by the Germans, and then reach Arnhem within 48-72 hours. Any deviation from the timetable, even slight, exponentially increased the pressure on the lightly-armed airborne troops along the route. Then there were the issues of resupply and logistics. Everything was hurriedly prepared.

Meanwhile, the Germans had not been idle. Field Marshal Walter Model, at his best in the midst of crisis, had been given command of German Army Group B as the debacle at Falaise played out. He quickly ended a chaotic retreat northward and established his headquarters at Oosterbeek, a western suburb of Arnhem. He put together Kampfgruppe, or battle groups, ad hoc forces commanded by capable officers, and brought scattered elements of the 15th Army northeast from the Scheldt estuary. Many of the units that Model collected had been completely written off by Allied intelligence.

Model's most influential move involved the withdrawal of General Wilhelm Bittrich's II SS Panzer Korps from France for rest and refitting. Bittrich's 9th and 10th SS Panzer Divisions had sustained severe losses in Normandy, but they were nevertheless formidable. Coincidentally, Model ordered Bittrich to settle near Arnhem, the focal point of Operation Market Garden. ■

Allied supply canisters that fell into German-held territory hang by their parachutes from trees near Arnhem. *(Creative Commons Bundesarchiv Bild via Wikimedia Commons)*

OMINOUS SIGNS

The meeting was heated from the start. General Bernard Montgomery had taken it upon himself to decide who would attend and who would not. He took the offensive from the beginning and railed against the broad front strategy.

General Dwight D. Eisenhower, Supreme Commander of Allied Forces in Europe, listened even as the feisty commander of 21st Army Group went on a rant. Some reports of the September 10, 1944, meeting relate that Montgomery produced a folder containing communiqués from Eisenhower and ripped it to pieces, demanding that the chief choose between his own forces and those of XII Army Group to the south, particularly the US Third Army under General George S. Patton, his bitter rival, for the lion's share of scarce supplies in order to support his airborne/ground assault into The Netherlands that came to be known as Operation Market Garden.

Eisenhower was patient, a master of coalition warfare, but at length he reached out, patting Montgomery's knee and admonishing, "Steady Monty! You can't speak to me like that. I'm your boss."

Montgomery then uttered, "I'm sorry Ike."

Still, his point was driven home, and Montgomery got the go ahead for Market Garden. An outgrowth of his earlier Operation Comet, Market Garden was incredibly ambitious and radically out of character for Monty. Nevertheless, if successful it might indeed kill dead the Third Reich within weeks and even end World War Two by Christmas 1944.

However, there were variables, even ominous signs, some known and others

British airmen report on their run over The Netherlands to deliver airborne troops to their glider landing zone during Operation Market Garden. *(Public Domain collections of the Imperial War Museums via Wikimedia Commons)*

unknown, that threatened Market Garden from the outset. During a whirlwind of preparations some real warning signs emerged. These were either dismissed or whitewashed amid an air of optimism.

Granted, senior Allied commanders had reason to be optimistic – but euphoric? The German Army did appear to be beaten, at least in the short run. Many of its finest divisions had been shattered in Normandy, while the headlong retreat from the encirclement at Falaise in August 1944 had led the Dutch to describe the

event as "Dolle Dinsdag," or "Mad Tuesday." Some civilians looked out their windows and saw the motley clusters of civilian automobiles, horse-drawn carts, kubelwagens, trucks, tanks, and German soldiers on foot having fled France, crossed into Belgium and then streamed toward the frontier of The Netherlands.

To many observers, civilian and military alike, the German Army looked beaten. A bold airborne/ground thrust like Market Garden might well finish the whole business with a rapid thrust into the Ruhr and the extinguishing of the

Troopers of the British 1st Airborne Division ready for boarding a Short Stirling transport aircraft in the opening hours of Operation Market Garden. *(Public Domain collections of the Imperial War Museums via Wikimedia Commons)*

American airborne troops prepare for an exercise jump at Aldermaston in Britain. (Public Domain US Army Air Forces via Wikimedia Commons)

German industrial base. But such a perception was unfounded. Adolf Hitler had dispatched his "Fireman," Field Marshal Walter Model, to the West to restore order, and he capably stopped the stampede and initiated a regrouping effort that happened to coincide with Montgomery's grand design. Coincidentally, Model made his headquarters in Oosterbeek, a western suburb of Arnhem, the ultimate target of the Allied effort.

Therefore, although the Germans in The Netherlands were taken by surprise initially, Model's moves had given them the organisation and poise that would stem the Allied tide. And then there was the element of sheer luck. Model, his capable subordinates Generals Kurt Student, newly appointed commander of the 1st Parachute Army, and Wilhelm Bittrich with his II SS Panzer Korps were positioned to thwart the advance of XXX Corps and reduce the British airborne toehold at Arnhem bridge.

The Allies possessed the element of surprise. They could also invest three airborne divisions to seize key bridges, and XXX Corps was a veteran combat formation that surely could manage the rapid run of more than 60 miles from the Meuse-Escaut Canal to the linkup at Arnhem. At the same time, supply issues dogged the British and Americans, and beside that constant constraint there was insufficient airlift to bring all three airborne divisions and the 1st Polish Independent Parachute Brigade to bear in a single wave. Follow-on airlifts of paratroopers, glider-borne troops, supplies, ammunition, medicine, and food would take time.

Weather conditions were perfect for the initial airborne insertion and kickoff of the ground advance on Sunday, September 17, 1944, but this uncontrollable aspect of any offensive manoeuvre deteriorated at the worst possible time, postponing subsequent air operations from resupply to troop insertion and even tactical air support as Market Garden unfolded.

Adding to the list of Allied concerns was the simple fact that XXX Corps was to proceed down a single road, often elevated above the surrounding polder country. The narrow penetration front made the spearhead inherently weak, and when opposition was encountered, the British vanguard would be required to halt, deploy infantry, clear the road of damaged or destroyed vehicles and then move on to each successive bridge. All

this, of course, depended on the ability of the US 101st and 82nd Airborne Divisions and the British 1st Airborne Division holding bridges that were intact after the parachute and glider insertions were accomplished in broad daylight. Airborne forces are inherently lightly armed and not intended to operate for extended periods without relief. The predicted 48-72 hours that 1st Airborne would be required to take care of itself at Arnhem depended on speed everywhere else, adherence to a rapid timetable, and the limited effectiveness of German resistance.

Then, the most immediate warning of all was downplayed, dismissed, and discarded. In the autumn of 1944, Major Brian Urquhart (no relation to 1st Airborne Division commander General Roy Urquhart) was the 23-year-old GSO 2 chief of intelligence on the staff of General Frederick "Boy" Browning, commander of the I Airborne Corps and deputy commander of the First Allied Airborne Army, charged with the tactical administration of "Market," the airborne phase of the Allied offensive.

Major Urquhart had already become alarmed when intelligence reports, some from the Dutch Resistance, strongly suggested the Germans had rallied under Field Marshal Model. Directives to units that the Allies had thought completely destroyed in Normandy were circulating. Among these was a disturbing message that indicated the presence of an assault gun regiment near Arnhem. As more reports filtered in, Urquhart was concerned with the prospect that II SS Panzer Korps was actually in The Netherlands and positioned to possibly annihilate any airborne force, ill-equipped to defend itself against tanks.

Urquhart voiced his concerns "to anyone who would listen on the staff," as he later characterised his effort. He met with General Browning and others on or about September 12, just five days before Market Garden was to begin and remembered, "They said that I should not worry unduly, that the reports were probably wrong, and that in any case, the German troops were refitting and not up to much fighting."

Undeterred, Urquhart received grudging permission for RAF Spitfires to conduct an aerial photo reconnaissance of the intended operations area. An abundance of photos were

Luftwaffe General Kurt Student led the 1st Parachute Army in the defence of Arnhem and other Allied objectives during Operation Market Garden. (Creative Commons Bundesarchiv Bild via Wikimedia Commons)

taken, but five shot from an oblique angle on an "end of the run" film strip clearly showed the presence of German armoured vehicles. Though conjecture surrounds the unit depicted – some modern analysts claim these were older PzKpfw. III tanks of an inferior formation rather than formidable PzKpfw. IVs and other armoured vehicles of an SS panzer division – Urquhart was convinced of the imminent peril they presented.

When Urquhart showed the photos to General Browning, he received a rather nonchalant reply. "I wouldn't trouble myself about these if I were you. They're probably not serviceable at any rate." Still, word of the photographic evidence reached the Americans, spurring General Eisenhower to dispatch his chief of staff, General Walter Bedell Smith, to inquire as to the danger. Any lingering concerns were shunted aside, though, and Major Urquhart was described as "suffering from acute nervous strain and exhaustion." He was told to take convalescent leave as soon as possible or face a court martial.

British troops man machine guns in a defensive position during Operation Market Garden. (Creative Commons Regional Archives Nijmegen via Wikimedia Commons)

German troops take up positions around Arnhem to stop the British airborne advance on the bridge over the Lower Rhine. *(Creative Commons Bundesarchiv Bild via Wikimedia Commons)*

the American drop zones, remembered that Market Garden came as a complete surprise.

"The 17th of September, 1944, was a Sunday," Student later commented, "a remarkably beautiful late summer day. All was quiet at the front. Late in the morning the enemy air force suddenly became very active... From my command post at Vught I was able to observe numerous enemy aircraft; I could hear the crash of bombs and fire from aircraft armaments and antiaircraft guns in my immediate vicinity. At noon there came the endless stream of enemy transports and cargo planes, as far as the eye could see..."

For better or worse, Montgomery's gamble was unleashed as warnings were set aside. At the same time, Dolle Dinsdag was over. Determined enemies, Allied and Nazi, were destined for an epic clash of arms. ■

There were doubters among Allied senior officers. Polish General Stanislaw Sosabowski was angered and vocal in his dissent, plainly stating that his paratroopers would be "slaughtered." While some officers laughed and talked of taking their golf clubs along on the Market Garden mission, Sosabowski scoffed at the notion that the German Army was a spent force. Even General Brian Horrocks, commander of XXX Corps, was sceptical. He recognised the daunting task before him. "The roads were all causeways, which are ideal for an armoured force to stop another from advancing. All you've got to do is to disable one tank, and that blocks the whole thing," he later remarked. "I simply did not believe that the Germans were going to roll over and surrender. Well, I didn't get anywhere with this. Everyone thought that I was hysterical, nervous, and so on."

While Allied preparations proceeded, Model was busy as well. He took steps to restore order among the varied German units in The Netherlands and expected an Allied attack. Its size and scope, however, were unknown in the beginning. General Student had taken command of the newly-formed First Parachute Army in early September. It was a hodgepodge of formations but numbered 30,000 soldiers. When the Allied offensive materialized, Model gave Student the 59th Infantry Division, which just happened to be on the road near Tilburg, and the 107th Panzer Brigade, diverted from its original order to defend Aachen against the US First Army.

Elsewhere, Model ordered several Kampfgruppen, ad hoc battle groups comprised of troops, armour, and artillery, into action against XXX Corps and the airborne advances. Headquarter units were pressed into the defence, and German officers regularly demonstrated great competence. At the same time, the Allies had turned their attention to Market Garden and failed to drive another 20 miles northward to cut off the retreat of the German 15th Army from the area surrounding Antwerp. As the clearing of the Scheldt estuary was postponed for Montgomery's venture, 86,000 German troops and their equipment

were withdrawn to prevent their encirclement south of the Scheldt. Elements of these forces would figure in the failure of Market Garden and the future fighting in The Netherlands.

And then, there were the two SS panzer divisions, the 9th Hohenstaufen and 10th Frundsberg, of II Panzer Korps under Bittrich. These battle-hardened but depleted forces were the key defenders in the undoing of Market Garden at Nijmegen and Arnhem.

Weather conditions favoured the Germans as the Allied thrust wore on, and the scope of Market Garden, though not known to Model initially, was revealed early. After an American glider was shot down, a German soldier inspected the wreckage and found the top-secret Market Garden plan in its entirety. Within hours, the complete blueprint was in General Student's hands and the intelligence coup was passed up the chain of command. Such are the fortunes of war.

On the morning of September 17, Field Marshal Model was enjoying lunch when word that British airborne troops were descending near his Arnhem headquarters. At the same time, Student, his headquarters situated in a cottage along the highway between Eindhoven and Nijmegen just eight miles from one of

A German soldier of a Luftwaffe field force wears a sprig of camouflage in his helmet near Arnhem. *(Creative Commons Bundesarchiv Bild via Wikimedia Commons)*

Billowing parachutes dot the sky as Allied airborne forces descend on drop zones in The Netherlands. *(Public Domain National Archives and Records Administration via Wikimedia Commons)*

Sherman tanks of the Guards Armoured Division, spearhead of XXX Corps during Operation Market Garden, are shown along a roadside in September 1944. *(Public Domain collections of the Imperial War Museums via Wikimedia Commons)*

1ST AIRBORNE DIVISION

British parachute troops walk along a road during a training exercise in Norwich, 1941. *(Public Domain collections of the Imperial War Museums via Wikimedia Commons)*

Soldiers of the Border Regiment prepare for Operation Ladbroke in Sicily with a folding bicycle in the foreground. *(Public Domain collections of the Imperial War Museums via Wikimedia Commons)*

From the time that General Roy Urquhart took command in January 1944, the 1st Airborne Division trained expectantly. Urquhart, a tough, experienced leader of men who ironically had never jumped from a plane and was prone to air sickness, nevertheless won the confidence of his officers and men while they honed their skills to razor sharpness.

But the June 6, 1944, D-Day invasion of Normandy went ahead without the Red Devils. The 6th Airborne Division had been chosen instead to spearhead the great airborne operation that opened the campaign to liberate Western Europe, and there was considerable disappointment throughout the ranks of the 1st Airborne.

One veteran remembered, "Our division felt 'out of it' when the 6th Airborne Division went on D-Day instead of us. Of course, they did extremely well, which was even more upsetting. Then, operation after operation was cancelled, but our officers told us we were being kept for 'something special.' There

Paras of Company C, 2nd Battalion return from the Bruneval Raid of February 1942. *(Public Domain United Kingdom Government via Wikimedia Commons)*

was a lot of speculation; jumping on Berlin and snatching Hitler was one rumour."

No one was more disappointed than General Urquhart, who said later, "The summer passed interminably, planning one operation after another, only to see each cancelled." Indeed, between D-Day and September 7, 1944, the Allied senior commanders planned and then cancelled 14 separate airborne operations. By autumn, Urquhart described his Red Devils as "hungering for a fight... there was a dangerous mixture of ennui and cynicism slowly creeping into our lives. We were trained to a fine edge and I knew that if we didn't get into battle soon, we would lose it. We were ready and willing to accept anything with all the 'ifs.'"

When the 1st Airborne Division was finally designated for the real thing, its objectives could hardly have been more ambitious. At Arnhem, where the road bridge that stretched across the Lower Rhine was the ultimate prize of Market Garden, there were also a pontoon bridge close by and two and one-half miles upstream and to the west of the city a railroad bridge that were to be seized as well. As the mission unfolded, it was discovered that a centre section of the pontoon bridge had floated away, making it unusable, while the Germans blew the railroad bridge sky high. It was, then, the fight for the road bridge, the 2nd Battalion's desperate temporary hold on the north end, and the valorous but unsuccessful attempt of the rest of the 1st Airborne Division to reach them that brilliantly

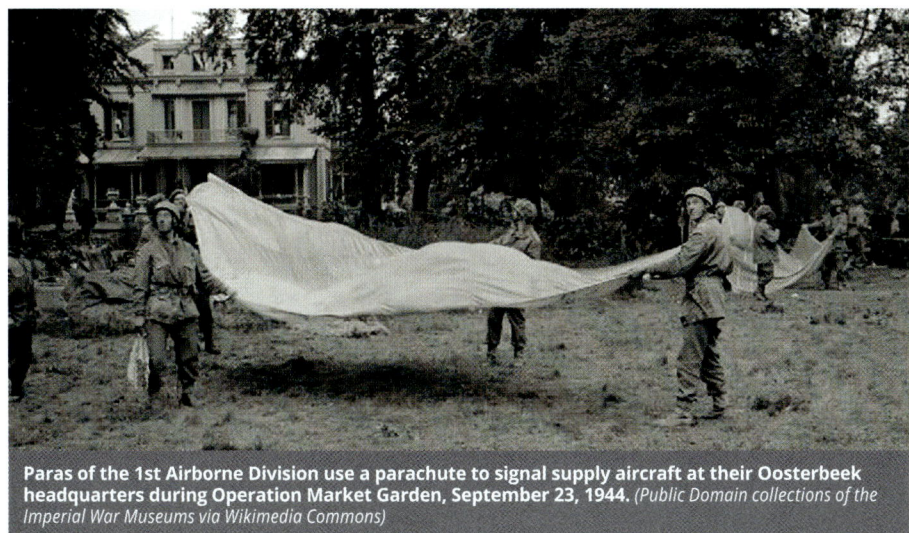

Paras of the 1st Airborne Division use a parachute to signal supply aircraft at their Oosterbeek headquarters during Operation Market Garden, September 23, 1944. *(Public Domain collections of the Imperial War Museums via Wikimedia Commons)*

Soldiers of the 1st Airlanding Light Regiment, Royal Artillery operate a 75mm pack howitzer. *(Public Domain collections of the Imperial War Museums via Wikimedia Commons)*

etched the names of the brave paras who fought in Market Garden among Britain's great heroes.

As the plan for the 1st Airborne Division and the accompanying Polish 1st Independent Parachute Brigade took shape, General Urquhart worried about reports of a buildup of German antiaircraft weapons in the vicinity of Arnhem that obviously would put transport and glider aircraft at greater risk. He also knew that the shortage of adequate air transport would require subsequent lifts, over three days, to bring the full strength of the 1st Airborne Division and the Polish brigade together on the ground.

Compounding his concerns was a lack of suitable drop and landing zones close to the bridges at Arnhem. The marshy terrain near the road bridge was a hazard for parachute troops who might come down in water over their heads and lose their kit, or even worse drown. The ground also would be unsafe for glider touchdowns, contributing to crashes that might injure or kill many airborne soldiers before they could even fire a shot in anger.

"My problem was to get enough men down on the first lift," Urquhart later assessed, "not only to seize the main bridge in the town itself, but also to guard and defend the drop zones and landing areas for the succeeding lifts. To seize

the main bridge on the first day my strength was reduced to just one parachute brigade."

Perusing maps of the southern Netherlands, one viable alternative landing area emerged. Broad, flat farmland suitable for both paratroops and gliders was located to the west and northwest of Arnhem. The only sticking point was sheer distance, six to eight miles from the road bridge across the Lower Rhine. Urquhart would have to make the best of a situation that was challenging from the outset. Elements of the 1st Airborne Division would have to dash for the bridge and hold it while the balance of available manpower came up as quickly as possible. Of course, there were the apparent concerns with assembling units and moving out rapidly, perhaps even in the face of enemy resistance.

And so, the Red Devils' Arnhem epic went forward on September 17, 1944.

The 1st Airborne Division had come into being after Prime Minister Winston Churchill's demand for an airborne force within the British military in 1940. Its lineage was that of No. 2 Commando, the 11th Special Air Service Battalion that was

redesignated the 1st Parachute Battalion, and then the raising of the 2nd and 3rd Parachute Battalions from volunteers already serving in the infantry ranks and aged 22 to 32. These units would form the 1st Parachute Brigade under the command of Brigadier Richard Gale.

General Frederick "Boy" Browning was named commanding officer of Parachute and Airborne Troops in October 1941, and in that same month the 1st Airlanding Brigade came together with the commitment of the 31st Independent Infantry Brigade Group and the four units that were subsequently assigned, the 1st Royal Ulster Rifles, 2nd Oxfordshire and Buckinghamshire Light Infantry, 2nd South Staffordshire Regiment, and the 1st Border Regiment. Browning took charge of training, equipment, and other requirements in the burgeoning force, and at year end his command was officially designated the 1st Airborne Division. The division was augment at Brown's insistence with the 2nd and 3rd Parachute Brigades, formed in June and November 1942 respectively.

The initial enemy action undertaken by elements of the 1st Airborne Division was Operation Biting, the February 1942 raid on the German Wurzburg radar station at Bruneval on the coast of French Normandy. Under the command of Major John Frost, destined to play a central role in the later fighting at Arnhem, Company C, 2nd Battalion, Parachute Regiment successfully completed the raid and brought back components that yielded vital intelligence. They even snatched a Luftwaffe signalman who provided information on the new radar's operation.

The 1st Airborne Division then contributed 30 engineers of the 9th Field Company to a glider mission dubbed Operation Freshman that targeted a heavy water production facility in Norway. On the night of November 19, 1942, the tow planes and gliders took off, but their mission ended in disaster as the gliders crashed, killing several engineers and seriously injuring others. Those who survived the landings were taken prisoner and executed by the Germans.

Troops of the 1st Airborne Division and Italian civilians pose with a captured Nazi flag in 1943. *(Public Domain United Kingdom Government via Wikimedia Commons)*

A war correspondent attached to the 1st Airborne Division types his despatch from a position in the forest near Arnhem, Operation Market Garden, September 18, 1944. *(Public Domain United Kingdom Government via Wikimedia Commons)*

In the spring of 1943, elements of the 1st Airborne Division transferred to North Africa, engaging in some operations as infantrymen. Transfers continued through August in preparation and support for Operation Husky, the Allied invasion of Sicily.

Two airborne insertions were conducted during Operation Husky, and both ran into difficulties. Operation Ladbroke, a glider mission to capture a bridge near the city of Syracuse, was initiated on July 9, 1943, and tragedy struck as 65 gliders were released from their tow planes prematurely. These crashed into the Mediterranean Sea, and at least 250 men were lost. Only a fraction of the force intended to take the Ponte Grande actually reached the objective. They held on for a considerable period of time, but when their relief did not show up on schedule and their number had dwindled from 87 to 15, these luckless glider men were compelled to surrender to Italian soldiers.

Meanwhile, the 1st Parachute Brigade undertook Operation Fustian to capture the Primosole bridge across the River Simeto. This mission was in trouble from the outset as both enemy antiaircraft guns and friendly fire took a toll on the transports. Pilots took evasive action, and the insertions that followed were scattered widely. Still, the airborne troops managed to capture the bridge temporarily before heavy counterattacks forced them to retire. Reinforcements arrived during the night, but three days of fighting were required before a bridgehead was secured.

In September, the 1st Airborne Division was transported by ship to the Italian mainland, participating in Operation Slapstick, a complementary action to Operation Avalanche, the main Allied landings at Salerno. The airborne troops captured the port of Taranto in the heel of the Italian boot and then Brindisi to the east on the coast of the Adriatic Sea. Advancing 125 miles to occupy Foggia, the 1st Airborne was relieved by infantry divisions of the V Corps, Eighth Army. The bulk of the 1st Airborne Division was withdrawn to Britain in December. Its commanding officer, General George Hopkinson, was killed in action in Italy, and he was temporarily replaced by Brigadier Ernest Down, previously commander of the 2nd Parachute Brigade.

After General Urquhart took command while numerous on-again, off-again airborne operations were being contemplated, his division was finally committed to Operations Market Garden in September 1944. During the desperate days that followed in The Netherlands, the 1st Airborne was decimated. Following its withdrawal from the shrinking perimeter at Oosterbeek, west of Arnhem, the depleted division, which lost about 8,000 men killed, wounded, or captured during Market Garden, did not see further action.

After World War Two in Europe ended, the 1st Airborne Division was sent to Norway and engaged in repatriating German prisoners of war and other duties. The division was disbanded in late 1945. ∎

After the Bruneval Raid, paras show Wing Commander Percy Pickard of No. 51 Squadron, RAF a German helmet they brought back. *(Public Domain collections of the Imperial War Museums via Wikimedia Commons)*

Four paras of the 1st Airborne Division take shelter in a shell hole near the division headquarters at Oosterbeek during Operation Market Garden, September 17, 1944. *(Public Domain United Kingdom Government via Wikimedia Commons)*

BRITISH AIRBORNE EVOLUTION

A Parachute Regiment trooper is shown in full combat gear while carrying a Sten gun at the ready during training. *(Public Domain collections of the Imperial War Museums via Wikimedia Commons)*

Soviet paratroopers board a transport plane in 1941. Sir Archibald Wavell was amazed when he witnessed an airborne demonstration in the Soviet Union. *(Public Domain civil code of the Russian Federation via Wikimedia Commons)*

General Archibald Wavell led a British military delegation to the Soviet Union in 1936, and his observation of a Red Army airborne exercise was nothing short of astonishing.

After seeing 1,200 Soviet troops parachute from planes to earth along with 100 machine guns and 18 light field artillery pieces, Wavell reported, "If I had not witnessed the descents I could not have believed such a thing possible." Still, by the outbreak of World War Two, the British Army had done virtually nothing to integrate airborne forces into its table of organisation and equipment.

When Prime Minister Winston Churchill asked for a note on the progress of developing airborne units in 1940 and declared that he wanted a corps of 5,000 paratroopers available by that winter, many military men and government officials were becoming aware of the successes achieved by their German enemy's parachute and glider forces. But in Britain there were no troops dedicated to such an endeavour, no training facilities, no weapons or equipment developed or modified for airborne usage, and no transport aircraft to deliver them into combat.

Churchill, however, was a prime mover in airborne development, but even in the spring of 1942, the sight of dedicated air transport was disheartening amid virtually no enthusiasm

within the RAF for developing dedicated airborne troop transports or aircraft meant to tow gliders. The extent of availability that season was only 12 outdated Whitworth Whitley bombers for parachutists and nine Hawker Hector biplanes that pulled aloft a few General Aircraft Hotspur gliders.

The early steps toward a viable airborne component within the British Army were energised with the 1940 appointment of Major John Rock to the task of raising such a force. As it turned out, the development of the British airborne occurred rapidly when given only some of the required resources, particularly as General Frederick "Boy" Browning became the foremost advocate of the airborne in the military. Nevertheless, early in the process there was a decided lack of interest on the part of the RAF in assisting with airlift pilot training or devoting precious aircraft to its development. The RAF establishment and Air Chief Marshal Sir Arthur "Bomber" Harris, chief of Bomber Command, were immersed in their bombing campaign against the Third Reich, prompting Browning to comment, "Bomber Command display no interest and carry out no training in parachuting or towing."

At length, Churchill did intervene, and progress was achieved. RAF Ringway in Cheshire became the site of the Central Landing School, and interestingly No. 1 Parachute Training School

was established there in June 1940. Thus, while the organisation and deployment of the burgeoning airborne forces would stay with the British Army, parachute training was initiated under the control of the Royal Air Force.

Details so minute as the shape of the actual parachute were worked out, and 35 men executed the first wartime airborne operation in British military history, Operation Colossus, in February 1941. By 1944, several independent parachute formations along with the 1st and 6th Airborne Divisions and the 2nd Parachute Brigade were formed. Meanwhile, the dearth of suitable aircraft was a source of continuous

A parachute trainee at RAF Ringway demonstrates an exit from the rear of a Whitworth Whitley bomber converted for airborne use. *(Public Domain collections of the Imperial War Museums via Wikimedia Commons)*

Two soldiers of the Parachute Regiment are shown during a training exercise in August 1942. Note the Sten gun one of them carries. *(Public Domain collections of the Imperial War Museums via Wikimedia Commons)*

concern that was somewhat alleviated by the introduction of the American Douglas C-47 Skytrain transport, which the British christened the "Dakota." With the Dakota, paras could actually jump out of a door in the fuselage rather than through a hole in the floor or some other improvised exit from an obsolete bomber.

The British paratrooper carried up to 100 pounds of personal effects, weapons, ammunition, and other necessities. During early operations paras jumped without weapons and recovered their arms from canisters dropped separately. Introduced in 1943, the kit bag became an indispensable addition to the airborne outfit. Strapped to the paratrooper's right leg, it was lowered by quick release once the parachute canopy deployed.

The airborne soldier typically wore webbing that included a waist belt and straps for the carrying of a haversack, ammunition pouches, a two-pint water bottle, entrenching tool, drinking mug, respirator, and spike bayonet for the .303-calibre Lee-Enfield Rifle No. 4 Mk I, the standard issue shoulder arm of the British military during World War Two. The bolt action No. 4 was fed by a 10-round box magazine, and an experienced operator could fire 20 to 30 aimed shots per minute. The paratrooper rifleman also carried a pair of No. 82 hand grenades, referred to commonly as Gammon bombs, and a Fairbairn-Sykes fighting knife. The rim of the standard British infantryman's helmet was removed for the parachutist's use, and the result was quite similar to the headcover used in the German Fallschirmjäger.

The standard parachute battalion was roughly 400 strong and included a headquarters group with three parachute or light airborne infantry companies, each of these including

a headquarters and three platoons totalling 117 men. The parachute rifle company was organised along the same lines as the infantry company, although sometimes fielding as many as 10 fewer men. Company headquarters consisted of the company commander, usually a major, and the second-in-command, usually a captain, both armed with the .45-calibre Colt M1911 pistol, and 13 enlisted personnel, while the platoons fielded a commanding officer, usually a lieutenant, and 33 enlisted men each. Each platoon included three rifle sections and a machine gun group.

A British soldier carries a Bren gun into action in The Netherlands in 1944. The Bren light machine gun was a standard weapon at platoon level in the British airborne. *(Public Domain collections of the Imperial War Museums via Wikimedia Commons)*

In addition to the No. 4 rifle, heavier firepower at the platoon level was provided with a pair of Bren Mk I light machine guns. These were license-built British versions of a proven Czech design that fired the .303-calibre round at a rate of up to 520 per minute fed from a 30-round detachable box magazine or 100-round detachable pan magazine. Platoon sergeants were often armed with the Sten Mk V submachine gun, which fired a 9X19mm Parabellum round from a 32-round detachable box magazine at a rate up to 600 per minute. Each section also included a mortarman who operated a single two-inch mortar and a sniper equipped with the No. 4 Mk I(T) sniper variant rifle.

At the battalion level, as many as 300 Sten guns were kept in reserve and could be issued liberally throughout the battalion. The Sten was cheap to produce, and though sometimes prone to jamming would provide welcome firepower at the lowest organisational level. Officers were usually among the first to be given the Sten prior to operational deployment since their standard weapon was the .45-calibre pistol. The Bren gun was the common base weapon in fire and manoeuvre ground tactics. Paratroopers transported the Bren gun into action in an "LMG Valise" carrying bag that was attached to their front. The paratrooper secured the bag around the neck and legs and then disconnected it by quick release after the parachute canopy opened to hang 20 feet below him during the descent.

For immediate engagement of strongpoints and enemy armoured vehicles, the primary weapon of the British airborne was the PIAT (Projector Infantry Anti-tank), an 83mm spring loaded spigot mortar that fired a high-explosive anti-tank round up to a distance of 350 yards. The PIAT entered service in Africa in 1943 and remained standard issue for British airborne units until 1950. Nine of these weapons were controlled at battalion level, and these were regularly parcelled out to the companies evenly for use at their discretion. Airborne artillery included the 75mm pack howitzer, and later with the introduction of larger Hamilcar gliders, the 6-pounder and 17-pounder field guns, their required towing vehicles, and even light tanks. ◼

A British soldier carries a PIAT over his shoulder. The PIAT was used by British airborne units against enemy armoured vehicles and strongpoints. *(Public Domain collections of the Imperial War Museums via Wikimedia Commons)*

82ND AIRBORNE DIVISION

Shortly after the United States entered World War Two on December 7, 1941, six airborne regiments were authorised in the US Army, and the formation of these regiments in turn facilitated the activation of the first airborne division in the Army's history as parachute infantry battalions were formed at Camp Mackall, North Carolina, Fort Benning, Georgia, and Camp Toccoa, Georgia.

The 82nd Infantry Division had fought with distinction in World War One and then stood down after hostilities ceased. On March 25, 1942, the 82nd was reactivated under then-Major General Omar Bradley, who later commanded XII Army Group in Europe. In August, the 82nd was redesignated as the first US Army airborne division, and Major General Matthew B. Ridgway took command at Camp Claiborne, Louisiana, as training commenced.

While many fine officers and soldiers gravitated toward the adventure of airborne service, one individual had more than a bit of a challenge realising his aspiration. Captain James M. Gavin, a 1929 graduate of the US Military Academy at West Point, applied for a transfer to the airborne while serving as an instructor at the academy. He had read newspaper accounts of the German airborne operations in Western Europe and Greece and asked for the change – which was promptly denied.

Gavin initiated a letter writing campaign to influential friends, including Lieutenant William T. Ryder, commander of the Army's first airborne test platoon who made the first official parachute jump by an active member of the US armed forces on August 16, 1940. Gavin also visited Washington, DC, several times to personally campaign for his transfer. In July 1941, his relentlessness was rewarded, and he completed jump school in August. Gavin went on to become one of the wartime legends of the US Army, an airborne trailblazer who rose to command the 505th Parachute Infantry Regiment (PIR) and the 82nd Airborne Division.

Nicknamed "All American," the 82nd Airborne Division experienced combat for the first-time during Operation Husky, the Allied invasion of Sicily, on July 9, 1943. The jump was widely scattered, while one transport crashed into the Mediterranean Sea and two others became so thoroughly lost that they returned to airfields in North Africa with their paratroopers still aboard. Two days later, an airborne reinforcement operation was met with withering friendly fire. In the tragic case of mistaken identity, more than 400 airborne troops and troop carrier personnel were casualties while 23 C-47 transport planes were shot down and 37 others damaged.

Meanwhile, scattered clusters of paratroopers came together, sometimes just a few of them under officers they did not know. Gavin, commanding the 505th PIR, led one such mixed bag of American soldiers in a spirited defence of Biazza Ridge. Other troopers managed to seize assigned objectives and improvised. Sixty paratroopers of the 3rd Battalion, 505th PIR joined up with Lieutenant Colonel Earl Taylor's 3rd Battalion, 45th Infantry Division and three 75mm pack howitzers of the 456th Parachute Field Artillery Battalion and moved out. Colonel Reuben Tucker's 504th PIR occupied the town of Castellammare on the afternoon of July 24, ending the 82nd Airborne participation in the Sicily campaign.

Operation Husky had been a learning experience, and numerous issues were addressed while counting the cost. Some senior officer clamoured for the cessation of airborne operations, and among them was General Lesley McNair, commander of US Army Ground Forces. General Ridgway strongly disagreed and pushed for an airborne role in Operation Avalanche, the Allied Fifth Army invasion of the Italian mainland at Salerno in September 1943. Although a high-risk airborne seizure of Rome was approved, it was cancelled at the last

Tanks of Allied XXX Corps roll toward Nijmegen as the 82nd Airborne fights for control of bridges across the River Waal during Operation Market Garden. *(Public Domain collections of the Imperial War Museums via Wikimedia Commons)*

At their RAF Cottesmore base, paratroopers of the US 82nd Airborne Division line up for coffee from an American Red Cross clubmobile. *(Public Domain Signal Corps Archive US Army via Wikimedia Commons)*

Paratroopers of the 504th Parachute Infantry Regiment, 82nd Airborne Division, place an artillery piece aboard a glider in 1943. *(Public Domain US Army via Wikimedia Commons)*

minute due to security concerns. Instead, the 504th PIR dropped on the Sele Plain, the 505th at Paestum, and elements of the 509th at Avellino to support General Mark Clark's beachhead after a ferocious German counterattack had nearly driven the Allies into the sea.

The successful support jumps in Italy silenced the airborne critics and helped ensure an airborne component for Operation Overlord, the Allied invasion of Normandy on June 6, 1944, which included the 82nd and 101st US Airborne Divisions and the British 6th Airborne Division. The 504th PIR remained in Italy after the bulk of the 82nd Airborne Division was withdrawn to England to rest and refit in preparation for Overlord. That spring, the 82nd received the 507th and 508th PIR to join the veteran 505th PIR and 325th Glider Infantry Regiment. The 82nd and the heretofore unbloodied 101st Airborne Division were assigned to secure the western flank of the Allied invasion lodgement on D-Day. The 82nd was to jump astride the River Mederet, seize crossings there and hold the area from the Merderet to the English Channel and the River Douve northward to the town of Sainte-Mere-Eglise.

While the 505th PIR took Sainte-Mere-Eglise and held crossings of the Merderet at Chef-du-Pont and La Fiere, then linking up with the 502nd PIR, 101st Airborne, the 507th and 508th PIR were to jump west of the Merderet and support the 505th. More than 900 transport aircraft and 500 gliders carried the 82nd Airborne into battle on the night of June 5-6, 1944, after its jump and landing zones had been pulled east due to a suspected concentration of German troops. Primary enemy resistance was expected from the 91st Airlanding Division, 1057th Grenadier Division, 6th Parachute Regiment, and 709th Infantry Division.

Prior to D-Day, Air Chief Marshal Sir Trafford Leigh-Mallory was so concerned with the risk of the airborne insertion that he recommended it should be scrapped and made the dire prediction that half the transport aircraft involved would be shot down along with 70 percent of the gliders. In the event, casualties were much lower among

Prior to departure during Operation Market Garden, paratroopers of the 82nd Airborne Division receive final instructions. *(Public Domain Signal Corps Archive US Army via Wikimedia Commons)*

the airborne than Leigh-Mallory anticipated, but the airdrop was buffeted by winds, and again the troopers were scattered widely.

American paratroopers groped in darkness and found one another in small groups, the troopers of both divisions mixed thoroughly. About 30 paratroopers of the 82nd dropped helplessly into the centre of Sainte-Mere-Eglise and were

killed or captured. One trooper dangled from a church steeple in the town and played dead for nearly three hours until taken prisoner.

Fierce firefights erupted across the area, and here and there numerous objectives were taken while others changed hands or remained in German control. Three intrepid troopers of the 508th PIR watched a battalion of enemy infantry with tank support assemble for a counterattack in the small village of Haut Gueutteville and then held up the advance for two hours in a remarkable feat of arms while their comrades occupied important high ground as the crossings of the Merderet at Chef-du-Pont and La Fiere were being contested. Sainte-Mere-Eglise was occupied quickly, but the Germans counterattacked the town repeatedly through the next day.

After several days of hard fighting, elements of the 82nd Airborne had linked up with adjacent divisions and begun a steady advance. The division was withdrawn to England in early July following just over a month in the line, and General Ridgway proudly reported, "...33 days of action without relief, without replacements. Every mission accomplished. No ground gained was ever relinquished." The All Americans had suffered 5,245 casualties in Normandy, but the division had burnished its reputation as a veteran, hard-fighting unit.

After absorbing replacements and refitting, the 82nd Airborne Division was tabbed for its role in Operation Market Garden and then the stubborn defence of the Nijmegen salient, dubbed "the

This Allied glider crashed in a field in France on D-Day, June 6, 1944. *(Public Domain US Army via Wikimedia Commons)*

Paratroopers of the 82nd Airborne Division trudge through snow during the Battle of the Bulge. *(Public Domain US Army via Wikimedia Commons)*

Paratroopers of the 82nd Airborne Division guard a large group of German prisoners captured during Operation Market Garden. *(Public Domain collections of the Imperial War Museums via Wikimedia Commons)*

Island." After 55 days in The Netherlands, the division had lost roughly 3,400 men killed, wounded, or captured. Its tired troopers were pulled from the line and ordered to old French Army facilities at Sissone and Suippes, France. Along with the 101st, resting at Mourmelon-le-Grand, it was the only available Allied reserve when the storm of the Nazi Ardennes Offensive broke on Saturday, December 16, 1944.

When the Germans fractured the thin American line in the Ardennes Forest, intent on reaching the Belgian port of Antwerp and driving a wedge between Allied armies north and south, General Dwight Eisenhower, Supreme Commander of Allied Forces in Europe, ordered the weary airborne troops into action again. As the Battle of the Bulge escalated, the men of the 82nd Airborne Division climbed aboard trucks and headed to the north shoulder of the great salient the Germans had driven into the Allied front.

General Gavin had taken command of the 82nd Airborne Division in August, and with General Ridgway in England observing the training of the newly arrived 17th US Airborne Division, he was also the temporary commander of XVIII Airborne Corps. Gavin issued orders to the 101st Airborne Division to prepare to move out and headed with the 82nd toward the town of Werbomont, Belgium, where good defensive ground was located. With Ridgway's return, Gavin led his division in establishing a defensive line. In the coming days, the German thrust was blunted, and the three regiments of the 82nd Airborne engaged in bitter fighting around the village of Cheneux.

In frequent combat through January 9, the 82nd Airborne gained ground until perilously

exposed against several German divisions, reluctantly pulled back, and then regained all the ground previously vacated. They had contributed mightily to the defeat of Hitler's last major offensive in the West. After suffering 2,000 casualties during the Battle of the Bulge, the division was order to a rear area around the towns of Chevron and Pepinster, Belgium. Gavin had already written proudly of the recent effort on December 31, 1944, "Our Army has a hell of a lot to learn, but at present these airborne troopers of this division are making monkeys out of the Germans opposing them. They are better trained and are far superior combat soldiers...."

In the waning months of World War Two, the 82nd Airborne Division fought as ground

troops in assaults against the German Siegfried Line, or West Wall, in February 1945. By April, the division was occupying positions on the west bank of the great River Rhine near Cologne, Germany. At any given time, General Ridgway had under XVIII Airborne Corps command several ground units as well as airborne troops. By May 2, the bulk of the 82nd crossed the River Elbe in company with the US 7th Armored Division. At the end of the war, the two divisions secured the flank of 21st Army Group at Ludwigslust, where General Gavin accepted the surrender of 140,000 troops of the German 21st Army.

During World War Two, the 82nd Airborne Division spent 422 days in combat and sustained nearly 9,000 casualties. ∎

General Matthew Ridgway and officers of the 82nd Airborne Division discuss plans in Sicily, July 25, 1943. *(Public Domain US Army via Wikimedia Commons)*

Pulling a sled loaded with ammunition, troopers of the 82nd Airborne Division move ahead through heavy snow during the Battle of the Bulge. *(Public Domain US National Archives and Record Administration via Wikimedia Commons)*

101ST AIRBORNE DIVISION

As C-47 transports deliver supplies to the 101st Airborne Division, parachutes plummet earthward and scatter across the ground. *(Public Domain US Army via Wikimedia Commons)*

Activated at Camp Claiborne, Louisiana, on March 25, 1942, the 101st Airborne Division came into being on the same day that its sister 82nd Airborne Division was created. The 101st was originally an infantry division formed in July 1918, but it did not see action during World War One. Revived in 1921, the division basically existed only on paper for the next 20 years.

When Major General William C. Lee, the first commander of the Screaming Eagles, addressed the original assembly of 101st personnel in 1942, he said to them, "The 101st has no history, but it has a rendezvous with destiny." Lee, the father of the American airborne, could not have been more prophetic in his pronouncement.

Prospective paratroopers endured a gruelling training regimen. Physical endurance was continually tested, and one of the most notable locations, made famous in the Stephen Ambrose book and subsequent television series *Band of Brothers*, was Camp Toccoa, located in the mountains of northeastern Georgia. Built by the Works Projects Administration in the late 1930s as a National Guard facility, Camp Toccoa became a primary training centre, the first 5,000 of an eventual 17,000 trainees arriving in July 1942.

During World War Two, the 501st, 511th, 517th, and the legendary 506th Parachute Infantry Regiments (PIR), 101st Airborne trained

there. One of the most imposing aspects of Camp Toccoa was 1,735-foot Currahee Mountain. Those who completed the running of that monolith remember the famed slogan, "Three miles up; three miles down!" and the war cry "Currahee!" which was said to have

A paratrooper of the 101st Airborne Division climbs aboard a C-47 transport prior to a mission. *(Public Domain US Army via Wikimedia Commons)*

translated from a Native American language as "stand alone." Another familiar cry among American paratroopers was the single word "Geronimo!" upon exit from an aircraft.

Trainees who completed five successful live jumps were presented the coveted silver winged airborne badge. The paratrooper was trained considerably beyond the skill set of the regular infantryman. He was required to be proficient with every available weapon up to platoon level, to maintain and rapidly pack a parachute, and to use explosives.

The US airborne division numbered roughly 8,500 men, about half the size of a standard infantry division. Its basic tactical unit was the parachute battalion, consisting of a headquarters company and three rifle companies totalling 535 men. The primary fire and manoeuvre ground unit was the squad, consisting of 12 troopers with two non-commissioned officers and 10 riflemen. The platoon included 37 troopers, and the company 130. The regiment consisted of three battalions, headquarters, and support personnel totalling 2,000. Originally, the division included three regiments, one parachute infantry and two glider infantry; however, that configuration changed during the course of World War Two.

The 101st Airborne Division trained rigorously from the spring of 1942 but did not experience combat for more than two years. Its baptism

Tents crowd the landscape at Camp Toccoa, Georgia, where elements of the 101st Airborne Division trained during World War Two. *(Public Domain US Army via Wikimedia Commons)*

A damaged C-47 transport lies in a field after crashing during delivery of supplies to the 101st Airborne Division. *(Public Domain US Army via Wikimedia Commons)*

of fire occurred during the airborne phase of Operation Overlord, the D-Day invasion of June 6, 1944. The division reached Britain in the autumn of 1943 with only the 502nd PIR and 327th Glider Infantry Regiment. Within weeks the 506th and 501st PIR augmented its strength. In Normandy, the 101st and 82nd Airborne Divisions were ordered to secure the western flank of the landing beaches.

Among the primary D-Day objectives were the narrow bridges, or causeways, that crossed marshes and lowlands just inland from Utah Beach, the westernmost of the Allied landing beaches. Securing four causeway exits from the beach itself would allow the US 4th Infantry Division to rapidly expand its lodgement in Normandy. The 502nd and 506th PIR, less one battalion, were to seize the causeways, while other elements of the 101st were to descend near the town of St. Martin-de-Varreville and destroy an emplacement of 122mm guns that might wreak havoc on Utah Beach, secure a lock on the River Douve near the town of Carentan and other objectives, and then link up with the US 4th Infantry Division approaching from Utah Beach.

Severe weather forced a 24-hour postponement of the D-Day operation, and when it commenced the weather remained far from ideal. The transport and glider aircraft approaching assigned drop and landing zones were buffeted by high winds, and German flak opened up with steady fire. Amid the difficult conditions, the insertion became scattered across a wide area. One entire stick of paratroopers from Company A, 502nd PIR was dropped into the English Channel and drowned. Others actually came down on Utah Beach, wading ashore after shedding their chutes and often losing all gear. General Don Pratt, assistant commander of the 101st, was among those killed in numerous glider crashes.

Radioman Hugh Pritchard came down in a marsh, momentarily plunging to the bottom in deep water with his pack and radio in a leg bag, 140 pounds of additional weight. His parachute billowed and dragged him to the surface and some distance afterward; only its collapse prevented Pritchard from drowning. Others were not so fortunate. In addition to the natural water hazards, the Germans had flooded many low-lying areas. At times troopers could not shed their heavy gear and drowned.

Here and there, paratroopers searched for one another, alone and in small groups. Troopers found themselves commingled, men of the 101st joining with men of the 82nd, and they set out as best as they could to achieve their objectives. The subsequent fight for the causeways was ferocious. Lieutenant Colonel Robert Cole, commanding the 502nd PIR, came down in an area assigned to the 82nd Airborne, but the officer proceeded to the expected position of the Soviet guns. After assembling a force of about 75 paratroopers, he found the guns had been moved, engaged in a sharp firefight that left 10 Germans killed, and then seized one of the causeways that was unguarded. Cole's troops ambushed Germans retreating from Utah Beach and linked up with the 8th Infantry Regiment, 4th Division at about 1 p.m. on June 6.

Elsewhere, the troopers of the 101st made significant contributions to the D-Day success. Elements of Lieutenant Colonel Patrick Cassidy's 1st Battalion, 502nd PIR cleaned out a group of buildings labelled as WXYZ on their maps, killing and capturing scores of Germans while also establishing a defensive line as planned. Troopers of the famed Easy Company, 506th PIR, led by Lieutenant Richard Winters, fought a textbook small unit action in silencing a battery of German 105mm guns at Brecourt Manor. Winters earned the Distinguished Service Cross in the fight. When D-Day came to a close, the 101st and 82nd Airborne Divisions had secured the western flank of the Allied invasion beaches, and the Screaming Eagles had suffered 1,300 killed or wounded.

During the week that followed, the 101st engaged in a terrific battle for control of Carentan, suffering heavy casualties but taking the crossroads town. Lieutenant Colonel Cole's bravery was conspicuous, and he earned the Medal of Honor, presented posthumously after his death during Operation Market Garden. Afterward, the 101st repulsed enemy counterattacks and held ground south of Carentan until relieved. After losing 4,670 men in Normandy during a month of sustained combat, the 101st was withdrawn to Britain.

General Maxwell Taylor, who had taken command of the 101st in May after General Lee suffered a heart attack, told his men, "You hit the ground running toward the enemy. You have proved the German soldier is no superman. You have beaten him on his own ground, and you can beat him on any ground."

Just weeks after its retirement to England to rest and refit after the fighting in Normandy, the 101st Airborne participated in Operation Market Garden, securing bridges and holding open

General Dwight D. Eisenhower, Supreme Commander of Allied Forces in Europe, talks with paratroopers of the 502nd Parachute Infantry Regiment, 101st Airborne Division prior to D-Day insertion. *(Public Domain US Army via Wikimedia Commons)*

Paratroopers of the 101st Airborne Division display a captured Nazi flag in Normandy. *(Public Domain US Army via Wikimedia Commons)*

Amid the initial confusion, General McAuliffe took the 101st, loaded aboard trucks, to the crossroads town of Bastogne, Belgium, where General Troy Middleton's VIII Corps was headquartered. McAuliffe obtained permission to remain at Bastogne, realising that holding the town would deny German forces a primary route of advance during their push to reach the bridges on the River Meuse and then the great port of Antwerp, Belgium, while driving a wedge between the Allied armies to the north and south.

During the critical ensuing days, the 101st held Bastogne along with elements of Combat Command B, 10th Armored Division, and other units against repeated German attacks. The situation was desperate as the paratroopers, short on ammunition, food, and winter clothing were hard pressed. At one point, a group of four Germans came to the Americans under a white flag and demanded the surrender of Bastogne's gallant garrison. McAuliffe was incensed and issued a reply that resonates in the history of the US Army.

A paratrooper of the 101st Airborne Division, right, enjoys a toast with another soldier at Berchtesgaden, Germany, in the last days of World War Two. *(Public Domain US Army via Wikimedia Commons)*

the northward route of XXX Corps during the airborne/ground offensive into The Netherlands. Although it was slated for withdrawal shortly after its role in Market Garden was completed, the 101st was called upon to defend the Nijmegen salient, or "the Island," due to a shortage of available infantry units. After 72 days in the line, the division was finally relieved, pulling back to rest at Mourmelon-le-Grand, France.

That respite was also quite short as the Germans launched their Ardennes Offensive on December 16, 1944, about 100 miles east of the 101st Airborne encampment. Along with the 82nd Airborne, the Screaming Eagles constituted the only readily available reserve to help stem the German onslaught that resulted in the Battle of the Bulge. With General Taylor attending a conference in Washington, DC, the division was under the temporary command of its artillery officer, General Anthony McAuliffe, who took early orders from General James Gavin, temporary commander of the XVIII Airborne Corps in the absence of General Matthew Ridgway, who was in England observing the training of the newly-arrived 17th Airborne Division.

General George S. Patton, Jr., presents the Distinguished Service Cross to General Anthony McAuliffe of the 101st Airborne Division for the defence of Bastogne. *(Public Domain US Army via Wikimedia Commons)*

He said simply, "To the German commander: "Nuts!" The American commander."

McAuliffe handed the typewritten note to Lieutenant Colonel Joseph Harper, commander of the 327th Glider Infantry Regiment, and remarked, "Will you see that it's delivered?" Harper grinned and responded, "I'll deliver it myself."

The epic stand of the 101st Airborne Division at Bastogne came to an end when the spearhead of the 4th Armored Division, Third US Army made contact with the defenders on December 26. During the fighting around Bastogne, the Screaming Eagles lost more than 1,600 casualties.

After gaining lasting fame during the Battle of the Bulge, the 101st Airborne Division moved into the French province of Alsace to conduct aggressive patrolling operations. By March 1945, the division was in the Ruhr mopping up pockets of German resistance and assisting with military government functions along the west bank of the River Rhine. At the end of April, the 101st was assigned to the US Seventh Army and participated in a sweeping advance through Bavaria, engaging in the race to occupy Hitler's mountain retreat at the Eagle's Nest, or Berghof, near the village of Berchtesgaden, and remaining in the vicinity during the last days of the war.

The 101st returned to France in August, and the use of two atomic bombs ended World War Two before any orders to prepare to deploy to the Pacific were received. When the division was deactivated in November 1945, it had served 214 days in combat and suffered more than 11,000 casualties while etching its name indelibly among the elite units of the US Army. ■

Transport aircraft drop supplies to the 101st Airborne Division at Bastogne during the Battle of the Bulge. *(Public Domain US Army via Wikimedia Commons)*

US AIRBORNE PROGRESS

airborne insertion, the seizure of objectives by lightly armed, fast moving formations, and their relief in a short period of time. Actually, the circular read, "Airborne troops should not be employed unless they can be supported by other ground or naval forces within approximately three days, or unless they can be withdrawn after their mission has been accomplished. No fire support, except from combat aviation, can be expected until contact is made with other forces."

The return on the investment of airborne forces could be calculated along with the risk, and when deemed appropriate, the paratroopers and glider troops were sent into action. They were equipped to perform their assigned tasks. They could hit hard and fast, but their very nature and makeup could not allow prolonged deployment in the field, often behind enemy lines, in the face of heavy and increasing enemy resistance.

The American airborne soldier was equipped to play his role in combat. Before heading into a fight, he was highly trained and expected to carry out orders without hesitation. He learned his craft through four phases of training, basic, individual technical parachute training, unit training, and combined training. Throughout the program, he could be disqualified for a breach

Heavily loaded American paratroopers prepare to exit their transport craft during training.
(Public Domain National Archives and Records Administration via Wikimedia Commons)

Combat loaded American airborne troops sit in the interior of a C-47 transport plane.
(Public Domain US Army Signal Corps Library of Congress via Wikimedia Commons)

The doctrine that governed deployment of US airborne forces in World War Two was codified in field manual *FM 30-31 Basic Field Manual: Tactics and Techniques of Air-borne Troops*, adopted on May 20, 1942.

Boldly, the field manual declared that airborne troops were the "spearhead of a vertical envelopment or the advance guard element of air landing troops or other forces." The primary mission of the airborne, then, was to take control of landing areas until relieved by stronger forces arriving by glider or other aircraft. Combat experience brought about a refinement of tactics, and in 1943, Training Circular No. 113 specified control of airborne troops under theatre commanders and then senior officers in areas of deployment.

With the refinement came several maxims that were to be followed with the commitment of airborne troops to combat. Among these were: the element of surprise must be present; parachute troops should not be used for missions that can be performed by other troops; the decision to use parachute troops should be made well in advance of the scheduled date of the operation; a comprehensive knowledge of the terrain involved in the operation is essential; local air superiority must exist; terrain objectives to be seized and held should lie in the path of the contemplated advance of friendly forces; and parachute troops should be relieved and withdrawn to their base as soon as practicable after the arrival of supporting ground forces.

In the actual use of paratroopers during World War Two, some incidents of modification – even disregard – of these maxims come readily to

mind, particularly in relation to Operation Market Garden and the Battle of the Bulge. Nevertheless, commanders and even individual soldiers always understood that the exigencies of war, the tactical situation on the ground, would not necessarily conform to the ideal as depicted in a manual. Training Circular No. 113 stated the obvious when considering the premise of

This display at the 82nd Airborne Division Museum, Fort Bragg, North Carolina, depicts some of the weapons used by US paratroopers during World War Two. *(Creative Commons Gary Todd via Wikimedia Commons)*

American soldiers fire a Browning M1919 .30-calibre machine gun in action against German troops. *(Public Domain US Signal Corps National Archives and Records Administration via Wikimedia Commons)*

The 75mm pack howitzer provided light artillery firepower to American airborne units in World War Two. *(Creative Commons via Wikimedia Commons)*

of instruction, including the refusal to go aloft for a scheduled jump, refusal to jump from a plane in flight, continued hesitancy or weak exits, tendency toward airsickness, hysteria, or extreme nervous condition prior to the jump, and more.

When a paratrooper had earned his coveted silver wings, he was quite familiar with every aspect of airborne warfare. His accoutrements were made available to accomplish his mission.

Every paratrooper was issued two-piece jump suits and jump boots. When fully equipped and ready, he carried a staggering array of materiel, and the field manual provided instructions for the location of each item from compass to gloves, rifle to hand grenades, ammunition, rations, map, pocketknife and toilet tissue. The average paratrooper carried 70 pounds of additional weight, and officers often carried kit weighing up to 90 pounds. If an individual trooper was assigned a specialised role, his burden might increase to 120 additional pounds. It was not uncommon for a fully laden trooper to require assistance to stand, walk, and to board an air transport plane. The paratrooper might also carry additional equipment in a canvas "leg bag" attached to the parachute harness and literally strapped to one of his legs.

The field manual specified that other items carried at times in addition to the standard kit included demolition equipment, signal equipment, bayonet, additional ammunition, medical equipment, and weapons components.

"The amount of equipment carried is limited to that which allows a safe rate of descent," it noted. "The type of equipment is limited by the fact that any protruding angular objects may foul the suspension lines of the canopy, and the possibility that such objects may cause serious injury to the parachutist, who may have to roll or tumble on landing." Additional supplies and equipment were sometimes dropped in one of numerous types of containers. These were tied together in an arrangement called a daisy chain.

The American paratrooper carried an array of standard weaponry that included the semiautomatic .30-calibre M-1 Garand rifle, one of the true war-winning weapons of the conflict, fed by an eight-round en bloc clip, and weighing nine and one-half pounds. Officers, headquarters and administrative personnel, and others sometimes carried the shorter and more compact .30-calibre M-1 Carbine, lighter at just over five pounds and fed by a detachable 15- or 30-round box magazine. The weight of the M1 Garand was its primary drawback, and

a canvas carrying case, called a "Griswold Bag," was issued for safe parachute deployment. When the rifle was placed in the bag, the stock was removed for easier carry, and the weapon could be quickly reassembled on the ground.

Heavier fire at the airborne squad level was provided by the .45-calibre Thompson submachine gun, which weighed 11 pounds but offered a high rate of fire at approximately 700 rounds per minute. The heavier M1918 .30-calibre Browning Automatic Rifle (BAR) was sometimes seen, but at more than 16 pounds it was quite a burden. The American paratrooper was further armed with Mk. 2 hand grenade, the familiar US pineapple explosive, the T2 rifle grenade, 60mm and 81mm mortars, the Browning M1919 .30-calibre light machine gun, the iconic Colt M1911 .45-calibre pistol, and additional ammunition.

One of the heaviest man-portable weapons often immediately available to paratroopers when confronted by enemy tanks, halftracks, or fixed strongpoints was the M1 rocket launcher, popularly known as the bazooka. The shoulder-fired weapon was normally operated by a team of two, and at 18 pounds it could be disassembled for easier carry. The bazooka fired a 60mm rocket capable of penetrating some armour and of destroying reinforced pillboxes and bunkers. The heaviest airborne artillery was the dependable 75mm pack howitzer, which was air transportable aboard a glider or delivered by parachute for rapid assembly in the combat zone.

The US airborne soldier was well-trained, well-equipped, and highly motivated. During combat, he exemplified a high degree of tactical dexterity and fighting proficiency. Inevitably, though, the airborne divisions were required at times to fight as infantry for extended periods, such as the defence of "the Island" in the wake of Operation Market Garden and deployment to the front lines by truck to bolster the Allied response to the German offensive during the Battle of the Bulge. ■

An American soldier rises to fire a bazooka at an enemy position. The shoulder-fired weapon was effective against tanks and strongpoints. *(Public Domain US Army via Wikimedia Commons)*

1ST INDEPENDENT
PARACHUTE
BRIGADE (POLAND)

When Poland was overrun in September 1939, many Polish soldiers and patriots evacuated the country and continued to fight the Nazis in the West. Then, with the fall of France in the spring of 1940 as many as 20,000 Polish soldiers were transported to locations in Scotland and other areas of the United Kingdom. These troops were under the control of General Wladyslaw Sikorski, prime minister of the Polish government-in-exile and commander-in-chief of its armed forces.

Among these expatriate military men, a number were accomplished in parachute training. Between the world wars, Poland had become a centre of parachute training and development, both in the military and among civilian enthusiasts. The Polish military became interested in the potential of airborne operations in the mid-1930s, probably prompted by concerns that the free city of Danzig, established under the terms of the Treaty of Versailles, might be a target for seizure by the aggressive Nazi regime in neighbouring Germany.

The Polish military established training facilities in several cities, and the primary installations were constructed at Bydgoszcz in the north of the country. Parachute towers were erected there, and the first training jumps took place in January 1939. In the spring, the Military Parachute Centre was established at the airfield in Bydgoszczc, and earlier a squadron of planes from the 4th Aviation Regiment had been allotted for airdrops. These aircraft were primarily the Fokker F.VII, also known as the Fokker Trimotor, a civilian airliner converted for military operations.

The first 80 Polish paratroopers completed their training in June 1939 after a rigorous course that included exercises in practice landings with the use of a trapeze from which the prospective paratroopers hung by their hands and rolled into forward, side and backward landings, jumps from the towers, and daylight and nocturnal live jumps from the Fokkers. The outbreak of World War Two disrupted plans for another 40 paratroopers to complete the training, but a number of the original graduates managed to escape the Nazi occupation.

At first, the Polish military personnel in the United Kingdom were concentrated in the vicinity of Glasgow, and plans for an expansion into armoured and airborne formations progressed with the support of then-Colonel

The flag of the 1st Independent Polish Parachute Brigade features its famous diving eagle. *(Creative Commons American1990 via Wikimedia Commons)*

Stanislaw Sosabowski, an advocate for the organisation of the airborne who would eventually lead the brigade into combat. Originally, the intent of this Polish military reconstitution was for the troops to fight in their homeland when an anticipated general uprising against the Nazis would one day be ignited.

In the autumn of 1941, the Polish airborne contingent was formalised initially as the Polish Parachute Brigade. By September, almost 400 Polish soldiers had received certification as parachutists by completing the British Army's training program at the Central Landing School, RAF Ringway, Manchester. The nucleus of the new parachute brigade was drawn from the 4th Rifle Brigade, although volunteers for airborne training came from many of the existing Polish units. Headquarters was established

Soldiers of the 1st Independent Polish Parachute Brigade prepare for ceremonies with the flag. *(Creative Commons Czeslaw Datka Republic of Poland via Wikimedia Commons)*

Troopers of the 1st Independent Polish Parachute Brigade read a map during exercises. *(Public Domain Republic of Poland via Wikimedia Commons)*

Polish paratroopers parade down a city street prior to their deployment in Operation Market Garden. *(Public Domain Poland National Digital Archives via Wikimedia Commons)*

In August 1944, the Polish Home Army initiated the Warsaw Uprising, and fighting erupted in the city's streets. The Poles in exile were anxious to return to their country and join the battle against the Nazis. However, the political situation was awkward amid restive relations between Prime Minister Winston Churchill and President Franklin D. Roosevelt in the West and Soviet Premier Josef Stalin in the East. Discussions at the highest levels had already occurred. General Sikorski had died in a plane crash a year earlier, and the loss of his influence had weighed on an agreement to transfer command of the brigade to the First Allied Airborne Army just weeks after the D-Day landings in Normandy. Many of the Polish paratroopers were disenchanted with the change, and promises that their brigade would eventually be airdropped to support the Warsaw Uprising rang hollow.

Subsequently, the brigade was relocated in the summer of 1944 to bases in East Anglia, closer to facilities of the British 1st Airborne Division in Wansford, Cambridgeshire. Soon enough, there were rumours and actual plans for the brigade to participate in airborne operations in France or Belgium. However, the rapid advance of Allied ground forces led to their cancellation or later revision. Finally, by mid-September 1944, the prospect of deployment became real for the officers and men of the 1st Polish Independent Parachute Brigade with Operation Market Garden. ◼

at Largo House in Leven, a seaside town in Fife in the Central Lowlands of Scotland.

The Poles built their training centre on the grounds of Largo House, constructing parachute towers and installing an assault training course that was nicknamed the "Monkey Grove." Static jumps were made from a tower that replicated one the Poles had previously built in their homeland. During the course of the war, troops from several countries, including the Free French, underwent basic airborne training under the supervision of the Poles while also completing the four-week course at RAF Ringway.

When the Polish soldiers completed their airborne training, they received a silver badge depicting a diving eagle and emblazoned on the reverse with the motto "For You My Country." The Poles were outfitted with the British airborne kit and standard uniforms, stencilling their distinctive eagle emblem in yellow on the rimless helmets and wearing unique badges and emblems that identified them as separate. Unlike the British airborne, they donned a grey beret that further set them apart from their hosts.

By 1944, the airborne unit had been renamed the 1st Polish Independent Parachute Brigade and numbered more than 3,000 men. On the eve of Operation Market Garden, the brigade consisted of three parachute battalions each with three companies, as well as engineer, medical, signals, and transport and supply companies, and anti-tank and light artillery batteries. In June 1944, the brigade is said to have received its unit's colours, hand sewn by a group of women in occupied Warsaw two years earlier, consecrated in a church in the Polish capital city, and then secretly sent to the paratroopers in the United Kingdom.

Although the original premise for the organisation of the Polish forces had been to fight the Nazis in Poland, the exigencies of war and political influence intervened. The logistics of transporting combat troops – particularly airborne forces – and deploying them from Western Europe to Poland appeared impractical while the limited availability of air transport was a prominent factor in changing the mission of the 1st Independent Parachute Brigade.

During training exercises in Scotland, Polish paratroopers fire a light mortar. *(Public Domain Poland National Digital Archives via Wikimedia Commons)*

A squad of Polish paratroopers conducts manoeuvres, one firing a Lee-Enfield rifle and another a Bren Gun. *(Public Domain Poland National Digital Archives via Wikimedia Commons)*

FIELD MARSHAL BERNARD L. MONTGOMERY

F ield Marshal Bernard L. Montgomery, the most prominent British soldier of World War Two, was without doubt a moulder and shaper of the course of the great conflict.

Montgomery's wartime career is marked with many milestones, those of courage and leadership in the midst of defeat at Dunkirk, triumph and discord in Sicily and Italy, sentinel victories in North Africa and Normandy, of rivalries with contemporaries, and of stubborn determination in every aspect of his command. He was the father of the ill-fated Operation Market Garden, and in the execution of that ambitious drive across the waterways of the southern Netherlands, he had hoped to crown his career with the war-winning master stroke the would seize the Ruhr, the industrial nexus of the Third Reich, and end the war by Christmas 1944.

Montgomery is remembered well for his extraordinary organisational skills. He was the cerebral and technical architect of the set piece battle. Such skills were often on display in the desert of North Africa and elsewhere. Therefore, the swiftness with which Market Garden came together and its aggressive, sensitive timetable are seen by historians as a striking departure from the field marshal's standard operating procedure. From risk averse to high stakes gambler, he believed in Market Garden, and even after its failure he defended the gains that were made.

In early September 1944, Montgomery had come up with a plan he called Operation Comet. Somewhat limited in scope, it involved the seizure of bridges in the southern Netherlands. Although it failed to receive enough support to be launched, Operation Comet was a primer for the expanded Market Garden that did move ahead, combining both British and American airborne strength with a critical thrust by the veteran XXX Corps on the ground.

Market Garden was perilous, risky business, but Montgomery believed in it. He was then persuasive enough to gain the approval of General Dwight D. Eisenhower, supreme commander of Allied forces in Europe. The sceptics, those who questioned the probability for success and even labelled the offensive as foolhardy, were shunted aside. Their concerns were muted by the lustre of the prize that Montgomery saw at Arnhem, a little town in Holland, where the last of several bridges would, when it was in his hands, serve as the conduit for the final dagger thrust that would bring down the black hearted Nazis.

Bernard Law Montgomery was born at St. Mark's Vicarage, Kennington Oval, London, on November 17, 1887, the son of Henry Montgomery, a minister of the Church of Ireland, and Maud Farrar Montgomery, many years junior to her husband. The mother was a domineering persona, mostly devoid of affection, who

Pictured in 1943, Field Marshal Bernard Montgomery was the author of Operation Market Garden. *(Public Domain collections of the Imperial War Museums via Wikimedia Commons)*

While commanding V Corps in England, General Montgomery meets with war correspondents. *(Public Domain collections of the Imperial War Museums via Wikimedia Commons)*

regularly beat her children. Upon her death in 1949, the field marshal declined to attend her funeral, and during her lifetime, he forbade his son, David to have any association with her.

The family lived several years in the British colony of Tasmania, and upon return to England Montgomery finished his education at King's College, Canterbury, and St. Paul's School, London, then opting for the Royal Military Academy, Sandhurst, and a military career. He was frequently in hot water for disciplinary infractions but managed to graduate in 1908. Although disappointed when his academic performance precluded assignment to the Indian Army, he accepted a commission in the Royal Warwickshire Regiment. While serving with the 1st Battalion in India, he rose to lieutenant.

With the outbreak of the Great War, Montgomery's 1st Battalion moved to France, and he was shot in the chest during action along the Belgian frontier in October 1914. He recovered, received the Distinguished

In this photo from October 1918, Minister of Munitions Winston Churchill attends a review of the 47th Division. The division's chief of staff, Lieutenant Colonel Bernard Montgomery is shown at extreme left. *(Public Domain collections of the Imperial War Museums via Wikimedia Commons)*

In this 1940 photo, 3rd Division commander Major General Bernard Montgomery stands at left with II Corps commander Lieutenant General Alan Brooke and Major General Dudley Johnson of the 4th Division. (Public Domain collections of the Imperial War Museums via Wikimedia Commons)

Perhaps the most famous photo of Montgomery depicts him peering from the turret of a tank in the North African desert, 1942. (Public Domain US Department of Defense via Wikimedia Commons)

and I thanked Heaven to have a commander of his calibre to undertake this march."

Montgomery assumed temporary corps command on the continent and then of V and XII Corps in England. In preparation for an anticipated Nazi invasion of the British Isles, he led South-Eastern Command. Through it all, he maintained an air of abruptness and disdain for those he deemed inadequate. Early in World War Two, Brooke wrote him a letter with an admonition. "I know you well enough also, Monty, to give you a word of warning against doing wild things. You have a name for annoying people at times with your ways, and I have found difficulties in backing you at times against this reputation."

Personality conflicts aside, Montgomery's star continued to rise. When General William "Strafer" Gott's plane was shot down in North Africa and he was killed en route to take command of the Eighth Army in Egypt, Monty was chosen as the alternative. His plane touched down in Cairo on August 12, 1942, and after months of planning, reinforcement, and replenishing of his troops along with the introduction of sufficient armoured vehicles, he executed the brilliant victory at El Alamein in October.

From there, Montgomery and Eighth Army pursued the German-Italian forces of Panzerarmee Afrika across hundreds of miles of desert, destroying the myth of legendary Field Marshal Erwin Rommel's invincibility. Operation Torch introduced a two-front war in North Africa, and by the spring of 1943, the Allies were masters of the African shores.

Montgomery went on to play a key role in Operation Husky, the Sicily campaign, and then the invasion of the Italian mainland. Along the way he and US General George S. Patton, Jr., clashed in epic fashion. Both men were arrogant and at times insufferable.

Monty was withdrawn from Italy in December 1943 to join the staff of General Eisenhower during the planning for Operation Overlord, the D-Day invasion of Normandy. He was selected to lead the Allied ground troops ashore on June 6, 1944, and his enthusiastic endorsement for going ahead with the invasion during appalling weather was inspirational to those around him. When Eisenhower asked each of his lieutenants for their opinion, Monty, without hesitation, crowed, "I would say go!"

During the fight for the crossroads and communications centre of Caen in Normandy,

Service Order for gallantry along with promotion to captain and then major, and ended the war as chief of staff of the 47th Division with the rank of lieutenant colonel.

Montgomery received steady promotion even during the languid interwar years. He was given greater responsibility, it seems, even by those who did not personally find his demeanour to their liking. He managed to wrangle a slot at the War College, Camberley, during a conversation at a tennis party with General Sir "Wully" Robinson, former Chief of the Imperial General Staff (CIGS). He held various staff positions, returning to Camberley as deputy assistant adjutant general and with his old 1st Battalion, Royal Warwickshire Regiment, and later as an instructor at the Military Staff College in Quetta, India. He was promoted

brigadier and given command of the 9th Infantry Brigade in the summer of 1937, but the death of his wife, Betty, that year cast a pall over the remainder of his personal life and probably led to a redoubling of his effort to advance in the military.

As the British Expeditionary Force was evacuating at Dunkirk in the dark, early days of World War Two, Major General Montgomery led the 3rd Division with tactical proficiency. General Alan Brooke, commander of II Corps and future CIGS, recognised talent while also acknowledging that Montgomery was possessed with a towering ego.

"There is no doubt that one of Monty's strong points is his boundless confidence in himself," wrote Brooke of the 1940 Dunkirk evacuation manoeuvres. "He was priceless on this occasion,

Montgomery plays with his pet puppies named 'Hitler' and 'Rommel' in France in 1944. (Public Domain collections of the Imperial War Museums via Wikimedia Commons)

Montgomery tried for weeks to take the town that had been an immediate D-Day objective. Some conjecture surrounds that lofty goal, but in the weeks that followed he did pull much of the German armoured strength upon his 21st Army Group, facilitating the breakout from the Normandy beachhead to the south during Operation Cobra.

Later that decisive summer, Montgomery's army group participated in the resounding defeat of the Germans at Falaise. Although he had been required to give up overall ground command as American General Omar Bradley took over 12th Army Group, Prime Minister Winston Churchill pushed through his promotion to field marshal.

By autumn, Montgomery and Patton had renewed their rivalry, and their persistent spats over supply priorities were a continuing thorn in Eisenhower's side. Still, 21st Army Group conducted operations to capture French ports on the English Channel coast and then the deepwater port of Antwerp, Belgium, a considerable distance up the estuary of the River Scheldt from the open sea.

When Antwerp was liberated on September 4, 1944, Montgomery was already contemplating

During a meeting with King George VI at his mobile headquarters in France on October 13, 1944, Field Marshal Montgomery points out a location on a map. Operation Market Garden had ended just weeks earlier. *(Public Domain collections of the Imperial War Museums via Wikimedia Commons)*

General Montgomery shakes hands with his bitter rival, US General George S. Patton, Jr., in Sicily. *(Public Domain US Army via Wikimedia Commons)*

his blueprint for Operation Comet and then Market Garden. Recent experience in Italy and Normandy had revealed the dangers of airborne operations, and even though the many Allied officers believed the German Army was a spent shell of a force, it was conceivable that a ground thrust into The Netherlands would meet stiff enemy opposition. Montgomery still believed the potential for success was worth the investment of precious lives and materiel.

Although there was considerable opposition, it was overcome. Once the die was cast there was no turning back. Even reports of a concentration of German tanks and armoured vehicles in the vicinity of Arnhem failed to derail the Market Garden express. It was in the event that the shortcomings of the plan were laid bare. Speed was of utmost importance. Lightly armed airborne troops could not be

expected to hold bridges indefinitely. There was the narrow single highway that XXX Corps was obliged to transit. There was adverse weather with which to contend. Resupply by air was an inherently haphazard proposition.

And, of course, the Germans would have something to do with the success or failure of the airborne/ground offensive. They did, in fact, display tremendous resilience after recovering from the shock at such Allied audacity. They blew bridges sky high. They stymied the progress of the 1st Airborne Division at Oosterbeek, bottled up the 2nd Battalion, Parachute Regiment at Arnhem, and at times slowed the XXX Corps advance to a standstill.

Nevertheless, Montgomery said that Market Garden was 90 percent successful. He defended the operation in his 1958 memoir and was its proponent to his dying day.

During the final months of the war, Montgomery led 21st Army Group in helping to eliminate the German salient during the Battle of the Bulge and across the Rhine. His troops encircled more than 350,000 enemy soldiers in the Ruhr Pocket, and on May 4, 1945, he accepted the surrender of enemy forces in northern Germany, The Netherlands, and Denmark.

After the war, Montgomery was a national hero. However, he never tamed his love of self. Churchill once said that the great commander was "in defeat, unbeatable: in victory, unbearable." He was free with his criticism of the performance of Eisenhower and other former Allied senior officers. Still, by the end of his career in 1958, he had received copious honours, succeeded Brooke as CIGS, and been raised to the peerage as Viscount Montgomery of Alamein.

Montgomery commanded the postwar British Army of the Rhine and served as Eisenhower's deputy in the early days of the NATO alliance. He never smoked or consumed alcohol while maintaining his Christian faith and died, one of the pivotal personages of World War Two, in Isington, Hampshire, aged 88, on March 24, 1976. ■

With the Brandenburg Gate in the background, Field Marshal Montgomery walks through Berlin on July 12, 1945. He is flanked on left and right by Soviet Marshals Georgi Zhukov and Konstantin Rokossovsky. *(Public Domain collections of the Imperial War Museums via Wikimedia Commons)*

GENERAL FREDERICK 'BOY' BROWNING

When the Horsa glider came to a skidding stop in a cabbage patch at the edge of the Reichswald forest, a wheel ripped away by an electric cable, its passengers were shaken but otherwise unhurt.

A single figure quickly emerged and bounded toward a clump of trees to relieve himself. Lieutenant General Frederick "Boy" Browning returned with a grin on his face and quipped, "I wanted to be the first British officer to pee in Germany." And so, the deputy commander of the Allied First Airborne Army had arrived in The Netherlands during the opening hours of Operation Market Garden.

Browning had been an advocate of Market Garden and ever since has borne a significant share of the blame for its failure. Actually, he had offered an honest assessment to Field Marshal Bernard Montgomery when the ambitious airborne/ground offensive was first presented to him on September 10. When Browning asked Montgomery how long the 1st Airborne Division was expected to hold the bridge across the Lower Rhine at Arnhem before relief would arrive in the form of XXX Corps, Montgomery replied, "Two days."

Browning countered that the "Red Devils" could hold for four days and then is believed to have uttered the succinct appraisal of Market Garden that has lived in history: "Sir, I think we may be going a bridge too far."

Nevertheless, Lieutenant General Browning offered support for Market Garden, even

After returning to England from Normandy in the summer of 1944, General Frederick 'Boy' Browning poses in front of a C-47 Dakota of RAF Transport Command. *(Public Domain collections of the Imperial War Museums via Wikimedia Commons)*

Lieutenant General Frederick 'Boy' Browning served as deputy commander of the Allied First Airborne Army during Operation Market Garden. *(Public Domain collections of the Imperial War Museums via Wikimedia Commons)*

after intelligence reports began to filter into headquarters that two powerful German SS panzer divisions were in the vicinity of Arnhem, their tanks and armoured vehicles potentially positioned to devastate the lightly armed paratroopers of the 1st Airborne Division. Browning was a brave officer, a decorated veteran of World War One, and he relished the opportunity to lead troops in combat on such a grand scale.

Criticism of Browning's performance before and during Market Garden began early. Some officers questioned the need for the deputy commander's headquarters to take to the field. Not only did it place a high-echelon command in harm's way, but it also deprived the Allied airborne forces of more than 30 gliders, critical transport vehicles for their troop deployment. Still, Browning packed his glider full. Among his personal belongings were three teddy bears and a print of Renaissance artist Albrecht Dürer's Praying Hands that he had carried since the Great War.

The unfolding of Operation Market Garden indeed defined the career of General Browning, a career worthy of tremendous praise but also subject to scrutiny and searing disapproval. Although the shadow of Market Garden looms over that career of more than 30 years, Browning is rightly considered the "father" of the British airborne forces. By the autumn of 1944, he had developed a reputation as a courageous soldier, persuasive lobbyist, capable administrator, and an officer willing to

General Browning observes airborne training at Netheravon, Wiltshire. Note the distinctive airborne shoulder flash that he introduced. *(Public Domain collections of the Imperial War Museums via Wikimedia Commons)*

pull strings to leverage strong relationships, both military and civilian, to achieve his objectives.

Known to his family as Tommy, Frederick Arthur Montague Browning was born December 20, 1896, in Kensington, London, the second child of wine merchant Frederick Henry Browning and Ann Alt, the daughter of distinguished scientist and author George Earl Alt. Educated at the Downs School in Winchester and prestigious Eton College, where he was an outstanding athlete but mediocre student, Tommy sat for the entrance examination to the Royal Military College, Sandhurst, in November 1914. He passed the English and French sections

General Frederick 'Boy' Browning escorts King George VI during a 1942 visit to Southern Command. Here the general describes the operation of a Jeep-mounted Vickers machine gun. *(Public Domain collections of the Imperial War Museums via Wikimedia Commons)*

General Browning confers with General Stanislaw Sosabowski, commander of the Polish 1st Independent Parachute Brigade. Their relationship was always contentious. *(Public Domain Republic of Poland via Wikimedia Commons)*

belt of the Grenadier Guards. He introduced the famed maroon beret and airborne shoulder flash depicting the Greek hero Bellerophon riding the winged horse Pegasus. He qualified as a glider pilot at age 46 but made only two parachute jumps, sustaining slight injuries both times.

In the summer of 1942, Browning travelled to the United States to confer with his American airborne counterparts. His somewhat haughty bearing set the tone of a tempestuous relationship with U.S. senior commanders that persisted throughout World War Two. He was impressed with American resources and training but at times seemed to be lecturing his hosts, although they had more airborne experience than the British. Browning later acknowledged that he may have come across as overbearing, but the damage was done.

In the spring of 1943, Browning relinquished direct command of the 1st Airborne Division to serve as Advisor on Airborne Training and Operations to the headquarters of General Dwight D. Eisenhower, Supreme Commander of Allied Forces in the Mediterranean and later

but failed History and Geography. Still, this was wartime, and Eton headmaster Edward Lyttleton was authorised to recommend individuals to the Army Council for appointment, which he did.

Tommy graduated from Sandhurst on June 16, 1915, the product of an accelerated program due to the need for officers in the field, and received a commission as a 2nd lieutenant in the prestigious Grenadier Guards. It is likely that he gained his nickname of "Boy" during this period as he bore a striking resemblance to another Guards officer already called "Boy" or possibly to distinguish himself from his father. On one memorable occasion future Prime Minister Winston Churchill was assigned as an officer in Browning's 2nd Battalion, arriving at the front without his greatcoat. Browning saw the shivering Churchill and offered his own. Churchill never forgot the kind gesture.

At the Battle of Cambrai in 1917, Browning assumed command of the remnants of companies whose officers had been killed or wounded in the heat of combat and consolidated gains of tactically important ground. He received the Distinguished Service Order, a rare acknowledgement for a junior officer, and some observers asserted that his heroism was only just short of the Victoria Cross. Promoted captain in 1920, Browning developed a sharp manner of speech and professionalism. Those who did not know him often mistook such conduct for arrogance and aloofness.

Although his temper was volcanic, it quickly subsided, and he was known throughout the army for his reputation of fairness.

Between the world wars, Browning served as an instructor at Sandhurst and competed in the bobsleigh competition in the 1928 Winter Olympics at St. Moritz, Switzerland. He was an outstanding hurdler, narrowly missing an opportunity to compete in earlier Olympic games, and his maintained a lifelong love of sailing. On July 19, 1932, Browning married acclaimed author Daphne du Maurier. They had three children, remained married for 33 years, and often led separate lives.

With the outbreak of World War Two, Browning was a brigadier in command of the Small Arms School. He narrowly missed combat during the Battle of France in 1940, but in October Prime Minister Churchill appointed him General Officer Commanding of the newly-formed 1st Airborne Division. Although the idea of airborne forces was in its infancy in Britain, its foundation already laid by other visionary officers, Browning capitalised on the opportunity to shape a division from its inception. His work ethic, organisational skill and dash make him worthy of the title "father" of the British airborne.

General Browning enacted a rigorous training regimen and was determined to make the airborne an elite force that exuded esprit de corps. He designed his own uniform with swagger stick and the polished Sam Browne

Lieutenant General Frederick 'Boy' Browning consults with Brigadier General James Gavin, commander of the US 82nd Airborne Division, during Operation Market Garden. *(Creative Commons collection of Regional Archives Nijmegen via Wikimedia Commons)*

all of Western Europe. While he had little direct influence on airborne operations, Browning rightly predicted that the glider portion of the airborne phase of Operation Husky, the invasion of Sicily that summer, would be disastrous. By August he was assessing the progress of the newly-formed 6th Airborne Division and became involved in discussions for the airborne phase of the D-Day invasion of Normandy.

As commander of the British 1st Airborne Corps, Browning led the 1st and 6th Airborne Divisions, the Special Air Service Brigade, the 52nd Lowland Division, and the 1st Polish Independent Parachute Brigade. When Eisenhower authorised the formation of the First Allied Airborne Army, he considered Browning for command. However, the post was instead given to American General Lewis Brereton – probably to fend off the vocal displeasure of American officers in their distaste for Browning. Appointment as deputy commander was no balm to Browning's wound, and it irritated General Matthew Ridgway, commander of the U.S. XVIII Airborne Corps. In the coming months, Browning's relationship with Brereton, Ridgway, and other U.S. officers steadily deteriorated. At one point, Browning offered to resign, only to back down when he discovered that Brereton was quite willing to accept.

Eager to deploy the First Airborne Army, Brereton was livid when he discovered that Browning had already conducted extensive talks with Montgomery and British 2nd Army Commander General Miles Dempsey behind his back and committed his airborne corps to Operation Comet, the forerunner of Market Garden. As tactical command for Market Garden was shaped, the personality clash made cooperation more difficult. At the same time, relations between Browning and General Stanislaw Sosabowski, commander of the Polish 1st Independent Parachute Brigade, reached

This photo of acclaimed author Daphne du Maurier, wife of General Browning, was taken about 1930. *(Public Domain автор неизвестен/ author unknown free use via Wikimedia Commons)*

General Browning addresses the crowd during a celebration of victory in Europe on the island of Ceylon in 1945. *(Public Domain collections of the Imperial War Museums via Wikimedia Commons)*

a low point. Ridgway's hard feelings were then compounded when Browning was chosen to run the airborne phase of Market Garden.

During the run-up to Market Garden, Browning was faced with the challenges of high-level command decision-making, and therein lies the substance of his harshest criticism. When intelligence officer Urquhart (no relation to the 1st Airborne Division commander) came to him with disturbing photographic evidence of the presence of the German 9th "Hohenstaufen" and 10th "Frundsberg" SS Panzer Divisions in the vicinity of Arnhem, Browning declined to raise the alarm that the enemy tanks and panzergrenadiers might pose a serious threat while they refitted in The Netherlands after being roughly handled in Normandy.

While Browning has borne much of the criticism – or blame – for allowing Market Garden to proceed, he was not the only Allied officer to become aware of the SS concentration around Arnhem, and he had no individual authority to call off the operation. Nevertheless, he suggested that Urquhart take sick leave due to "nervous strain and exhaustion" and did not speak up.

Further, once Browning's headquarters was on the ground in The Netherlands it was proven wholly unprepared for tactical operations. He admitted to the handicap and wrote, "My staff is almost more inefficient than I could possibly imagine now [that] we are in the field – I suppose it's due to people being pushed up the tree too quickly without sufficient experience..."

One bright spot that emerged from the ordeal of Market Garden was the cooperation between Browning and Brigadier General James M. Gavin, the 37-year-old commander of the U.S. 82nd Airborne Division, during operations around Nijmegen. Browning's chief of staff Brigadier Gordon Walch, reported, "The mutual trust and respect shown by General Boy and General Jim Gavin working closely together... was particularly good to see."

Still, in the wake of the Market Garden, Browning sought the relief of General Sosabowski

ostensibly due to issues with their working relationship. However, some historians believe that Browning served up Sosabowski as a potential scapegoat for the setbacks experienced in attempting to reinforce the 1st Airborne Division at Arnhem. Interestingly, Montgomery placed no public blame on Browning for the failure, but Browning received no further promotion in its aftermath.

Browning was soon posted as chief of staff to Admiral Lord Louis Mountbatten in Southeast Asia Command, and his performance received praise. After the war, he served as Military Secretary and then as Treasurer to the Household of Princess Elizabeth. He formally retired from the military in April 1948, then served as treasurer to the Duke of Edinburgh with a spacious office in Buckingham Palace.

A heavy smoker and avid drinker, Browning suffered a severe decline in health during his later years, including a nervous breakdown in 1957. He is thought to have contemplated suicide during an extreme bout of depression and retired from public life at age 62. He died of a heart attack on March 14, 1965, at Menabilly estate in Cornwall.

When eminent historian and author Cornelius Ryan began research for his bestselling book *A Bridge Too Far* in 1967, he contacted Daphne du Maurier, who offered that Browning had expressed regret for the loss of life during Market Garden, although he had rarely spoken of the period.

Daphne supposedly considered Ryan's treatment of her husband fair and reasonable. However, the film adaptation of the book was not so generous. Released in 1977, the film *A Bridge Too Far* featured actor Dirk Bogarde as General Browning, and the screenplay casts the airborne commander as a "fall guy," more so than many other officers who were perhaps equally or even more responsible for the failure of Operation Market Garden.

One former associate summed up the movie experience squarely in defence of General Browning. "He was not like that at all and could not have commanded such widespread loyalty if he had been." ■

General Browning looks on as King George VI inspects rations issued to airborne troops during a 1944 visit to headquarters of the 1st Airborne Division. *(Public Domain collections of the Imperial War Museums)*

General Roy Urquhart is seated at centre in this photo of the 1st Airborne Division headquarters staff taken sometime in 1944. *(Public Domain United Kingdom Government via Wikimedia Commons)*

GENERAL ROY
URQUHART

Major General Roy Urquhart, commander of the 1st Airborne Division, stands in front of his headquarters during Operation Market Garden. *(Public Domain collections of the Imperial War Museums via Wikimedia Commons)*

Cut down by German machine-gun fire as he observed an assault against an enemy strongpoint during fighting in Italy on September 9, 1943, Major General George Hopkinson, commander of the 1st Airborne Division, was the only British airborne general killed in World War Two.

After word of Hopkinson's death reached the headquarters of the I Airborne Corps,

General Urquhart salutes during a review of troops in late 1945. *(Creative Common Fotograaf Onbekend / Anefo via Wikimedia Commons)*

Allied 1st Airborne Army, discussions began immediately as to a capable replacement. When the most likely successor to Hopkinson, Brigadier Eric Down, was sent to form a new airborne division in India, the airborne command establishment was in a quandary.

Reports indicated that Brigadier Roy Urquhart had commanded the 231st Infantry Brigade with great skill in Sicily and Italy. There was just a wrinkle or two… Urquhart had never parachuted from an airplane or ridden into combat aboard a glider… and he was prone to air sickness. No matter. Urquhart was the man for the job. General Frederick "Boy" Browning, deputy commander of the 1st Airborne Army, made the decision.

No one was more surprised by the appointment than Urquhart himself. He believed, and rightly so, that the airborne had been a close-knit enclave within the British Army and that officers selected to senior command had historically been appointed from within. Nevertheless, newly-promoted Major General Urquhart took charge of the 1st Airborne Division on January 7, 1944.

When he assumed the post, Urquhart, a 43-year-old Scotsman, felt duty bound to qualify as a parachutist. He approached Browning about the matter and received a characteristically blunt reply. Browning looked Urquhart up and down, taking not of his rather bulky physique, and commented, "I shouldn't worry about learning to parachute. Your job is to prepare this division for the invasion of Europe. Not only are you too big for parachuting but you

are also getting on." Urquhart was six feet tall and weighed a substantial 200 pounds.

Despite Browning's admonition to prepare the Red Devils for combat, the immediate job for Urquhart was to earn the respect of the officers and men of the 1st Airborne Division. The new commander felt he was being scrutinised at every turn, and one of his subordinates had even been unofficially informed that when Urquhart failed to achieve command and control confidence that the division would be passed on to him. It is, therefore, a tribute to the constitution of the man that had never jumped that he did indeed gain that vital confidence of the "Red Devils" from officers to individual rank-and-file.

Sergeant Roy Hatch, a glider pilot, said that Urquhart was "a bloody general who didn't mind doing the job of a sergeant." Colonel John Frost, who earned everlasting fame in command of 2 Para at Arnhem, remembered the early days of Urquhart's command tenure in England, offering that he "...was not a man to court popularity and, largely owing to the way the Division was dispersed all over Lincolnshire, we did not see him as much as we would have liked, but he very soon earned our complete respect and trust. In fact, few generals have been so sorely tested and have yet prevailed."

Urquhart was true to form during the opening hours of Operation Market Garden. When a young signalman asked for help dragging a heavy radio battery from a supply trench, he had turned to the nearest soldier and Urquhart obliged. After the first battery was brought out, the signalman asked for help with a second. Again, the general pitched in. Finally, the young signalman realised that his helper was Urquhart himself and offered an apology. The general simply replied, "That's all right son."

Robert Elliott "Roy" Urquhart was born in Shepperton, Middlesex, on November 28, 1901, the son of a Scottish physician, and attended St. Paul's School in London and the Royal Military Academy, Sandhurst. He was commissioned as a 2nd lieutenant in the Highland Light Infantry in 1920, made first lieutenant in two years, and then five long years later was promoted captain, symptomatic of the slow rate of promotion in the peacetime, inter-war British Army. He served in Malta, Palestine, and India and became Deputy Assistant Quartermaster General of the Indian Army in the spring of 1939.

With World War Two well underway, Urquhart transferred to England from Egypt in 1941 as a staff officer with the 3rd Infantry Division. Promoted lieutenant colonel, he commanded the 2nd Battalion, Duke of Cornwall Light Infantry and then took charge of the 231st Infantry Brigade before returning to Britain as a staff officer with the XII Corps. Then came the fateful appointment to lead the Red Devils.

General Urquhart, seen over the right shoulder of Field Marshal Bernard Montgomery, walks with a group of officers during a visit to the 133rd Parachute Field Ambulance at Oakham, March 1944. (Public Domain Paradata UK via Wikimedia Commons)

During preparations for Operation Market Garden, General Urquhart continually lobbied for as many transport aircraft as possible. When he put in a request, he was regularly told that the American airborne divisions were receiving larger numbers of planes due to the fact that they were going in closest to the XXX Corps start line. The 101st in particular, would be inserting the bulk of its manpower in the first lift to help assure the capture of the important bridges during the early hours of the "Garden" ground phase of the offensive. Failure to do so might have meant that the airborne forces further north would be cut off and annihilated. Therefore, Urquhart was insistent that most important equipment should be loaded for the initial insertion of the 1st Airborne Division, specifically referencing anti-tank weapons.

In the event, just about everything that could go wrong for the Red Devils during Market Garden did. Urquhart's command was inserted eight miles from the Arnhem bridge. Covering that distance was, in itself, a handicap, and the commander apparently did not vigorously oppose the plan. Communications difficulties emerged when it was discovered that radio equipment was largely inoperable. When Urquhart ventured away from his division headquarters in the field, he was cut off and spent some desperate hours hiding from the Germans in various houses on the outskirts of Arnhem. When Operation Market Garden was over, the effort to capture the bridge across the Lower Rhine had failed after nine agonizing days. However, Urquhart and the 1st Airborne Division had fought bravely. Colonel Frost's 2 Para, the only battalion to reach the bridge at Arnhem, became legendary in its dogged fight.

After sustaining heavy losses in Market Garden, the 1st Airborne Division did not see combat again during World War Two. When the war ended, Urquhart led the division to Norway, where its troopers handled the repatriation of German prisoners and facilitated the reestablishment of the Norwegian government.

Major General Urquhart retired in 1955 after holding several divisional commands, service as General Officer Commanding Malay Command, and then leading British troops in Australia. He died on December 12, 1988, at the age of 87. Portrayed by distinguished actor Sean Connery in the motion picture *A Bridge Too Far*, he had served as an advisor during its filming. ■

Proudly wearing his medals, General Roy Urquhart stands at right as Queen Beatrix of The Netherlands pats future King Charles III on the back during commemorations of the Battle of Arnhem in 1984. (Creative Commons Rob Croes / Anefo via Wikimedia Commons)

During ceremonies commemorating the 1944 fighting at Arnhem, General Urquhart stands at far right with other dignitaries at the Church of St. Eusebius, also known as the Grote Kerk, in the city. (Creative Commons Rob Croes for Anefo via Wikimedia Commons)

GENERAL BRIAN HORROCKS

The veteran commander of XXX Corps remembered the instant when he realised that Operation Market Garden would end with the decimation of the 1st Airborne Division at Arnhem.

"It was the blackest moment of my life," said General Brian Horrocks years later. Always leading men with panache, he was not accustomed to such loss. With the inception of Market Garden, he had been more than willing to take on the fight up the narrow road to relieve the three airborne divisions holding the highway open from northern Belgium to the Lower Rhine. Still, he had some concerns.

The terrain would pose a challenge, and then, of course, there were the Germans even though intelligence reports said their fighting prowess was rather feeble and they had few tanks to oppose the strength of XXX Corps. "I was uneasy that this vast operation was starting on a Sunday," he commented afterward. "Not, I am afraid, on account of any religious scruples, but because no attack which I had launched on a Sunday had ever been completely successful."

Horrocks further assessed, "I knew that it would be a very tough battle; especially so, owing to the nature of the country, with its numerous water obstacles and the single main road available for thousands of vehicles; but failure never even entered my head."

Actually, until Market Garden, the XXX Corps commander had rarely tasted failure, military or otherwise, and when he had seen setbacks his resilience was remarkable.

Born at Ranniket, a remote hill station in British India, on September 7, 1895, Brian Gwynne Horrocks, was the son of an Army doctor from Lancashire. His father, Willaim Heaton Horrocks,

Seated inside the turret of a Covenanter tank, General Brian Horrocks confers with an officer during 9th Armoured Division exercises in the summer of 1942. *(Public Domain collections of the Imperial War Museums via Wikimedia Commons)*

was knighted for service as Director of Army Hygiene during World War One. His mother was of Irish descent. Educated in England preparatory schools, Brian enjoyed sports more than academics, ranking near the bottom of his class at the Royal Military Academy, Sandhurst. Passing through on the eve of the Great War, he received a 2nd lieutenant's commission in the Middlesex Regiment just before the outbreak of hostilities.

While leading the 16th Platoon of the famed "Die-Hard" Regiment during the First Battle of Ypres in October 1914, Horrocks was seriously wounded in the stomach and taken prisoner. He remained a POW for most of the next four years, save intermittent periods of freedom due to numerous escape attempts following his recovery. Returning home in 1919, the young officer spent four years of back pay in just six weeks and later volunteered for service during the Russian Civil War. He received the Military Cross and was captured by the Bolsheviks.

Once repatriated, Captain Horrocks held several command posts, competed in the modern pentathlon in the 1924 Paris Olympic Games, and succeeded in entering the Staff College at Camberley on his fourth attempt to gain admission. By the late 1930s, he had been promoted lieutenant colonel and, somewhat ironically, became responsible for organising academic courses for aspiring staff officers from the Territorial Army.

While commanding XIII Corps in North Africa, General Brian Horrocks stands with his mentor, General Bernard Montgomery and a group of officers. *(Public Domain collections of the Imperial War Museums via Wikimedia Commons)*

General Brian Horrocks was generally praised for his conduct as a commander throughout World War Two. *(Public Domain collections of the Imperial War Museums via Wikimedia Commons)*

While commanding XIII Corps, General Brian Horrocks stands at far right along with General Bernard Montgomery, commander of Eighth Army, and Generals Oliver Leese and Herbert Lumsden of XXX Corps and X Corps respectively. *(Public Domain collections of the Imperial War Museums via Wikimedia Commons)*

When World War Two broke out, Horrocks was quickly in the midst of it. Commanding a battalion of the Middlesex Regiment, he had been in France only about an hour when he met his future mentor, General Bernard Montgomery, then commanding the 3rd Infantry Division. Elevated to brigadier, Horrocks engaged with Montgomery frequently, and his command of the 11th Brigade was noted by both Montgomery and General Alan Brooke, commander of the II Corps and future Commander of the Imperial General Staff. Horrocks evacuated from Dunkirk to Ramsgate aboard a small Dutch watercraft, manning a Lewis machine gun during the perilous crossing of the English Channel.

After command of the 9th Brigade, 3rd Division in England during preparations to defend against a German invasion, Brigadier Horrocks served Eastern Command for five months before promotion to major general and command of the 44th Division, again tasked with guarding English shores. He was commanding the 9th Armoured Division during training in northern

England when he was summoned to Cairo, Egypt, by Montgomery in mid-August 1942.

Montgomery trusted Horrocks, whom he nicknamed "Jorrocks," with command of the XIII Corps during the build-up prior to the decisive Battle of El Alamein against General Erwin Rommel and the vaunted Afrika Korps. Horrocks handled XIII Corps through the pivotal battle and subsequently led X Corps and then IX Corps in Tunisia. Following the Allied victories in North Africa and Sicily, he prepared IX Corps to take part in the invasion of the Italian mainland in September 1943.

But the corps commander never reached the Italian shore.

One day while discussing upcoming operations, Horrocks and the commander of the 46th Division stepped into a dusty street in Bizerte, Tunisia. Seemingly out of nowhere, a German fighter plunged toward them, firing its machine guns. Horrocks was grievously wounded in the chest and stomach, the bullet piercing a lung and intestines and exiting near his spine. Clinging to life, he underwent numerous operations, evacuated to Cambridge Hospital in Aldershot, Hampshire, and was sidelined for 14 months.

Although Horrocks had not fully recovered, Montgomery, leading the Allied 21st Army Group in Normandy, called him back into action on July 31, 1944. In command of XXX Corps, Horrocks served under General Miles Dempsey, commander of the British 2nd Army. However, his worth was always well-known to his patron Montgomery. Horrocks led XXX Corps through the encirclement of German forces at Falaise and its dash through northern France into Belgium, from the River Seine to the great port of Antwerp, sometimes covering 50 miles per day. He fought off a bout of fever and illness in August that was no doubt related to his earlier wounds.

On September 4, XXX Corps received an order to halt for "refit, refuel, and rest."

Then came the orders for Operation Market Garden. Horrocks had correctly surmised that the going would be tough, and the XXX Corps

Shown at right, General Brian Horrocks crosses a footbridge over the River Maas in late 1944. He is accompanied by General Bernard Montgomery and an unidentified officer. *(Public Domain collections of the Imperial War Museums via Wikimedia Commons)*

pace toward Arnhem was at times glacial. When the gallant offensive came to an end, he accepted the circumstances and took responsibility for the shortcoming of the ground phase. "If we were slow then the fault was mine because I was the commander… The sense of desperate urgency was there all right. There could be no doubt about that, and it was not for want of trying that we failed to arrive in time…"

No blame was levelled at Horrocks for the Market Garden failure. He retained command of XXX Corps, attached to General Henry Crerar's First Canadian Army through the bitter Battle of the Reichswald. Returned to Dempsey's 2nd Army in the spring of 1945, Horrocks led XXX Corps across the great River Rhine and into Germany, capturing the port of Bremen at the end of April.

After World War Two, Lieutenant General Horrocks served as General Officer Commanding Western Command and then as chief of the British Army of the Rhine before ill health forced him from the service in 1949. As a civilian, Horrocks served as Gentleman Usher of the Black Rod in the House of Lords for 17 years. He authored two memoirs and numerous articles while also becoming a television personality, hosting a documentary series on World War Two battles. He served as a military consultant for the 1977 feature film *A Bridge Too Far*, and his role was played by actor and personal friend Edward Fox.

Lieutenant General Horrocks died on January 4, 1985, at age 89. Inexplicably, following his funeral service his ashes remained unburied for nearly four decades before the Princess of Wales's Royal Regiment rendered honours at St. Paul's Church, Mill Hill, in 2022.

He is remembered as one of the most capable of British Army senior officers during World War Two, and he earned high praise from his American allies. General Dwight D. Eisenhower, Supreme Commander of Allied Forces in Europe, called Horrocks "the outstanding British general under Montgomery." Brigadier General James Gavin, commander of the US 82nd Airborne Division who served under Horrocks in The Netherlands in 1944, commented that he was "the finest general officer I met during the war, and the finest corps commander." ■

General Brian Horrocks confers with officers on the docks at Bremen, Germany, 1945. *(Public Domain collections of the Imperial War Museums via Wikimedia Commons)*

LIEUTENANT COLONEL JOHN FROST

Lieutenant Colonel John Frost led 2nd Battalion, Parachute Regiment in the gallant fight at Arnhem Bridge. *(Public Domain United Kingdom Government via Wikimedia Commons)*

SS troops, a concentration of military strength unrecognised by Allied intelligence, gather in Arnhem during Operation Market Garden. *(Creative Commons Bundesarchiv Bild via Wikimedia Commons)*

An inspirational leader and one of the most famous British soldiers of World War Two, Lieutenant Colonel John Frost led the gallant fight of the 2nd Battalion, Parachute Regiment at the north end of the highway bridge at Arnhem.

Despite the many setbacks that occurred and the difficulty of his force's predicament, Frost displayed courage and command presence that made the sacrifice at Arnhem a "nearer run thing" than it might otherwise have been. Outnumbered and outgunned, the paratroopers clung desperately to their positions in Arnhem – too distant for relief from the remainder of the 1st Airborne Division halted at Oosterbeek or the tanks and troops of the 2nd Army's XXX Corps traversing the embattled route to the tactically vital lodgement at the Lower Rhine.

By the autumn of 1944, such a heroic performance by Frost and 2 Para were not in any way surprising. Their military bearing, devotion to duty, and willingness to give their lives for their country were already evident. Frost had personally been involved in some of the most hazardous operations of the war and lived to tell the tale.

In February 1942, then-Major Frost had taken Company C, 2nd Battalion into Nazi-occupied France to execute Operation Biting. The airborne contingent was ordered to parachute into the area around Bruneval in Normandy and assault a German radar station there, retrieving components of a new type of radar detection system called Wurzburg. Frost and his 120 men, dropped in three groups of 40 at five-minute intervals, performed brilliantly, capturing a single Luftwaffe prisoner of war with valuable information on

the operation of the radar apparatus while also taking photographs and carrying off several components for study in Britain.

Company C lost three men killed, six wounded, and six taken prisoner. Strangely, just six raiders were given medals for the action. Frost was among them, receiving the Military Cross.

John Frost was born on December 31, 1912, in British India. He was the son of an army officer and attended Wellington College, Berkshire, where his academic progress was sluggish at best. Transferred to the Monkton School, Somerset, he made a better showing and then opted for a military career, attending the Royal Military Academy, Sandhurst. He graduated in 1932 and posted as a 2nd lieutenant with the Cameronians (Scottish Rifles), rising to 1st lieutenant in 1935. During the Arab Revolt, he served in Palestine and received promotion to captain. Meanwhile, World War Two erupted, and Frost returned to Britain in September 1941 to serve with the 10th Cameronians of the Territorial Army.

Disenchanted with the doldrums of coastal duties, Frost determined to apply for the Staff College, Camberley, but that initiative was derailed with an opportunity that came in the form of a notice from the War Office asking for volunteers to become officers in the newly formed Special Air Service. Without knowing exactly what the SAS was but surmising that it must be related to the Commando style of warfare, he was somewhat surprised to

find that he had joined a unit then developing an airborne component. The 11th Special Air Service Battalion had been redesignated the 1st Parachute Battalion in September 1941, and the 2nd and 3rd Battalions were recruited from volunteers like Frost, who was assigned to 2nd Battalion. At first, the prospect for Frost to become an airborne warrior did not look promising. His commanding officer pronounced, "I can't imagine any sensible person choosing you to be a parachutist. You ought to keep your feet firmly on the ground."

Despite the early challenges, Frost completed parachute training and was posted as commander of C Company, 2nd Battalion, Parachute Regiment

After the end of World War Two pedestrians and cyclists cross the Arnhem bridge in peace. *(Creative Commons Dutch National Archives via Wikimedia Commons)*

Lieutenant Colonel John Frost and 2nd Battalion, Parachute Regiment train for Operation Biting in February 1942. *(Public Domain collections of the Imperial War Museums via Wikimedia Commons)*

Urquhart placed his utmost confidence in the officer. "I knew that Frost of all people would press on rapidly if it were humanly possible," Urquhart wrote, "…a six-footer with an anxious moon face and permanent worry lines across his forehead, he relished a fight and had become one of the most capable battalion commanders in airborne forces. Despite a deceptively slow-motion air, Frost had developed a very fine tactical sense."

In the event, Frost and 2nd Battalion, the only substantial airborne unit to reach the highway bridge, performed above and beyond the call of duty and sacrifice when isolated at the north end of the span, hanging on for more than three days in heavy combat against strong and almost continuous German pressure. When the battle at the bridge was over and the wounded Frost went into captivity along with other stout-hearted paras, he said to Major Douglas Crawley, commander of B Company, "Well, Doug, I'm afraid we haven't got away with it this time." The reply came, "No sir. But we gave them a damn good run for their money."

Frost received a Bar to his DSO, and the citation read in part: "It was only when the enemy, having burned the defenders out of each house in turn, set fire to Brigade Headquarters House, where there were nearly 300 wounded that had to be surrendered, that co-ordinated defence ceased. Lt Col Frost though wounded on Wednesday morning, showed the greatest courage and determination throughout the battle. It was largely due to his fine leadership that the position was maintained intact for over three days."

Frost was liberated from a German prison camp in March 1945. He served in numerous command posts with the airborne forces, Territorial Army, and leading the 52nd Division for three years. He retired in 1968 with the rank of major general and died at age 80 in West Sussex on May 21, 1993.

Actor Anthony Hopkins gave a rousing portrayal of Frost in the 1977 film *A Bridge Too Far*, and in 1978, the road bridge at Arnhem was renamed "John Frostbrug," the "John Frost Bridge," in his honour – although those who knew him noted his reluctance to accept such recognition. ■

with the rank of major. It was an all-Scottish unit, and its combat readiness was sufficient that it was chosen to conduct Operation Biting, the first offensive mission of the Parachute Regiment during World War Two, and glean as much intelligence as possible about the new Wurzburg radar.

Following the Bruneval Raid, Frost was promoted acting lieutenant colonel and elevated to command of 2nd Battalion. In North Africa in late 1942, the battalion was ordered to attack airfields in Tunisia roughly 30 miles south of the capital of Tunis. Upon reaching the target area, it was discovered that the airfields had been abandoned. An expected rendezvous with an armoured column failed to materialise, and the battalion was stranded 50 miles behind Axis lines, its only alternative to strike out on foot. Fighting its way to friendly territory, the battalion lost 266 men in the effort, just 160 surviving the ordeal. Frost received the Distinguished Service Order (DSO) for heroism on February 11, 1943.

That summer, the 2nd Battalion jumped into Sicily to take possession of Ponte di Primosole, a key road bridge. During the jump the battalion was scattered across a large section of the island, and fewer than 300 men actually managed to form up to capture the bridge. Their hold was

brief as the small command was assailed by the bulk of the German 4th Parachute Regiment and compelled to temporarily give up the bridge until support arrived. After participating in Operation Slapstick, the Eighth Army landing at Taranto on the Italian mainland in September 1943, the 1st Airborne Division was withdrawn to Britain for rest and to absorb replacements.

By early September 1944, General Bernard Montgomery's Operation Market Garden was rapidly taking shape. General Roy Urquhart planned the dispositions of his 1st Airborne Division and chose the 2nd Battalion to capture the road bridge at Arnhem, taking over after Jeeps of the Reconnaissance Squadron had raced ahead to occupy it. The Reconnaissance Battalion was then to be relieved by Frost's 2nd Battalion and subsequently more airborne troops.

Frost was the most experienced battalion commander in the 1st Airborne Division, and

Lieutenant Colonel John Frost stands at right during commemoration ceremonies in Arnhem. P.C. Kruijff, a Dutch Resistance member, is speaking. *(Creative Commons Nico Kramer via Wikimedia Commons)*

The Arnhem highway bridge was renamed 'John Frost Bridge' by the Dutch people in 1978. *(Creative Commons W.wolny via Wikimedia Commons)*

LIEUTENANT COLONEL J.O.E. VANDELEUR

The inscription on the headstone is simple: "J.O.E. V. 1903 – 1988 ONCE AN IRISH GUARDSMAN".

However, there was much more to the man. Lieutenant Colonel John Ormsby Evelyn Vandeleur was inevitably to be known far and wide by the joining of his initials as "Joe." A colourful and memorable officer of the British Army, he led the tip of the XXX Corps spear across the Belgian frontier and into The Netherlands during Operation Market Garden and had already established himself as capable tactical commander.

During Market Garden, Vandeleur commanded the Irish Guards Battle Group that included his own 3rd Battalion and the 2nd Armoured Battalion commanded by his cousin, Lieutenant Colonel Giles Vandeleur. By the time the vanguard of XXX Corps jumped off from its starting point at Neerpelt, Belgium, elements of the Irish Guards had been through terrific combat in Norway, France, North Africa, Italy, and Normandy.

Joe Vandeleur was born on November 14, 1903, in the Nowshera District along the northwest frontier of British India, now part of Pakistan, where his father, Colonel Crofton Bury Vandeleur, was stationed. Educated at Cheltenham College and the Royal Military Academy, Sandhurst, Joe was commissioned in the Irish Guards in 1924. He was detailed to the Sudan Defence Force for three years, 1928-1931, and commanded a company given camels for transport as well as a motor machine gun battery. Transferred to Egypt, he was then assigned to the 1st Battalion in Palestine and experienced combat during efforts to curb hostilities between the Jewish and Arab populations.

Joe Vandeleur took command of the 3rd Battalion, Irish Guards in 1941, and the 2nd and 3rd Battalions landed in Normandy on June 25, 1944, fighting through to the breakout from the beachhead. On August 2 at the French town of Maisoncelles, he earned the Distinguished Service Order for heroism. The citation reads, "...He carried out a successful attack to clear the village, gaining his objective and subsequently in very confused circumstances and in very close country successfully held off counterattacks by tanks and infantry,

Tanks of the Irish Guards proceed down the road toward Nijmegen during Operation Market Garden. *(Creative Commons Dutch National Archives via Wikimedia Commons)*

This marker commemorates the heroism of the Irish Guards Battle Group under Lieutenant Colonel Joe Vandeleur at the Meuse-Escaut Canal. *(Creative Commons Les Meloures via Wikimedia Commons)*

including one attack by some 100 infantry on his Battalion HQ, where he personally directed operations, beating off and severely handling the Germans at close range with the personnel of the Battalion HQ. His conduct on this occasion was the greatest possible inspiration to the troops under his command."

The advance continued rapidly through open country and across the River Seine on August 29. The Irish Guards roared into Belgium and took part with the rest of the Guards Armoured Division in the liberation of Brussels on September 3.

Vandeleur had assumed command of the Irish Guards Battle Group prior to the action, and his first order to the combined unit was memorable: "Enemy Information – one word, chaos. Our intention: The Irish Group will dine in Brussels tomorrow night!" The following night by 9 p.m., the battle group was, in fact, in Brussels. True to his word, Lieutenant Colonel Vandeleur found the largest café on the main square of the city. Just as the commanding officer sat down with his staff,

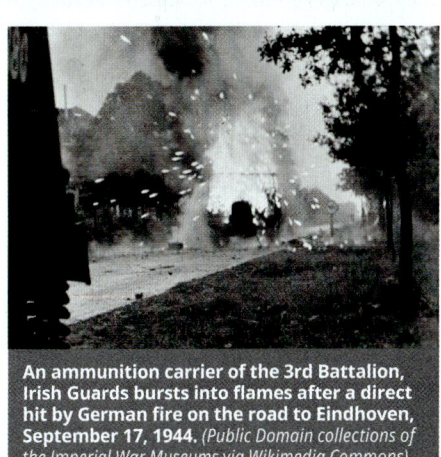

An ammunition carrier of the 3rd Battalion, Irish Guards bursts into flames after a direct hit by German fire on the road to Eindhoven, September 17, 1944. *(Public Domain collections of the Imperial War Museums via Wikimedia Commons)*

a message was received that the Germans were still putting up a fight in a house a short distance down the street. "They were fixed up quickly, and we returned to dinner," Vandeleur later quipped.

The campaign moved into northeast Belgium, and Vandeleur's battle group reached the Dutch frontier on the evening of September 10. In a swift assault the Irish Guard Battle Group captured the vital high, wooden bridge across the Meuse-Escaut Canal at the De Groote Barrier near the town of Lommel. Vandeleur knew that the Germans were likely to blow the bridge at any time and had been alerted that a pair of 88mm guns were located in nearby defensive positions. Nevertheless, he sent tanks and infantry to seize the span. The defenders were quickly overwhelmed, unable to bring their 88s to bear, and the three available engineers disarmed the explosives that had been wired to the bridge. The Irish Guards suffered only three wounded in

A Sherman tank of the Irish Guards takes up a position in a Dutch town beside a demolished bakery on the second day of Operation Market Garden, September 18, 1944. *(Creative Commons Willem van de Poll Dutch National Archives via Wikimedia Commons)*

the attack, and a Bailey bridge was soon thrown across the canal to allow greater traffic flow.

Lieutenant General Brian Horrocks, commander of XXX Corps, remarked, "I was so impressed with Vandeleur's brilliant and inspiring leadership that I gave orders for the De Groote Bridge to be called 'Joe's Bridge.'" The action earned Vandeleur a bar to his DSO, and the citation reads in part, "He had ready a party of infantry with sapper assistance to draw the demolition charges in the bridge and this he immediately rushed across under heavy covering fire from tanks. The charges were rendered innocuous, and before the enemy even realised what was happening the Irish Guards armour was streaming over followed by more infantry. Lieutenant Colonel Vandeleur's drive and initiative in getting not only his tracked vehicles but also his infantry carrying lorries over appalling going, and subsequent speed of his advance when he at last reached a road, alone made the capture of the bridge possible."

Four days after the capture of the Meuse-Escaut Canal bridge, orders were passed for the Irish Guards Battle Group to spearhead the XXX Corps drive up the narrow road to Arnhem and link up with the Red Devils of the 1st Airborne Division holding the bridge across the Lower Rhine. Vandeleur's troops were accustomed to being in the thick of the fight, and the position beyond the canal crossing was to serve as an ideal jump-off point during Operation Market Garden.

The Irish Guards Battle Group crossed the Dutch-Belgian border in strength at 3 p.m. on September 17, 1944, and contended with difficult conditions almost from the outset. Four battalions of German troops, two parachute and two from the 9th SS Panzer Division, soon blocked the narrow, elevated roadway and disabled or destroyed several tanks. After rocket-firing Hawker Typhoon fighter bombers screamed in to provide air support, the Germans finally fled their positions, abandoning their weapons. The road was cleared, and XXX Corps rumbled forward, but there were more

challenges ahead, more periodic firefights while negotiating the roadway, delays at Son and Nijmegen, and the eventual termination of the ground offensive within a few miles of Arnhem.

After Operation Market Garden, Vandeleur went on to command the 129th Infantry Brigade and the 32nd Guards Brigade. He attained the rank of colonel while active and was presented the honorary rank of brigadier upon retirement in 1951. He married twice, and both wives predeceased him. There were no children. During his later years, Vandeleur served as a military consultant for the feature film *A Bridge Too Far*, his character played by actor Michael Caine.

Joe Vandeleur lived his later years quietly in Pinkney's Green, Maidenhead, Berkshire, where he died peacefully on August 4, 1988, at the age of 84. ■

Brigadier J.O.E. Vandeleur's grave marker bears a simple inscription. *(Creative Commons Jack 1956 via Wikimedia Commons)*

This modern image depicts Joe's Bridge and the terrain surrounding the Meuse-Escaut Canal. *(Creative Commons Les Meloures via Wikimedia Commons)*

GENERAL MAXWELL D. TAYLOR

Nearly three decades after Operation Market Garden was over, General Maxwell D. Taylor, then commander of the 101st Airborne Division, recalled an episode during the offensive when he was dismayed with a sergeant who had fired mortar rounds at the Germans.

Even though the rounds had landed accurately, Taylor felt compelled to provide instruction. "When the sergeant had finally got his rounds on target and I had commended to him a thorough review of the mortar manual, I climbed down the ladder and into the courtyard just in time to rendezvous with a small German shell which exploded a few yards away, raising a cloud of dust and sending me rolling with a small fragment lodged in the sitzplatz," the general wrote in his 1972 book *Swords and Plowshares*. "When I opened my eyes, there was my bug-eyed sergeant hanging out the window of the belfry calling to his radio operator, 'Joe, I think the Krauts got the old man in the tail.' That is how I got my Purple Heart."

Taylor, whose Screaming Eagles had quite an assignment during Market Garden, seizing bridges and holding a stretch of road that became known as "Hell's Highway" for 15 rugged miles, had said of the ambitious plan and his division's critical role prior to departure, "With luck, we can make it." Even after the precision jump into the landing zones on September 17, 1944, that Taylor termed, "unusually successful; almost like an exercise," the fighting was fierce during the following hours. Five days later, the division was hanging onto its section of the corridor down which XXX Corps was to travel toward Arnhem, battling heavy counterattacks from enemy troops and tanks. After the linkup with XXX Corps, the 101st Airborne still had to hold the road.

Prior to the airborne insertion, Taylor remembered the scattered, chaotic night-time jump into Normandy during the D-Day landings and agreed with General Lewis Brereton, commander of the Allied First Airborne Army, that the Market Garden jump should take place in daylight. Allied air superiority would minimise the risk of German fighter plane interception and allow for swifter assembly once on the ground – perhaps shortening time to move out by an impressive

In this 1961 photo, Maxwell Taylor, former commander of the 101st Airborne Division and senior military leader, confers with President John F. Kennedy. *(Public Domain Abbie Rowe US Government via Wikimedia Commons)*

two-thirds. Although German flak might be more problematic, the tradeoff was deemed worthwhile. Taylor also specified that his airborne battalion drop and glider zones should be grouped closely together to facilitate their rapid movement toward the bridge objectives, each of which were to be seized on the first day of Market Garden.

By the autumn of 1944, Maxwell Taylor was a proven leader of men, and he had demonstrated personal courage during the drama of the pre-invasion hours of Operation Avalanche, the Allied invasion of Italy at Salerno in September 1943. Prior to the invasion, an airborne seizure of Rome had been contemplated. Taylor, who

During the Korean Conflict, General Maxwell Taylor greets other officers prior to a conference on the military situation. *(Public Domain National Archives and Records Administration via Wikimedia Commons)*

While serving as ambassador to South Vietnam, Maxwell Taylor talks with General William Westmoreland, commander of US forces in the country. *(Public Domain National Archives and Records Administration via Wikimedia Commons)*

General Maxwell Taylor jumped into The Netherlands and led the US 101st Airborne Division in Operation Market Garden. *(Public Domain United States Government via Wikimedia Commons)*

spoke several languages and was in command of the 82nd Airborne Division at the time, was asked to secretly enter the capital of Axis Italy, contact the new Italian Prime Minister, Marshal Pietro Badoglio, and assess the risk of such an airborne operation. Taylor wore his uniform to avoid being shot as a spy if captured and completed the clandestine mission, delivering the message "situation innocuous" that cancelled Operation Giant II and averted disaster, even as some transport planes were already in the air.

Maxwell Taylor was born on August 26, 1901, in Keytesville, Missouri, and took the examination for both the US Military and the US Naval academies. He graduated from West Point ranked fourth in the class of 1922 and served in Hawaii with the Corps of Engineers. After transferring to the Field Artillery, he completed the Command and General Staff College and served as an attaché with the American embassy in Tokyo, Japan. He reached the rank of major in July 1940 after completing the US Army War College.

Taylor served as a battalion commander and in the War Plans Division of the Army while reaching the rank of brigadier general in 1942 and assuming command of the 82nd Airborne Division, recently converted from an infantry division as the first parachute division in the US Army. After he completed the secret mission to Rome, General Dwight D. Eisenhower, Supreme Commander of Allied forces in Europe, commented, "...the risks he ran were greater than I asked any other agent or emissary to take during the war."

While preparations for the airborne phase of the June 6, 1944, D-Day invasion were underway, General William C. Lee, commander of the 101st Airborne Division, suffered a heart attack. Taylor stepped up to lead the division into its first combat and received promotion to major general. He jumped into Normandy and led the 101st in hard fighting to secure obstacles behind the designated invasion beaches along with the heavy combat against German parachute troops

to secure the crossroads town of Carentan, France. When the 101st was withdrawn from combat after a month, the division had suffered more than 4,600 killed, wounded, or captured.

After absorbing replacements and reequipping, the Screaming Eagles were deployed in Operation Market Garden and the subsequent defence of the Nijmegen salient, popularly referred to as "the Island." During the epic 101st defence of the Belgian crossroads town of Bastogne during the Battle of the Bulge in late 1944, Taylor was attending a conference in Washington, DC, and the division was ably led by its artillery commander, General Anthony McAuliffe. Although he had missed the difficult but stirring chapter of the 101st and its World War Two participation, Taylor termed the defence of Bastogne the "finest hour" of the division.

After World War Two, Taylor became superintendent of the US Military Academy and oversaw the written establishment of the institution's honour code. He commanded Allied troops in West Berlin during 1949-1951 and rose to lieutenant general as Deputy Chief of Staff for Operations and Administration in Washington. During the Korean War, Taylor led the US Eighth Army under the United Nations banner and commanded Allied forces in Japan.

From 1955-1959, General Taylor served as Army Chief of Staff. He deployed the 101st Airborne Division to Little Rock, Arkansas, during the desegregation of the public schools there and retired from the Army in 1959 amid disagreements with President Eisenhower regarding the makeup and readiness of the Cold War era Army. He became a trusted advisor to President John F. Kennedy after the 1961 Bay of Pigs fiasco and was recalled to active duty on the cusp of the Cuban Missile Crisis.

General Taylor was elevated to Chairman of the Joint Chiefs of Staff and became a shaper of US foreign policy, military preparedness

during the Cold War, and the conduct of the war in Vietnam until retirement in 1964 and was promoted to full general on the retired list. He also served as ambassador to South Vietnam and in various advisory roles in the administration of President Lyndon Johnson.

During his later years, General Taylor was a consultant and author. He died on April 19, 1987, at age 85. He was portrayed by actor Paul Maxwell in the 1977 feature film *A Bridge Too Far* that related the story of Operation Market Garden. ∎

Photographed during his tenure as chairman of the Joint Chiefs of Staff, General Maxwell Taylor was a military leader and presidential advisor of the Cold War and Vietnam eras. *(Public Domain Department of Defense via Wikimedia Commons)*

During a visit to nuclear research facilities at Oak Ridge, Tennessee, General Taylor stands third from left with General Lunsford Oliver, General Lewis Brereton, and General Leslie Groves. *(Public Domain US Department of Energy via Wikimedia Commons)*

GENERAL JAMES M. GAVIN

Only five weeks prior to Operation Market Garden, James M. Gavin was handed command of the US 82nd Airborne Division. On August 8, 1944, the decorated combat veteran took over the division as General Matthew Ridgway transitioned to command the XVIII Airborne Corps.

Gavin surveyed the triangular piece of The Netherlands his division was to occupy during Market Garden and quickly understood that he had too few men to accomplish every objective assigned simultaneously. He saw the high ground surrounding his landing zones as key to holding them open against German counterattacks, and he saw the crossings of the River Maas at Grave and seven others, some of them to the south around Groesbeek and Wyler, and the northernmost of the eight spans at Nijmegen.

The capture of the road bridge across the River Waal at Nijmegen was critical, but when Gavin discussed the situation with General Frederick "Boy" Browning, deputy commander of the First Allied Airborne Army, the two agreed that it would be seized last in succession. If the lower crossings were not taken and the high ground not secured due to enemy resistance, then it did not matter whether the Nijmegen bridge was in the hands of the 82nd Airborne Division. If the opportunity looked promising, however, Gavin might still dispatch some troops to take it.

In the event, Gavin did order a single battalion, the 1st of the 508th Parachute Infantry Regiment, to seize the Nijmegen bridge "without delay after landing." A misinterpretation of the order down the chain of command brought the belated effort to nil after the Germans arrived in force and stopped the effort in darkness on the first night of Market Garden.

The Nijmegen bridge was not captured until the evening of the 20th, and only then with the heroic crossing of the Waal by the 3rd Battalion, 504th PIR and the assistance of XXX Corps in clearing the streets and houses in the town. Some historians point to the delay at Nijmegen as a major contributing

General James Gavin wears the two-star rank of major general with the shoulder patch of the 82nd Airborne Division prominently displayed. *(Public Domain US Army via Wikimedia Commons)*

factor in the overall failure of Operation Market Garden. Indeed, it was a setback, but it was only one of numerous factors in the outcome.

James M. Gavin was the adopted son of Martin and Mary Gavin. His father was a miner in the coal country of Pennsylvania. Born March 22, 1907, James worked at various jobs from a young age and went to school only through eighth grade. Nevertheless, he decided early that he wanted a military career and ran away to New York in 1924, enlisting in the Army without consent of his parents, although he wrote a letter telling them he was fine and not to worry.

Young Gavin served in the Panama Canal Zone and was promoted to corporal within six months. He yearned to attend the US Military Academy and studied at an Army school in preparation for the written examinations. He entered West Point in the summer of 1925 after affirming that he was 21 years old, rather than his actual age of 18. He graduated in 1929, standing 185th among 299 cadets and spent the next three years at Camp Douglas, Arizona, with the 25th Infantry Regiment.

General Bernard Montgomery presents General James Gavin with the Distinguished Service Order in March 1945. *(Public Domain United Kingdom Government via Wikimedia Commons)*

Paratroopers of the US 82nd Airborne Division check their gear before a jump during World War Two. *(Public Domain US Army via Wikimedia Commons)*

Trucks roll past a damaged section of the road bridge over the River Waal at Nijmegen in early 1945. *(Creative Commons Dutch National Archives via Wikimedia Commons)*

After completing the Infantry School at Fort Benning, Georgia, and serving with the 28th and 29th Regiments at Fort Sill, Oklahoma, Gavin spent 18 months in the Philippines, and received promotion to captain and command of Company K, 7th Infantry Regiment, 3rd Division at Vancouver Barracks in Washington state.

Gavin was among the first US Army paratroopers, commanding a company of the 503rd Parachute Infantry Battalion, then an experimental unit. Promoted major, he was tasked with developing tactical airborne doctrine and wrote the field manual *FM 31-30: Tactics and Technique of Air-Borne Troops*. By August 1942, he was promoted colonel and given command of the 505th PIR. He led the 505th in its first combat deployment during Operation Husky, the Allied invasion of Sicily, in July 1943, after delivering a stirring written letter of encouragement to his command that read in part: "...The term

General James Gavin (right) talks with General Matthew Ridgway during the Battle of the Bulge, December 1944. *(Public Domain US Army via Wikimedia Commons)*

'American Parachutist' has become synonymous with courage of a high order. Let us carry the fight to the enemy and make the American Parachutist feared and respected through all his ranks. Attack violently. Destroy him where ever found. I know you will do your job. Good landing, good fight, and good luck. COLONEL GAVIN"

The paratroopers were strewn across Sicily, and Gavin had no idea where he had come to earth, later admitting that he was unsure whether he was even on the island. He finally assembled a few troopers and struck off in the direction of gunfire. Later, at the defence of Biazzo Ridge, his small force, including some from other outfits who had strayed in, Gavin led a tenacious fight and earned the Distinguished Service Cross, his country's second-highest award for courage in combat.

In December 1943, while preparations were underway for the D-Day invasion, Gavin was promoted brigadier general and made deputy commander of the 82nd Airborne Division under General Ridgway. In the predawn hours of June 6, 1944, the 82nd Airborne participated in another widely dispersed drop across the Cotentin Peninsula, the 505th being one of the few formations that made an accurate jump, securing its objective, the town of Sainte-Mere-Eglise, as well as bridges across River Merderet. The paratroopers fought to hold the vital town against German counterattacks and later withdrew to England. Gavin received a second Distinguished Service Cross for action at the town of le Motey, France, three days after the D-Day jump.

During Operation Market Garden, the 82nd Airborne Division fought well in capturing its assigned objectives, and the cooperation shown between Gavin and Browning was a bright spot in British-American relations, which

were often tempestuous. Still, the Germans held the Nijmegen bridge far too long. During his jump into the Netherlands, Gavin landed hard and fractured two discs in his back.

The 82nd Airborne Division held key ground on the northern shoulder of the German penetration during the Battle of the Bulge and then participated in the reduction of the salient through January 1945, ending World War Two on the River Elbe at Ludwigslust. The Pacific War ended as plans were being implemented to transfer the division in preparation for the invasion of Japan.

After World War Two, Gavin, nicknamed "Jumpin' Jim," was instrumental in the introduction of the all-Black 555th Parachute Infantry Battalion into the 82nd. He gained a reputation as an officer who made no distinction among soldiers based on race. He served as the Army chief of research and development, influencing the evolution of doctrine involving the helicopter, which was prominently utilised during the Vietnam War. However, he decried an erosion of funding for the Army and its "deteriorating" condition. He retired in 1958 with the rank of lieutenant general.

As a civilian, Gavin was a successful corporate executive and served as Ambassador to France in the administration of President John F. Kennedy. He opposed the Vietnam War and was asked to consider a third-party candidacy for president in 1968 but declined to enter the political arena. He died aged 82 on February 23, 1990.

In his New York Times obituary, the paper called Gavin "...a 'hands-on' commander who was constantly on the go. At the front, he made a point of talking to soldiers of all ranks and questioning them closely on their roles. He developed a habit, to which he clung for the rest of his life, of rising at 4 A.M. and starting his work day shortly afterward."

General Gavin led from the front and became a true pioneer in the sphere of airborne combat. ■

Lieutenant General James M. Gavin, who led the 82nd Airborne Division in Operation Market Garden, sat for this portrait in 1964. *(Public Domain United States Army via Wikimedia Commons)*

GENERAL STANISLAW SOSABOWSKI

Photographed in 1939, Major General Stanislaw Sosabowski escaped from the Nazis and formed the 1st Independent Parachute Brigade in Britain. *(Public Domain Republic of Poland via Wikimedia Commons)*

At the age of 50, General Stanislaw Sosabowski completed the entire eight parachute jumps required to earn his wings. Commander of the Polish 1st Independent Parachute Brigade, Sosabowski was always just that – as independent as possible. He was fiery and opinionated, and as the day of Operation Market Garden approached he voiced his opposition to the risky endeavour.

Sosabowski was born in Stanislau, Austria-Hungary, on May 8, 1892, which is today located in Ukraine. He was a Polish nationalist and fought the armies of Imperial Russia during World War One after being drafted in the Austro-Hungarian Army. After the Great War, he volunteered to serve in the army of the newly independent Poland. During the German invasion of Poland in 1939, his 21st Infantry Regiment acquitted itself bravely against overwhelming opposition. Sosabowski was captured but managed to escape. Making his way to France, he led troops of the Polish 4th Infantry Division. Then, with the Nazi victory in France in the spring of 1940, he was among roughly 6,000 Polish soldiers evacuated to Great Britain.

After much of the officer cadre of the 4th Infantry Division was assigned to the embryonic 4th Rifle Brigade, the nucleus of a reconstituted 4th Infantry Division, Sosabowski was permitted to form the 1st Independent Parachute Brigade with headquarters at Largo House in Scotland. During this period, Major General Sosabowski aspired to deploy his brigade in its homeland when the time came to liberate Poland from the Nazis. However, his unit was placed under British command via the terms of an agreement reached between the Polish government in exile and the British government.

From that time, Sosabowski maintained a prickly relationship with the British military, including his direct superior, Lieutenant General Frederick "Boy" Browning, commander of the I Airborne Corps and deputy commander of the Allied First Airborne Army. The brigade was held in reserve during the D-Day landings of June 1944, and its paratroopers were frustrated when they were not deployed to Poland during the Warsaw Uprising that began in August.

By September, as plans for Operation Market Garden were being formulated, Sosabowski became an early critic. The 1st Independent Parachute Brigade was slated to join the 1st Airborne Division in the capture of the road and railway bridges at Arnhem, but its commander was gravely concerned about the distance from the British drop zones to the city itself as well as the potential for heavy German resistance despite early intelligence briefings that indicated minimal enemy units in the area.

Compounding Sosabowski's concerns, bad weather delayed the insertion of his brigade. Leading elements parachuted near Driel on September 19, and the remainder followed two days later. Some of the Poles were dropped in the wrong place, and others came down in zones already under control of the Germans. They were under fire immediately and suffered heavy casualties. Sosabowski attempted repeatedly to cross the Lower Rhine and reinforce the embattled British paras at Arnhem, but due to heavy casualties and German resistance only about 200 men succeeded. The Polish paratroopers held on, linking up with XXX Corps and assisting in the evacuation of the decimated 1st Airborne Division as Market Garden ended.

Although his command had fought bravely, Sosabowski was targeted as a scapegoat for the failure of Market Garden. Under British

General Sosabowski posed for this portrait in 1942. He earned his parachute wings at the age of 50. *(Public Domain Republic of Poland via Wikimedia Commons)*

pressure, he was relieved of command in December 1944. When his paratroopers undertook a hunger strike in protest, Sosabowski's personal plea ended the dissent.

After World War Two, the communist government in Warsaw stripped Sosabowski of his Polish citizenship. However, he managed evacuate his wife and son Peter, blinded during the Warsaw Uprising, to safety in Britain in 1947. Essentially a man without a country, Sosabowski spent the last years of his life living in West London and working in an assembly plant for CAV Electronics in the suburb of Acton. He died on September 25, 1967, and two years later his remains were repatriated to Poland and buried in the Powazki Military Cemetery in Warsaw. ∎

General Sosabowski's final resting place is located in the Polish capital of Warsaw. *(Creative Commons Cezary Piwowarski via Wikimedia Commons)*

9TH SS PANZER DIVISION
HOHENSTAUFEN

Panzergrenadiers and a Sturmgeschutz III self-propelled assault gun are shown in an Arnhem street after Operation Market Garden. *(Public Domain SS-Kriegsberichter via Wikimedia Commons)*

Arnhem was a weigh station for the battered 9th SS Panzer Division "Hohenstaufen," a short-term stopping point on the way to Germany, where the formation was intended to absorb replacements and reequip with new armoured vehicles.

Weary after weeks of virtually uninterrupted fighting in Normandy, Hohenstaufen crossed the border between Belgium and The Netherlands and reached the area north of Arnhem from September 7-9, 1944. Led by SS Standartenführer (Colonel) Walter Harzer, the 9th SS, along with its sister division 10th SS "Frundsburg," comprised the II SS Panzer Korps. Led by SS Obergruppenführer (Lieutenant General) Wilhelm Bittrich, II Korps was assigned to the Sixth Panzer Army, Army Group B under Field Marshal Walter Model.

The departure date for Germany had been set as September 17, with some of the 9th's serviceable artillery and armoured vehicles that remained transferred to the 10th prior to departure. However, before the trains bound for the Fatherland could be boarded fully the entire movement was interrupted by Operation Market Garden. Timing governed most every aspect of Market Garden, and in this case it worked solidly against the Allies. Although seriously depleted after suffering heavy losses in Normandy, Hohenstaufen was ordered to reform and fight the incursion.

Activated in December 1942, the 9th SS Panzer Division Hohenstaufen consisted mostly of conscripts gathered from former members of the

An officer of the 9th SS Panzer Division Hohenstaufen issues orders in the field. *(Creative Commons Bundesarchiv Bild via Wikimedia Commons)*

Hitler Youth, young men who in many cases were barely 18 years of age. Roughly 30 percent of its manpower consisted of volunteers, and the officer cadre was drawn from the 1st SS Panzer Division Leibstandarte Adolf Hitler. Its first commander was General Bittrich, and though originally organised as a panzergrenadier division the addition of a battalion of superb PzKpfw. V Panther medium tanks upgraded its status to a full panzer division.

The 9th SS trained in France at Mailly le Camp, a rather bleak plain east of Paris, and in March 1943 it was given the honorary title of "Hohenstaufen," in tribute to the royal dynasty that had provided kings of Germanic states and the Holy Roman Empire during the 12th and 13th centuries. Initially based in the Mediterranean under the command of Obergruppenführer Paul Hausser, the 9th SS, 20,000 strong, was transferred to the Eastern Front and combined with the 10th SS Panzer Division to form the II SS Panzer Korps, 4th Panzer Army prior to engagement at Tarnopol in an effort

Shown behind their halftrack in Normandy, panzergrenadiers and tankers of the 9th SS Panzer Division count and clean their available equipment. *(Public Domain Johannes Dornn via Wikimedia Commons)*

to free the 1st Panzer Army, encircled there by the Soviet Red Army. Through the mud and rains of the spring, the linkup with the surrounded German forces was accomplished in early April 1944.

A panzergrenadier of the 9th SS Panzer Division Hohenstaufen mans a machine gun as the division goes into action. *(Creative Commons Bundesarchiv Bild via Wikimedia Commons)*

Self-propelled flak guns of the 9th SS Panzer Division Hohenstaufen move along a road near Arnhem. *(Creative Commons Bundesarchiv Bild via Wikimedia Commons)*

After the Allied landings in Normandy on June 6, the II SS Panzer Korps was pulled from a planned offensive against the Soviets in Ukraine and relocated to the West. The rail and road transfer into France was harried by Allied aircraft that exacted a heavy toll in men and machines. The situation deteriorated such that large-scale movement from Poland was limited only to night time.

At the end of June, Hohenstaufen fought the British 21st Army Group in Operation Epsom during the protracted battle for the city of Caen. Subjected to heavy Allied air attack and the pounding of Allied artillery on land joined by the large-calibre guns of naval warships offshore, the division lost as much as 20 percent of its tanks and armoured vehicles. Still, Hohenstaufen fought doggedly, claiming the destruction of 62 British tanks, twice its own combat losses. The bitter battle for Hill 112 again led to heavy casualties as the critical high ground changed hands several times. In stopping Allied progress and participating in a substantial counterattack that ended in July, the 9th lost more than 100 tanks and self-propelled assault guns.

Fighting continued through the summer in Normandy, and Hohenstaufen accounted for dozens of Allied tanks destroyed, but in the process suffered the loss of nearly half its panzergrenadier strength. In August, the Allies unleashed Operation Cobra, and the US Third Army broke out of its constraints in the Norman hedgerow country to begin a dash across France. Reduced to roughly one-third of its original fighting capacity, the 9th SS Panzer Division fought to open a corridor of escape as German force were becoming trapped in a pocket by Allied forces converging from the north and south near Falaise.

After the issue was decided in Normandy, the 9th SS fought as a rearguard for the withdrawal of German forces to the northeast. After a hard fight at Cambrai, in which Hohenstaufen claimed to have destroyed 40 American tanks, the withdrawal into The Netherlands was completed. To deter attacks by enemy fighter bombers during daylight, the division is believed to have displayed flags and other deceptive recognition markers indicating falsely that it was an Allied formation.

When the scope of Operation Market Garden was fully realised, the Germans were taken aback. Recovering from the shock, officers ordered those tanks, vehicles, and equipment of the 9th SS Panzer Division already loaded aboard rail cars to be rapidly offloaded and thrust into action. Colonel Harzer assembled a battle group that was subsequently divided into several such combat units that blocked the eastward advance of the 1st Airborne Division from its drop and landing zones through the western suburb of Oosterbeek and on to Arnhem as well as opposing the 2nd Battalion, Parachute Regiment at the north end of the Arnhem road bridge.

Field Marshal Model augmented the 9th SS with troops of other units as he could, and by September 21, the fighting at the bridge and in the city of Arnhem was over. The Hohenstaufen medical detachment cooperated with the British during several cease-fires, and its commanding officer, Sturmbannführer Egon Skalka, displayed great humanitarianism during the transfer of more than 1,200 wounded British paras to German medical facilities.

When the threat of Operation Market Garden had passed, Colonel Harzer received the Knight's Cross for his role in stemming the Allied airborne offensive. The 9th SS Panzer Division was finally withdrawn to Germany at the end of September.

Even after its replenishment, Hohenstaufen was in a weakened state with some components understrength as much as 50 percent. Many of the replacements received were from inexperienced Luftwaffe field units, but the fighting force did substantially grow in numbers. By December 1944, the division was deployed in preparation for the Ardennes Offensive with the Sixth SS Panzer Army under the command of Obergruppenführer Josef "Sepp" Dietrich, tasked with the recapture of the Belgian port of Antwerp.

During the subsequent Battle of the Bulge, the advance of the 9th SS Panzer Division was halted by the US 82nd Airborne Division at the town of Bra, Belgium, before turning south and engaging in heavy fighting during late December while attempting to seize the crossroads town of Bastogne, Belgium, then occupied by the US 101st Airborne Division and Combat Command B, 10th Armored Division. As the Ardennes Offensive lost its momentum, the division was withdrawn to Germany.

In the spring of 1945, Hohenstaufen was ordered to Hungary in the effort to relieve the garrison at Budapest, then surrounded by the Red Army. By the end of March, unfavourable weather and Soviet counterattacks had ground the relief effort to a halt and threatened to cut off the entire Sixth SS Panzer Army. The division managed to withdraw into Austria and surrendered in early May to US forces during the general capitulation that ended World War Two in Europe. ∎

The 9th SS Panzer Division Hohenstaufen was identified with this crest during World War Two. *(Public Domain original creator unknown Nazi Germany via Wikimedia Commons)*

Brigadeführer Heinz Harmel stands with officers of the 10th SS Panzer Division Frundsberg on the Eastern Front. *(Creative Commons Bundesarchiv Bild via Wikimedia Commons)*

10TH SS PANZER DIVISION
FRUNDSBERG

One of the most memorable armed clashes of Operation Market Garden occurred on September 18, 1944, as the Reconnaissance Battalion of the 9th SS Panzer Division Hohenstaufen had come under the temporary command of the 10th SS Panzer Division Frundsberg.

Commanded by Hauptsturmführer Viktor Gräbner, the Reconnaissance Battalion attempted to sweep across the highway bridge over the Lower Rhine at Arnhem and secure both ends, wiping out the British 2nd Battalion, Parachute Regiment which had occupied houses and gardens at the north end of the span inside the town itself. Grabner ordered 22 armoured vehicles forward along with panzergrenadiers, and the assault soon came under a torrent of fire from the paratroopers.

While elements of the 10th SS Panzer Division kept up a supporting fire from the south end of the bridge and the area of a brick-making business, the two-hour battle ended in a rout of Gräbner's battalion. Twelve vehicles were destroyed, and 70 SS panzergrenadiers, including Gräbner, were killed in action.

At the same time, elements of the 10th SS Panzer Division were organising to secure the rail and road bridges across the River Waal at Nijmegen; the road bridge was the longest tied-arch span in Europe at the time at 1,960 feet. The division was also ordered to bar the forward movement of the British 2nd Army's XXX Corps, moving as rapidly as possible to affect a link-up with the airborne troops at Arnhem. When the Frundsberg battle

groups proceeded toward their assigned tasks, they ran into the three parachute regiments of the US 82nd Airborne Division initially, holding the Waal road and railroad bridges and anxiously anticipating relief with the arrival of XXX Corps.

The 10th SS Panzer Division Frundsberg was created on paper at the same time as its sister, the 9th SS Panzer Division Hohenstaufen, by decree of Adolf Hitler on December 19, 1942. The Fuhrer intended to form a new panzer reserve in the West to replace the SS Panzer Korps consisting of the 1st SS Panzer Division Leibstandarte Adolf Hitler, 2nd SS Panzer Division Das Reich,

and 3rd SS Panzer Division Totenkopf, which was headed to the Eastern Front in early 1943.

The 10th SS Panzer Division was formed from conscripts and volunteers, many of these aged about 18, born in the year 1925, and raised from the Reichsarbeitsdienst (RAD) – the Nazi compulsory labour service. Another component, roughly an expected 5,000 men, were to come from among ethnic Germans who lived outside the national borders. Recruiting became a challenge, and the number expected from the RAD and other sources aged about 18 was increased, also with disappointing results.

An abandoned Panther tank sits on a roadside near Tarnopol, where the 10th SS Panzer Division Frundsberg fought in 1943. *(Public Domain sconosciuto via Wikimedia Commons)*

Sturmbannführer (Major) Ernst Tetsch commanded a Panther tank battalion of the 10th SS Panzer Division during Operation Market Garden. *(Creative Commons Bundesarchiv Bild via Wikimedia Commons)*

Finally, the recruiting was opened to young men born in 1923 or 1924. The effort to muster enough manpower was extended further to the border police and even to those of appropriate age who had previously been deemed unacceptable until standards were lowered.

The core of officers was drawn from other Waffen SS units, and the 10th SS Panzer Division, originally created as a panzergrenadier formation, was upgraded to full panzer division status in the autumn of 1943 under the command of Standartenführer (Colonel) Michael Lippert. Originally, the panzergrenadier formation was given the title of "Karl der Grosse" in honour of Emperor Charlemagne. However, in November the honorary title was changed to "Frundsberg" in reference to Georg von Frundsberg, a military commander of the 15th-16th centuries during the reigns of Holy Roman Emperors Maximilian I and Charles V.

After training for more than six months under the command of Gruppenführer (Major General) Lothar Debes and then Gruppenführer Karl Fischer von Treuenfeld, the first combat experience for Frundsberg occurred on the Eastern Front near the 9th SS in the area of Tarnopol attempting to link up with the 1st Panzer Army, which was fighting its way out of encirclement by the Soviet Red Army. The formations made contact in early April, and Brigadeführer (Brigadier General) Heinz Harmel took command as the division defended a line along the River Bug until June 12, when orders were received to transfer to Normandy to counter the Allied D-Day invasion.

Although its fighting strength had been depleted to just over 13,500 men, the east-west movement required more than 60 trains. At least one of them derailed during the transit, killing or injuring a large number of soldiers. Although the division reached the French frontier on June 18, Allied tactical air attacks took a considerable toll, and Frundsberg was delayed another week in deploying to the front. The division was embroiled in the fight for Hill 112 near Caen, and the battle raged for days.

Hohenstaufen had suffered considerable casualties and was pulled out of the line on July 15, leaving Frundsberg to cover an extensive area. With at least 2,000 of its own panzergrenadiers and tankers killed, wounded, or captured, Frundsberg was withdrawn at the end of the month for just a few days before returning to action in early August. Gains were made against the British, but subsequent advances in the vicinity of Chenodolle in the northwest were thrown back by heavy artillery and Allied fighter bombers.

Within days, the 10th SS Panzer Division was reoriented toward the axis of the American advance near Mortain and committed to the reserve of the XLVII Panzer Korps. The situation in Normandy was deteriorating rapidly, and Frundsberg was heavily engaged as the withdrawing German forces tried to hold the corridor from Argentan to Falaise. The division was in the centre of the cauldron as the Falaise Pocket began to close rapidly and only managed to extricate itself during sustained combat with a perilous crossing of the River Dives.

As the Falaise Pocket slammed shut in mid-August, trapping about 50,000 German troops, Frundsberg fell back to the northeast, crossing the River Seine at Oissel at the end of the month. During the following weeks, the division conducted a fighting withdrawal across the River Somme and eventually into Belgium and The Netherlands, where it laagered in anticipation of the transfer of some tanks and armoured vehicles from Hohenstaufen in preparation for the latter to move to Germany by rail for refitting.

This young SS soldier was captured during the fighting in Normandy in 1944. The 10th SS Panzer Division suffered heavy losses in the fighting at the Falaise Pocket. *(Public Domain Copyright expired. As a pre-1946 Canadian image via Wikimedia Commons)*

The ensuing fight for Nijmegen and the bridges was a dramatic, costly affair as the Brigadeführer Harmel maintained some support for Hohenstaufen at Arnhem and sent forces rapidly southward toward the critical bridges across the Waal. Frundsberg fought the 82nd Airborne Division house to house and street to street in Nijmegen, holding a vital traffic circle at the foot of the Waal road bridge. Finally, the vanguard of XXX Corps arrived and joined the American paratroopers in clearing Nijmegen and capturing the bridge in concert with a river-borne assault by the 3rd Battalion, 504th Parachute Infantry Regiment.

After the failure of Operation Market Garden, Frundsberg was engaged in the counteroffensive to reduce "the Island," also known as the Nijmegen salient. The division was then engaged in Alsace and relocated to the Eastern Front where it fought the Red Army in Pomerania and then Saxony. In the last days of World War Two, the remnants of Frundsberg surrendered to US forces in Czechoslovakia. ■

Brigadeführer Heinz Harmel led the 10th SS Panzer Division Frundsberg during Operation Market Garden. *(Creative Commons Bundesarchiv Bild via Wikimedia Commons)*

The 10th SS Panzer Division Frundsberg was identified with this crest during World War Two. *(Public Domain original creator unknown Nazi Germany via Wikimedia Commons)*

GENERAL WILHELM BITTRICH

General Wilhelm Bittrich stands at far right during a visit to the concentration camp at Mathausen along with Reichsführer SS Heinrich Himmler in June 1941. *(Creative Commons Bundesarchiv Bild via Wikimedia Commons)*

General Wilhelm Bittrich, commander of the II SS Panzer Korps, was probably the first high-ranking German officer to recognise that the Allies were intent on seizing numerous bridges across the waterways of the southern Netherlands during Operation Market Garden. As such, he became a key leader in the effort to contain the Allied offensive, particularly in the surrounding and eventual surrender of elements of the British 1st Airborne Division at Arnhem.

Bittrich's panzer corps, comprised of the 9th SS Panzer Division Hohenstaufen and the 10th SS

During a gathering of high-ranking SS officers, General Wilhelm Bittrich is visible over the shoulder of Reichsführer SS Heinrich Himmler. *(Creative Commons Bundesarchiv Bild via Wikimedia Commons)*

Panzer Division Frundsberg, had been roughly handled during the Normandy campaign in the spring and summer of 1944. The corps had fought the British, under Field Marshal Bernard Montgomery, in their attempts to capture the road and communications nexus at Caen and later defended at Falaise during the desperate efforts of the Seventh and Fifth Panzer Armies to avoid encirclement.

When the Normandy fight had been clearly lost, the II SS Panzer Korps was relocated to a sector of the southern Netherlands that was considered relatively quiet. While Bittrich's area of operations encompassed the towns of Eindhoven northeast to Arnhem, a road distance of roughly 52 miles, it was believed that the ranks of his weary panzergrenadiers might take on replacements and the two divisions' depleted armoured strength might be somewhat replenished. At the time of its movement in early September, Bittrich's command could muster only about 6,000 soldiers within its two combat divisions, and a relative handful of tanks were all that remained when many had been destroyed or abandoned in Normandy due to lack of fuel.

Although his divisions were widely dispersed, Bittrich responded quickly to the Allied airborne insertions of September 17, 1944, sending the 10th SS Panzer Division to confront the US 82nd Airborne Division and the armoured spearhead of XXX Corps at the highway and railroad bridges across the River Waal in Nijmegen and the 9th SS Panzer Division to stall the British 1st Airborne Division in its attempt to seize the bridge across the Lower Rhine at Arnhem. The heavy German resistance was unexpected, checking the progress of Market Garden sufficiently to render the offensive a strategic failure.

Wilhelm Bittrich was the son of a travelling salesman, born in the city of Wernigerode, Saxony, on February 26, 1894. With the outbreak of World War One, he volunteered for service with the German Army, fighting on the Western Front with the 77th Infantry Regiment and in Italy. He was seriously wounded in 1914 and received promotion to reserve lieutenant in the autumn of 1915. He earned the Iron Cross 1st and 2nd Class for bravery under fire and in 1916 transferred to the Luftstreitkrafte, Imperial Germany's air force, for pilot training. Assigned to Jagdstaffel (Fighter Squadron) 37, he shot down three Allied aircraft.

After the Great War, Bittrich joined the paramilitary Freikorps and earned a living as a sports instructor and real estate promoter. By the mid-1920s, he was serving as a flight instructor, training commercial and recreational pilots in Stettin and later Munich. During the period of covert German military training and rearmament in violation of the Treaty of Versailles, he joined the Reichswehr, the German Army of the inter-war period, and was ordered to Lipezk in the Soviet Union, where future Luftwaffe pilots were being trained. He became a member of the Sturmabteilung (SA), or Storm Troopers, and then the Schutzstaffel (SS) in the summer of 1932 and joined the Nazi Party on December 1.

Promotion came rapidly, and after entering the SS with the lowly rank of recruit, he advanced to Hauptsturmführer (Captain) by June 1934 and was involved with the formation of the SS Standarte Germania, later a component of the 5th SS Panzer Division Wiking. He commanded a battalion of the

General Wilhelm Bittrich commanded II SS Panzer Korps in The Netherlands and led the response to Operation Market Garden. *(Creative Commons Bundesarchiv Bild via Wikimedia Commons)*

SS Regiment Deutschland and participated in the military operations related to the annexation of Austria in 1938. In the spring of 1939, he was assigned to the headquarters of the SS Leibstandarte Adolf Hitler, the Fuhrer's personal bodyguard.

Prior to the invasion of Poland in 1939, Bittrich was elevated to the rank of SS Standartenführer (Colonel). He served as chief of staff to Leibstandarte commander Obergruppenführer (Lieutenant General) Sepp Dietrich. He also served in France and temporarily commanded the 2nd SS Panzer Division Das Reich in 1941, after its commander, Obergruppenführer Paul Hausser, was wounded. Promoted Brigadeführer (Brigadier General), Bittrich commanded the 8th SS Cavalry Division Florian Geyer, engaged in security operations in occupied areas of the Eastern Front. He took command of the 9th SS Panzergrenadier Division and oversaw its reconfiguration as a full panzer division in the autumn of 1943, subsequently leading the division against the Red Army until June 1944. A month later, he was given command of the II SS Panzer Korps with the rank of Gruppenführer (Major General).

After the bitter fighting in Normandy and the withdrawal of his corps into The Netherlands, Bittrich saw the imminent threat posed by Operation Market Garden. He advised his direct superior, Field Marshal Walter Model, to order the bridge across the Waal at Nijmegen destroyed. However, Model declined, intending to use the span to facilitate a major counterattack against the Allies. Bittrich did not consider such an option as viable due to the condition of his command, although it fought viciously to counter the Allied moves against the bridges at Nijmegen and Arnhem.

During the heavy combat at Arnhem, Bittrich authorised a three-hour cease fire at the request of the encircled 1st Airborne Division in order to remove wounded from the combat area and transfer them to German medical facilities. He reportedly approved the cease-fire without concurrence from higher command and was criticised for the gesture later. Nevertheless, his skilful handling of the 9th SS Panzer Division at Arnhem effectively thwarted the Market Garden offensive.

Through early October 1944, Bittrich led his command in attacks on the Nijmegen salient and the area dubbed "the Island." He was sceptical of Model's tactics and rightly

General Wilhelm Bittrich confers with other officers during Operation Market Garden. Field Marshal Walter Model stands at left. *(Creative Commons Bundesarchiv Bild via Wikimedia Commons)*

General Wilhelm Bittrich strolls with other Nazi officers during their visit to the concentration camp at Mathausen in 1941. *(Creative Commons Bundesarchiv Bild via Wikimedia Commons)*

concluded that the effort to dislodge the Allies would ultimately fail. He later led the II SS Panzer Korps during the Battle of the Bulge. In early 1945, his command was transferred to the

Eastern Front and fought in Hungary and in the defence of Vienna. Withdrawing his depleted force westward, Bittrich was captured on May 8, 1945. He had previously received both the oak leaves and swords to the Knight's Cross.

Bittrich was held in prison for eight years and stood trial in France in 1953 for war crimes related to the execution of 17 members of the Resistance in the city of Nimes. During the proceedings, it was proven that he had not issued orders for the executions and had actually initiated action against the perpetrators. Still, as a senior officer he was held responsible and sentenced to five years in prison. The sentence was considered completed due to his prior incarceration. A second trial for complicity in other war crimes led to conviction and a five-year sentence, but he was released shortly afterward. In his later years, the former SS officer became active in veterans organisations in Germany. He was portrayed in the 1977 feature film *A Bridge Too Far* by actor Maximilian Schell.

Bittrich died in Wolfratshausen, West Germany, on April 19, 1979, at the age of 85. When asked about the epic struggle at Arnhem, he said of the heroic 1st Airborne, "In all my years as a soldier, I have never seen men fight so hard." ■

During fighting in France, General Wilhelm Bittrich gestures while meeting with a group of staff officers. *(Creative Commons Bundesarchiv Bild via Wikimedia Commons)*

FIELD MARSHAL WALTER MODEL

At mid-day on September 17, 1944, Field Marshal Walter Model, commander of German Army Group B, sat down to lunch at the Hotel Tafelberg in Oosterbeek, a western suburb of Arnhem. Moments later, his meal was interrupted with disturbing news. Allied airborne troops were descending earthward a few miles away, their transport planes and billowing parachutes clearly visible.

Immediately, Field Marshal Model concluded that he was personally being targeted for capture in a daring airborne raid. After terrific fighting and the narrow escape of much of his command from the debacle in Normandy, Model had been given permission to pull back his remaining strength into The Netherlands to rest and refit. He made his headquarters at Oosterbeek, roughly 62 miles from the front line, where the Allies had halted their ground campaign in Western Europe for a time, primarily due to supply and logistics difficulties.

While Model took up residence at the Hotel Tafelberg and his staff at the nearby Hotel Hartenstein, some officers were certain that a major operation was brewing. Allied reconnaissance flights over the area and bombing missions had both recently increased. When Market Garden was finally unleashed, the alarming message reached Model at 1:40

Seated in a Kubelwagen, Field Marshal Walter Model visits troops near Aachen, Germany. He initially believed that Operation Market Garden was a kidnapping attempt. *(Creative Commons Bundesarchiv Bild via Wikimedia Commons)*

p.m., just 10 minutes after the first British paratroopers came to earth in the vicinity of Arnhem. According to historian Antony Beevor, Lieutenant General Hans Krebs, Model's chief of staff, exclaimed, "This will be the decisive battle of the war," to which Model replied, "Don't exaggerate like that. It's clear. Get to work."

Model and his staff took to their heels, quickly evacuating the hotels. As the field marshal feared he might be captured, General Willi Bittrich, commander of the II SS Panzer Korps later related the story of the rapid flight. "Model ran to his bedroom and stuffed his things into his suitcase. He rushed down and crossed the street. His suitcase fell open and all of his underwear were across the street. Helped by his men, he got them together a second time and ran off."

Piling into several staff cars, Model and his entourage sped away from the perceived direction of the British airborne incursion. One of the cars flagged down a German major who was riding a bicycle, and an officer peered through a window asking for directions to General Bittrich's headquarters. Only after the car had sped off did the major realise that the senior officer wearing the immaculate leather coat had been Field Marshal Model himself.

Bittrich recalled that Model arrived at his corps headquarters around 3 in the afternoon and declared, "I'm looking for a new headquarters. They almost caught me!"

While such an account of Model's somewhat shaky reaction to the British threat makes good reading, it seems a bit out of character for a veteran military commander who had demonstrated coolness during time of peril on many occasions. By the autumn of 1944, Model was a holder of the Knight's Cross with oak leaves and swords in recognition of service rendered

Crouching near the front lines beside an SS soldier, Field Marshal Walter Model compiled an impressive combat record. *(Public Domain Unknown German Army photographer via Wikimedia Commons)*

in stabilising the situation on the Eastern Front in the face of a relentless onslaught by the vengeful Soviet Red Army. He had earned the confidence of Adolf Hitler not only as a battlefield commander, but also as an ardent Nazi and gained the nickname of the Führer's "Fireman."

Born on January 24, 1891, in Genthin, Prussia, Model was the son of a music teacher. He joined the German Army as an officer cadet in 1909, and mobilised with the 52nd Infantry Regiment

Field Marshal Walter Model commanded German Army Group B on the Western Front. *(Public Domain Republic of Poland via Wikimedia Commons)*

during World War One. He was seriously wounded at Arras in the spring of 1915 and recovered to receive the Iron Cross First Class that autumn. He was wounded at least two more times and spent weeks recovering in hospital.

At the conclusion of the Great War, Model's outstanding service helped him to secure an officer's post in the interwar Reichswehr. He was promoted colonel in late 1934, and despite a somewhat turbulent initial reaction to Naziism he remained in the military and reached the rank of major general and corps level command by the eve of World War Two.

Model served as chief of staff of the IV Corps during the conquest of Poland. A staff officer of the Sixteenth Army, he received promotion to lieutenant general in April 1940, and took part in the Battle of France, as well as the planning for Operation Sea Lion, the later aborted invasion of the British Isles. His first senior command came with the 3rd Panzer Division on the Eastern Front, and his tanks advanced 250 miles to the banks of the River Dniepr in two weeks during Operation Barbarossa. Moving south into Ukraine with an expanded command that also included the 1st Cavalry Division, he participated in the envelopment of Kiev and subsequently the last drive on Moscow as the winter of 1941 halted operations.

In the wake of a massive Soviet counteroffensive that pushed the Germans back from Moscow, Model was given command of the Ninth Army in the Rzhev salient, skilfully parrying Red Army attempts to reduce the German lodgement. He earned praise and the oak leaves to his Knight's Cross for that effort. After the failure of Operation Citadel and the Battle of Kursk, Model took on the command of an additional army and executed brilliant counterattacks that thwarted Soviet offensive movements. For outstanding performance in command of Army Group North in the area of Leningrad, Model received promotion to field marshal in March 1944. He also commanded Army Group North Ukraine

Field Marshal Walter Model is shown at centre while serving on the Eastern Front in 1941. *(Creative Commons Bundesarchiv Bild via Wikimedia Commons)*

and Army Group Centre, displaying competent and inventive tactical and strategic planning.

As the debacle in Normandy played out in August 1944, Model was reassigned to take over OB West, German High Command on the Western Front, and Army Group B after Field Marshal Gunther von Kluge was implicated in the July 20, 1944, assassination plot against Hitler and committed suicide. Model brought the remnants of the German forces in Normandy out of the Falaise area. As Field Marshal Gerd von Rundstedt took command of OB West, Model retained command of Army Group B, withdrawing into The Netherlands.

During Market Garden, Model reacted quickly, alerting German forces in the areas of Allied airborne and ground operations and organising the defensive movements that upset the British and American timetable. His one apparent tactical

Field Marshal Model watches workers constructing a fortification on the Atlantic Wall in Normandy, 1944. *(Public Domain Poland National Digital Archives via Wikimedia Commons)*

error was his refusal to allow the destruction of the highway bridge across the River Waal at Nijmegen, intending to use it in counterattacking the Allies at an opportune moment that really never materialised. He declined to blow the bridge despite General Bittrich's advice to do so.

Model remained in command of Army Group B, leading skilfully during the fighting in the Hurtgen Forest and for control of the city of Aachen. With Rundstedt, he planned the Ardennes Offensive of December 1944 that led to the Battle of the Bulge, even though he was not in favour of an offensive on such a large scale with limited resources.

In the last days of World War Two, Model finally fell out of Hitler's good graces as Army Group B was encircled in the Ruhr. He committed suicide at the age of 54 on April 21, 1945. ■

Field Marshal Walter Model (left) surveys a map with OB West commander Field Marshal Gerd von Rundstedt and Army Group B Chief of Staff General Hans Krebs. *(Creative Commons Bundesarchiv Bild via Wikimedia Commons)*

DUTCH
RESISTANCE AND
COVERT OPERATIONS

The young ladies smiled and explained that they were merely looking for mushrooms in the wooded area near the Dutch city of Eindhoven. The German soldiers who questioned them bought the story and allowed them to continue on their way.

In actuality, the women were members of Group Sander, one of several Resistance enclaves working against the Nazis. Group Sander had regularly helped downed Allied airmen to elude capture and return to Britain, coordinating their efforts with the Belgian Resistance. In early September 1944, just days prior to Operation Market Garden, Margarethe Kelder and another female had been asked to search a wooded area to confirm the presence of a German antiaircraft battery, and their quick explanation of an innocent search for mushrooms allowed

them to complete their task. Their report was relayed up the chain of communication.

Although it evolved slowly, Dutch Resistance to Nazi occupation was quite active by the autumn of 1944 and regularly providing intelligence to the Allies. In the run-up to Market Garden, Allied Intelligence had also been provided with ULTRA signal intelligence reports of decrypted German communications. Some of these early reports confirmed the belief widely held among senior officers that the enemy was thoroughly beaten after its defeat in Normandy. However, there were subsequent ULTRA reports that provided a changing perspective, indicating an increasing number of enemy troops – even the arrival of the II Panzer Korps – in the vicinity of Arnhem and that the enemy situation had stabilised from one of retreat to one of defence.

Crown Prince Bernhard became the leader of the Dutch armed forces in exile during World War Two. *(Creative Commons author unknown via Wikimedia Commons)*

A member of the Dutch Resistance points to a possible location of German soldiers as he guides British paras during Operation Market Garden, *(Public Domain collections of the Imperial War Museums via Wikimedia Commons)*

Among other potentially significant ULTRA reports that might impact Market Garden was the confirmation that the German 15th Army had withdrawn thousands of troops and their weapons from a precarious position south of the River Scheldt into The Netherlands where some units had become available to General Kurt Student as he formed the 1st Parachute Army. Other ULTRA decrypts indicated the Field Marshal Walter Model, commander of German Army Group B, had located his headquarters at Oosterbeek, a western suburb of Arnhem, where the primary objective of Market Garden, the road bridge across the Lower Rhine, was located. As later ULTRA reports indicated a changing picture of the German situation in the southern Netherlands, such information was apparently given cursory review or dismissed out of hand as Market Garden gained momentum.

At the same time, reports from the Dutch Resistance were received and considered. The SOE (Special Operations Executive) and OSS (American Office of Strategic Services) were involved in strategic intelligence gathering via Dutch contacts and provided information to the Special Forces Headquarters (SFHQ), a component of SHAEF

Crown Prince Bernhard (right) confers with General Bernard Montgomery (centre), commander of 21st Army Group, and General Brian Horrocks, commander of XXX Corps. *(Public Domain collections of the Imperial War Museums via Wikimedia Commons)*

Jedburghs, operatives of the Special Operations Executive and Organization of Strategic Services, gather for instructions. Jedburghs participated in Operation Market Garden. *(Public Domain National Archives and Records Administration via Wikimedia Commons)*

(Supreme Headquarters Allied Expeditionary Force. During Market Garden the SOE and OSS cooperated in the deployment special operations teams known as Jedburghs with each airborne division. These teams did serve as liaisons between the Allied forces and the Resistance and gathered tactical Dutch intelligence reports. Additionally, 27 Royal Dutch Commandos were attached to the three airborne divisions to minimise the language barrier along other duties.

Depending on the source consulted, the Dutch Resistance during World War Two was either well organised or a disjointed collection of groups that rarely cooperated or communicated with one another, each pursuing its own tactical or strategic agenda. Regardless, there is no doubt that the Resistance played a role in the eventual defeat of the Nazis and might well have had greater influence on the course of Operation Market Garden had concerns not arisen among the British command establishment.

In September 1944, at least four major Resistance groups were operating against the Nazis in the occupied Netherlands. After Queen Wilhelmina and the Dutch government fled into exile in Britain in the spring of 1940, the Resistance had begun to take shape. Many of those involved were ordinary citizens, members of the intelligentsia, or personnel of the Dutch armed forces who had not been able to escape their country before the Nazis had solidified their hold. Crown Prince Bernhard rose as a popular figure among the Resistance and the Dutch populace, offering his services to the Allied intelligence community in Britain and then serving as head of the country's armed forces in exile.

Several factors influenced the British appraisal of Dutch intelligence information, including early scepticism surrounding the loyalties of Bernhard, a former member of the Nazi party who actually denied that fact throughout his life. However, by 1940 the crown prince had renounced his association with the Nazis, openly criticized Adolf

Dutch Resistance fighters pause for a photograph in the town of Winterswijk after its liberation on March 31, 1945. *(Creative Commons Julius Jääskeläinen via Wikimedia Commons)*

Hitler, and been cleared for service with the Allies. Two of his foremost advocates were King George VI and Prime Minister Winston Churchill.

Besides this substantial complication, there was an active Dutch Nazi Party with which to contend. German intelligence also rapidly established itself in the occupied country, and the political agendas of the various Resistance factions countered their interest in cooperating with one another. Methods of operation varied as well. For example, the Council of Resistance in the Kingdom of the Netherlands was committed to sabotage and acts of violence against the occupiers while the Order Service was more politically motivated.

The greatest obstacle to British acceptance of Dutch intelligence stemmed from the early success of a German counterintelligence effort called Operation North Pole. Agents of the Abwehr, German Military Intelligence, compromised the Dutch Resistance in early 1942 with the capture of numerous agents. The Germans then used their captured radios and codes to transmit false information to the SOE. Thoroughly taken in, the SOE continued to send agents and supplies into The Netherlands, often directly into the hands of the enemy. The deception was not discovered

A group of Dutch Resistance fighters pauses in a wooded area. The Dutch Resistance provided tactical support during Operation Market Garden. *(Creative Commons Werkgroep Doc. '39-'45 historische kring Dalfsen via Wikimedia Commons)*

In the autumn of 1944 the Dutch Resistance organised a railroad strike that slowed German troop movements. *(Public Domain Dutch National Archives via Wikimedia Commons)*

Dutch Resistance fighters destroyed offices in use by the German occupation forces in Amsterdam in March 1943. *(Public Domain Politie Amsterdam via Wikimedia Commons)*

until the summer of 1943 with the escape of two agents who made their way back to Britain and reported the catastrophe to the authorities.

After the damage inflicted in Operation North Pole was realised, the British were reluctant to accept virtually any intelligence offered by the Dutch Resistance. During a meeting on September 6, 1944, just 11 days before Market Garden began, Prince Bernhard met with General Bernard Montgomery, commander of Allied 21st Army Group and architect of the operation, and presented compelling reports gleaned from the Resistance on German troop strength, armour, and dispositions in the areas that fell within the Market Garden zone of operations. Bernhard was dismissed with little fanfare.

Nevertheless, Allied officers were aware of the Resistance reports even as Market Garden proceeded. The September 14, 1944, daily intelligence summary circulated by General Roy Urquhart to the officers of the 1st Airborne Division warned, "Rather fragmentary Dutch reports confirm that there are twenty thousand German troops east of the Ijssel (a tributary of the River Rhine)...where tanks have previously been reported. The same sources also state that defences are being prepared along the line of the Ijssel which is a very formidable river obstacle."

The following day, the I Airborne Corps, led by General Frederick "Boy" Browning who was also in command of the airborne forces committed to Market Garden, published its own appraisal of German strength in the southern Netherlands and took a decidedly different tone in regard to Dutch Resistance reports. "ENEMY opposition to the development of Resistance has been strong in HOLLAND as a result of this situation in the country and the extensive penetration of the population during the years before the war," it read. "It has therefore been impossible to develop a widespread network of Resistance in HOLLAND with...communications working to the UK. The organisation [Orde Dienst] has, however, been in existence for a considerable time and is thought to have been penetrated by the Germans...."

General Urquhart, concerned by the Dutch reports, took it upon himself to confirm the presence of German tanks in the vicinity of the 1st Airborne Division drop zones near Arnhem. He later remarked, "To convince Browning of the danger, I decided to try to get actual pictures of the German armour near the 1st Airborne Division's dropping zones, and asked for oblique photographs to be taken of the area at a low altitude by the acknowledged experts in this art, an RAF Spitfire squadron...The pictures when they arrived confirmed my worst fears. There were German tanks and armoured vehicles parked under the trees within easy range of the 1st Airborne Division's main dropping zone. I rushed to General Browning with this new evidence, only to be treated once again as a nervous child suffering from a nightmare."

Prior to Market Garden, Dutch Resistance operatives had maintained good communications via telephone, including a secret line that was open even during the German occupation. Sources indicate that access to this telephone system was offered to the 1st Airborne Division when it was on the ground. However, the British declined. Had they availed themselves of this communications tool, advanced warning of enemy movements and other information might have assisted in the defence of the Arnhem bridgehead.

At the same time, American airborne units on the ground in The Netherlands had little awareness of the security issues that caused concern among senior commanders. The Americans were willing to provide Dutch Resistance fighters with weapons and ammunition. During Market Garden, some Resistance members acted as guides, pointed out enemy positions, and even took their places alongside Allied troops and fought the Germans directly.

One intriguing aspect of the Dutch Resistance role in Market Garden is the possibility that the entire operation was compromised by a double agent working for the Germans. Christiaan Lindemans was a shadowy figure who may have been employed by British intelligence as early as 1940. However, he was captured and turned, possibly to save his brother, who was being held prisoner by the Germans. Lindemans is believed to have betrayed a number of Belgian Resistance operatives in Antwerp, where he may also have gained knowledge of the upcoming offensive. Although his role as an informant has not been confirmed, he may have passed sensitive information on Market Garden to the Germans after returning to The Netherlands.

Conjecture surrounds the entire episode, including whether the Germans actually acted on information received from Lindemans or did not consider it credible. In any case, Lindemans was arrested by the Allies in October 1944 and committed suicide in prison in 1946 while awaiting trial.

In the execution of Operation Market Garden, the Dutch Resistance network was not leveraged to its fullest, particularly in the Arnhem area. In some cases, Resistance personnel were utilized only as a need arose. Their tactical contribution was tangible evidence of strong commitment to the Allied cause, but their strategic value, particularly in intelligence gathering, was squandered amid the controversies and scepticism that often arise in wartime. ■

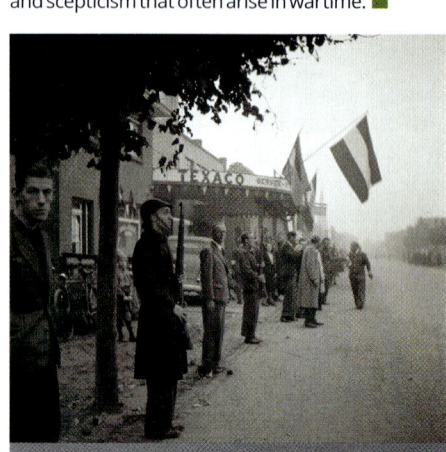

Members of the Dutch Resistance form a guard of honour to welcome their Allied liberators in the city of Nijmegen, September 21, 1944. *(Creative Commons Dutch National Archives via Wikimedia Commons)*

AIR TRANSPORT

I t was an awe-inspiring sight. Allied air power was on full display in the opening hours of Operation Market Garden, the largest airborne offensive of its kind in history to date.

Five thousand aircraft, including bombers and fighters executing tactical support missions, were aloft on September 17, 1944, but the most incredible spectacle was the air insertion, the "Market" phase of the operation that was singularly impressive as transport planes, some with paratroopers aboard and others towing 2,500 gliders laden with men and equipment, caused military personnel and civilians alike to gaze upward.

The airborne carpet at times seemed to drone overhead endlessly, stretching from horizon to horizon. Such a display of sheer military magnitude was seldom seen, and the daylight insertion of men and materiel was executed accurately, more so than the planners of Market Garden had thought possible and to the growing consternation of the astonished Germans.

Even so, in their display of strength the American IX Troop Carrier Command and British RAF Transport Command were hard pressed to deliver the means to fight the Germans in support of the XXX Corps drive toward Arnhem. The combined force included 1,438 Douglas C-47 transports, nicknamed Skytrain by the Americans and Dakota by the British, 327 converted glider-towing British bombers, and more than 2,100 CG-4 Waco, Airspeed Horsa, and General Aircraft Hamilcar gliders.

Still, the entire complement of Allied troops and supplies would require multiple airlifts. Although senior commanders wanted the insertion to be completed in a single day with two or more missions if necessary, General Lewis Brereton, commander of the First Allied Airborne Army, would commit to only one lift on the first day of Market Garden. Subsequent waves of airborne troops and equipment would have to be delivered on an ambitious schedule over the course of several days while the forces already on the ground were fighting the enemy.

Prophetically, General Roy Urquhart, commander of the British 1st Airborne Division had asserted, "An airborne division is designed to fight as a whole

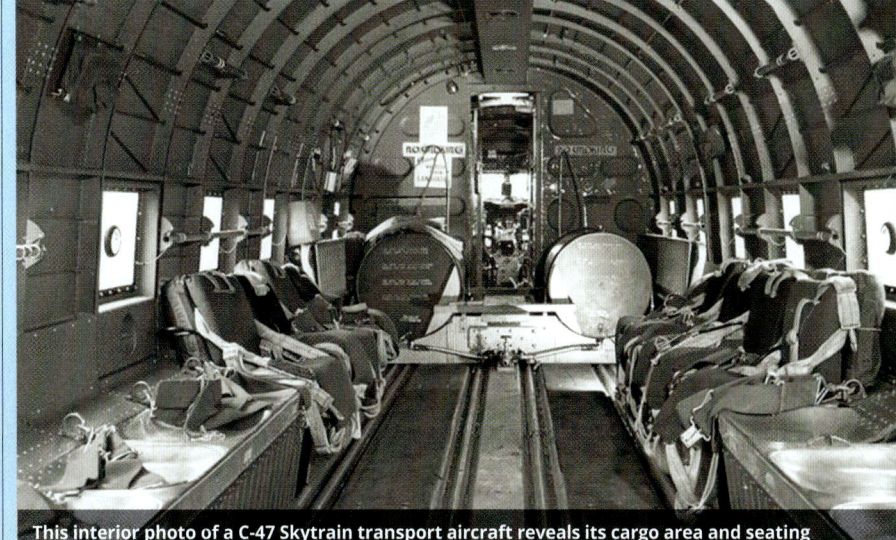

This interior photo of a C-47 Skytrain transport aircraft reveals its cargo area and seating arrangement. *(Public Domain US Air Force via Wikimedia Commons)*

and should be dropped or landed as such," but to his dismay the Red Devils were slated for insertion in three separate airlifts over three days, which in itself would seriously hamper the division's combat efficiency. Weather delays and the absence of available landing zones, some falling into the Germans, complicated matters even further.

Brereton took a pragmatic approach. There would be losses to German antiaircraft fire, possibly fighter interdiction, mechanical issues, maintenance, and accidents. The IX Troop Carrier Command, which would provide the paratrooper aircraft for all three airborne divisions, could muster fewer than 2,100 pilots, and these would be fatigued after their initial sorties. General Paul Williams, head of IX Troop Command and leader of the overall transport effort, voiced his "concerns about aircrew fatigue and the time needed to undertake aircraft maintenance and repair battle damage." In the event, only about 60 percent of the full combat strength of the US 82nd and 101st and the British 1st Airborne Divisions would be delivered on the first day.

Many of the C-47s that dropped paratroopers on September 17 would be used in subsequent airlift operations as tow planes

C-47 Dakota air transports drop paras of the 1st Airborne Division during Operation Market Garden, September 17, 1944. *(Public Domain collections of the Imperial War Museums via Wikimedia Commons)*

A restored C-47 Skytrain transport flies above the Duxford D-Day Air Show in 2014. *(Creative Commons Airwolfhound via Wikimedia Commons)*

This photograph, taken from inside a Horsa glider, shows Short Stirling bombers with gliders in tow. *(Public Domain collections of Imperial War Museums via Wikimedia Commons)*

for gliders. The squadrons of No. 38 Group and No. 48 Group RAF would supply their converted glider-towing bombers from the first day onward. When bad weather did intervene, postponing supply and reinforcement drops for hours and even days, the situation in the ground combat areas deteriorated, particularly in the vicinity of Arnhem, where the weary paras of the 1st Airborne Division sometimes looked on helplessly as supplies were parachuted into drop zones that had indeed been overrun by the Germans.

When the great formations of transport aircraft approached hostile territory in clear skies on September 17, enemy antiaircraft guns boomed. Some planes went down in flames, and others were heavily damaged. During the course of Market Garden, 377 Allied aircraft of all types were lost, many of them C-47s shot down or written off as unflyable and gliders that crashed and broke apart on landing. Preparations for the Market phase of the offensive into The Netherlands were essentially completed in only one week, while earlier airborne operations in Sicily, Normandy, and southern France had been fine-tuned during months of preparation. Nevertheless, the performance of men and machines in the Market Garden airlift was outstanding.

When General Dwight D. Eisenhower, Supreme Commander of Allied Forces in Europe, wrote his post-World War Two memoir *Crusade in Europe*, he credited the bulldozer, the two and one-half ton truck, the landing craft, and the C-47 as critical in achieving final victory. The C-47, a military version of the Douglas DC-3 passenger liner that first flew in 1935, was indeed a war winner. During the conflict, more than 10,000 of the aircraft were produced, and it rendered incredible service in every theatre of operations.

A single C-47 was capable of carrying up to 18 fully equipped paratroopers or a cargo payload of up to three tons. The heaviest weapon it could transport was the 75mm pack howitzer, so this became the standard artillery field gun of the US airborne forces. The C-47 could absorb tremendous punishment and stay in the air, and its crew of four, pilot, co-pilot, radio operator, and navigator loved their plane and praised the ease with which it flew.

The versatile C-47 required a runway of only 3,000 feet for take-off, and though its average cruising airspeed of 150 miles per hour was slow, its range was an impressive 1,500 miles and its service ceiling was 26,400 feet. When time came for its human cargo to exit through a fuselage

A Waco CG-4 glider is shown aloft during training exercises in 1943. *(Public Domain National Museum of the US Air Force via Wikimedia Commons)*

door, the Skytrain could slow to 110 miles per hour and remain aloft while providing a stable jump platform. The fuselage door was seven feet wide, allowing paratroopers laden with up to 100 pounds of combat kit to exit easily. At peak production in mid-1943, American industry was producing more than 100 C-47s per month, continually attempting to satisfy the demand for the transport and its follow-on C-53 variant that was not configured to carry cargo, only to deliver airborne troops. In the spring of 1945, the larger C-46 Commando entered service in the European theatre, but not in sufficient numbers to supplant the ubiquitous Skytrain.

RAF Transport Command employed several converted bomber types for airborne transport before largely giving way to the C-47 Dakota. The bombers, however, continued to function in the glider-towing role. The Short Stirling, the first four-engine bomber introduced with the Royal Air Force, made its initial flight in May 1939, and as British airborne operations took shape it served as an airborne troop transport and glider tow in its Stirling IV configuration. Other bomber types in airborne and glider service included the twin-engine Armstrong Whitworth Whitley and Albemarle and the Vickers Wellington among others.

Gliders were significant components of Allied airborne capability, and thousands were involved in operations in the European theatre. The US airborne primarily relied on the Waco CG-4 glider, which was dubbed Hadrian by the British. Gibson Appliance, Ford Motor Company, and Cessna Aviation were among the 15 companies that produced the CG-4 from 1942 forward, and nearly 14,000 were completed. Constructed primarily of wood and canvas with some metal components, the Waco was flown by a pilot and co-pilot. It was more than 48 feet long, stood nearly 13 feet high, and had a wingspan of more than 83 feet. The glider made its combat debut in Sicily in July 1943, and carried a respectable payload of 13 assault troops and their equipment or a single Jeep or 75mm pack howitzer. It was loaded through a hinged section of the nose.

British paras are shown seated inside a Horsa glider prior to a mission during World War Two. *(Public Domain collections of the Imperial War Museums via Wikimedia Commons)*

Its cargo unloaded, a Hamilcar glider sits abandoned in a field during Operation Market Garden. *(Public Domain United Kingdom Government via Wikimedia Commons)*

German soldiers inspect the wreckage of a Waco glider that has come down in Normandy. *(Creative Commons Bundesarchiv Bild via Wikimedia Commons)*

The Royal Air Force fielded the General Aircraft Hotspur, which was produced from 1940 to 1943 in anticipation of its use in an assault role. More than 1,000 were built by the end of its production run, but it became clear that larger glider models were required for major airborne operations. As World War Two progressed, the Hotspur was relegated to a training role, and many of the British pilots and aircrew who flew during Market Garden received some glider training in the Hotspur.

Perhaps the most famous Allied glider of World War Two was the Airspeed Horsa, which was introduced in 1941 with approximately 3,800 built by the end of the conflict. London furniture manufacturer Harris Lebus built roughly 2,700 of these, while Airspeed produced 700 and Austin Motors Ltd. another 365. The Horsa was used by British and Commonwealth forces across the globe, as well as the US Army Air Forces. Named for the legendary warrior who conquered Britain in the 5th century, the prototype Horsa took its first flight in September 1940. Towed aloft by a Whitley bomber, it performed well and landed with little difficulty. The wood and canvas glider progressed from drawing board to production in a remarkable 11 months.

Crewed by a pilot and co-pilot, the Horsa was capable of carrying up to 25 combat ready troops, a pair of quarter-ton trucks, or a single 105mm howitzer along with its crew and quarter-ton towing truck with a complement of ammunition. Even as the Horsa was being manufactured, improvements were suggested and implemented, including a hinged nose for ease of loading, a reinforced floor, tow attachment modifications, and a stronger twin nose wheel.

In 1942, General Aircraft began working on a larger glider, nicknamed the Hamilcar in homage to the legendary Carthaginian war leader Hamilcar Barca. The Hamilcar entered service in mid-1944 and was designed to carry heavier cargo, including 17-pounder anti-tank guns and supporting equipment or light tanks. The Hamilcar was imposing among other contemporary glider types with a payload capacity of eight tons, wingspan of 110 feet, height of just over 20 feet, and length of 68 feet. Flown by a pilot and co-pilot, more than 30 Hamilcars were employed in Operation Market Garden to carry supplies, trucks and Jeeps, and artillery pieces into battle. General Aircraft built 344 Hamilcar gliders from 1942 to 1946. ◾

Carrying Tetrarch light tanks, Hamilcar gliders come in for a landing in Normandy in June 1944. *(Public Domain collections of the Imperial War Museums via Wikimedia Commons)*

101ST AIRBORNE IN ACTION

Brigadier General Anthony McAuliffe, artillery commander of the 101st Airborne Division, addresses glider pilots before their mission during Operation Market Garden on September 18, 1944. *(Public Domain US Air Force via Wikimedia Commons)*

Since its baptism by fire during D-Day and the Normandy campaign, the US 101st Airborne Division had been recovering from weeks of hard fighting in France. Absorbing replacements and re-equipping, the division was in England from mid-July 1944 until its deployment during Operation Market Garden.

With the formulation of British Field Marshal Montgomery's bold plan for an air-ground offensive into The Netherlands, the Screaming Eagles were briefed on their critical role in opening the ground corridor for XXX Corps to roll forward, crossing key bridges that would facilitate a dagger thrust into the Ruhr.

Under the command of General Maxwell Taylor, the 101st was to secure the southernmost bridges along the route into the Netherlands. These spanned the Wilhelmina Canal at the town of Son, while other targets of the 101st included a pair of bridges across the River Dommel at St. Odenrode, four spans crossing the River Aa at Veghel, and others across the Willems Canal. Another 101st objective was the Dutch town of Eindhoven, a population centre along the 15-mile stretch of roadway that the 101st had to hold open for XXX Corps to transit. By the time their experience during Operation Market Garden was over, the route was known to the paratroopers as Hell's Highway.

The sky over Western Europe was clear on September 17, 1944, and the parachute insertion of the 101st Airborne into The Netherlands was accomplished in broad daylight. The airdrop was virtually flawless, only two of battalions of the

General Maxwell Taylor commanded the 101st Airborne Division during Operation Market Garden. *(Public Domain ibiblio.org via Wikimedia Commons)*

101st failing to come down in their designated drop zones. In Normandy, the pilots of transport aircraft had reacted erratically to heavy German flak, veering off course and scattering their human cargoes across the Norman countryside. For Market Garden, their flight path had intentionally been laid out to expose the C-47

Colonel Robert F. Sink commanded the 506th Parachute Infantry Regiment during Operation Market Garden and later rose to the rank of lieutenant general. *(Public Domain US Army via Wikimedia Commons)*

transports to minimal German flak, flying over mostly Belgian airspace and limiting the distance over ground held by the enemy to only 65 miles.

The 101st Airborne was supplied with 424 C-47s of the IX Troop Carrier Command along with 70 tow planes and gliders. The first C-47s carrying pathfinders of the 101st lifted off at

their advance toward the bridges. A railroad bridge over the Aa was already secured by a few of Kinnard's men by the time he reached the outskirts of the town. The 2nd Battalion captured three bridges intact in the vicinity of Veghel, and the 3rd Battalion covered the regiment's rear with the capture of the village of Eerde and cutting of the Veghel-St. Odenrode highway.

Within three hours, the 501st PIR had taken all of its assigned objectives for September 17, but Kinnard had moved out of his drop zone in such haste that much of the 1st Battalion's equipment had been left behind. He had ordered Captain

Colonel John 'Iron Mike' Michaelis led the 502nd Parachute Infantry Regiment in The Netherlands and rose to the rank of four-star general and commander of US forces during the Korean War. (Public Domain US National Archives and Records Administration via Wikimedia Commons)

10:25 a.m. and others followed at 10-minute intervals. The 442nd and 435th Troop Carrier Groups managed to get 45 aircraft aloft in five minutes and 32 in the air and in formation within 15 minutes respectively. This time, the pilots held their courses and braved the antiaircraft fire to make the accurate delivery. Although the 424th Troop Carrier Wing dropped 42 sticks of the 1st Battalion, 501st Parachute Infantry Regiment (PIR) three miles northwest of its designated drop zone, the tight drop pattern facilitated the rapid assembly of 90 percent of the battalion's troopers within 45 minutes.

The 506th PIR was dropped right on target by aircraft of the 442nd and 436th Troop Carrier Wings with only one transport plane shot down in transit. Within an hour, the regimental command post was established and 2,200 men had been dropped with such accuracy that the 506th was 80 percent functional. The 502nd came down accurately with the exception of its 1st Battalion and was also operational within the hour. Altogether, the jump was likened to an exercise, and the war journal of the 506th commented that it was "an ideal jump, better than any combat or practice jump executed." Only 24 troopers were injured during the airdrop.

In fine form, the three regiments of the 101st Airborne Division set out for their objectives. The 506th, under Colonel Robert Sink, was ordered to capture a bridge over the Wilhelmina Canal and then occupy Eindhoven. Colonel John Michaelis was to lead the 502nd in establishing a perimeter around its drop zone north of the 506th for use as a glider landing zone, take one of the bridges over the River Dommel, and then others across

the Wilhelmina Canal near the town of Best. The 501st, under Colonel Howard Johnson, was ordered to take four road and rail bridges across the Willems Canal and the River Aa near Veghel.

Lieutenant Colonel Harry W.O. Kinnard, commanding the 1st Battalion, 501st PIR, moved out quickly toward Veghel, some of the troopers riding bicycles or commandeering trucks to speed

Paratroopers of the US 101st Airborne Division inspect the wreckage of a glider after it crashed in The Netherlands. (Public Domain US Army Signal Corps via Wikimedia Commons)

W.S. Burd with 46 men to bring the equipment forward along with the few paratroopers that had been injured in the jump, knowing that the pace of such a movement would be slow. A heavy German counterattack soon had Burd in a fix. His 101st troopers were fighting for their lives and occupying a single building when Kinnard received word that they were about to be overrun. Colonel Johnson granted permission to send a platoon to Burd's aid, but the effort failed and the trapped troopers were captured along with the equipment.

Meanwhile, Lieutenant Colonel Patrick F. Cassidy assembled his 1st Battalion, 502nd PIR quickly despite the bit of confusion with its landing. He pushed the battalion forward, and the Screaming Eagles swept into St. Odenrode, which commanded a major highway and a bridge over the River Dommel. They took the town quickly, killing 20 Germans and capturing 58 enemy soldiers.

General Taylor realised that the rail and road bridges over the Wilhelmina Canal near the town of Best were not in the direct line of advance for XXX Corps and had not been designated as primary objectives. Nevertheless, he believed the capture of at least one bridge at Best was critical to shoring up the defensive perimeter of the 101st Airborne. It could also be used as an alternate route across the canal should the road through Son become blocked.

American intelligence reports indicated that only a few German troops defended Best. Therefore, a single company, Company H, 3rd Battalion, 502nd PIR, was handed the assignment to take a 100-foot-long concrete road bridge and a nearby railroad span across the Wilhelmina Canal at Best, four miles west of the main highway route assigned to XXX Corps. Company H had already lost a number of men in earlier fighting, but Captain Robert E. Jones ordered his

Corporal Jaap Bothe of the 101st Airborne Division, formerly a resident of Rotterdam, The Netherlands, talks with a Dutch farmer who is giving a ride to American paratroopers near the town of Son, September 19, 1944. (Public Domain Signal Corps Archive via Wikimedia Commons)

troopers to move out. Moments later, intense German fire erupted. Jones sent a patrol forward under Lieutenant Edwin L. Wierzbowski, and this handful of troopers got within sight of the highway bridge – as close as 15 feet – before it was forced to dig in. The torrent of enemy shells and bullets had reduced Wierzbowski's force to only three officers and 15 men.

As the afternoon of the 17th waned, Lieutenant Colonel Robert G. Cole, commander of the 3rd Battalion, 502nd PIR, set out with the rest of his battalion to find Jones and Company H at about 6 p.m. However, darkness halted the effort before contact was established. The following morning, Cole talked over the radio with the pilot of a spotter plane assisting in the effort. The pilot requested that orange recognition panels be placed on the ground near the battalion command post, and Cole, who had earned the Medal of Honor for valour in Normandy, decided to oblige. The officer raised his head slightly, shielding his eyes from the sun and looking overhead for the spotter plane. Seconds later, a single shot echoed across the landscape. Cole was shot dead by a German sniper's bullet fired from the window of a farmhouse roughly 300 yards distant.

The fight for control of Best lasted another two days, and much to the consternation of the Americans, the Best road bridge was blown up by the Germans around noon on the 18th. Best, it turned out, was being defended by a much stronger contingent of enemy forces than anticipated. For a while, rumours circulated that the road bridge at Best had been captured and that Company H had been annihilated. In actuality, Wierzbowski's little patrol was surrounded, and at times reinforcements sent to their aid had no idea where the beleaguered Company H was located. Eventually, a much larger Allied force was needed to subdue the German defenders at Best. At least two more infantry battalions and British tanks

eventually got the job done. During the fighting on September 18-19, Private First Class Joe E. Mann earned a posthumous Medal of Honor.

Just south of Son, the three battalions of the 506th PIR converged on the town. General Taylor accompanied the 1st Battalion as it rushed toward the Wilhelmina Canal road bridge and came under heavy fire from German 88mm guns at the edge of the Zonche Forest. As the other two battalions of the 506th, under the command of Colonel Sink, approached the area, they were also pounded by 88mm artillery fire.

When paratroopers of the 506th finally reached the Son bridge, the Germans blew the span sky high, almost in the faces of the Americans. Still, the 101st had made tremendous progress. By nightfall on the 17th, the Screaming Eagles were in possession of Veghel, St. Odenrode, and Son.

The advance on Eindhoven was slowed considerably by the destruction of the Son bridge, but by evening on the 17th XXX Corps had halted six miles away at Valkenswaard. The ground phase of Operation Market

Colonel Howard Johnson commanded the 501st Parachute Infantry Regiment during Operation Market Garden. He was killed in action in October 1944. (Public Domain US Army via Wikimedia Commons)

Paratroopers of the US 326th Medical Company, 101st Airborne Division talk with members of the Dutch Resistance in the town of Veghel during Operation Market Garden. (Public Domain Central Intelligence Agency via Wikimedia Commons)

Hell's Highway to be clear of German resistance after a few hours of combat on September 18.

That morning, the 506th moved forward, destroying a pair of German 88mm guns and entering Eindhoven. Everywhere they had encountered Dutch civilians, the paratroopers were greeted with spontaneous celebration, and in Eindhoven the revelry was particularly notable. Throngs of jubilant Dutch men, women, and children took to the streets, rejoicing in their apparent liberation, waving their country's flag, dancing and singing, and offering bread, cheese and wine to the paratroopers. One American officer remembered the scene years later. "The reception was terrific," he remarked. "The air seemed to reek with hate for the Germans.

A paratrooper of the 101st Airborne Division makes a hard landing during Operation Market Garden. *(Public Domain US Army via Wikimedia Commons)*

Airborne troops of Company E, 506th Parachute Infantry Regiment, consult a map along with Dutch civilians during Operation Market Garden. *(Creative Commons MoldesRules via Wikimedia Commons)*

Garden had come up against stiff German resistance along its single narrow road. In some places the road was elevated and the British tanks were perfectly silhouetted against the sun, making them easy targets for German anti-tank gunners. Further, each time an enemy machine gun chattered or a squad of enemy infantry opened fire, the XXX Corps column was required to halt and deploy its own infantry to deal with the obstacle.

The fighting to open the corridor for the XXX Corps advance had been difficult and the 502nd PIR had run into stiff resistance in the vicinity of Best. However, this objective was secondary. Senior commanders of the 101st Airborne, therefore, expected their stretch of

Dutch civilians dance in the streets of Eindhoven, The Netherlands, after paratroopers of the US 101st Airborne Division entered the city during Operation Market Garden. *(Public Domain collections of the Imperial War Museums via Wikimedia Commons)*

Allied armoured vehicles and trucks pass through the crowded streets of Eindhoven, The Netherlands, on September 20, 1944. *(Public Domain collections of the Imperial War Museums via Wikimedia Commons)*

The troopers of the 506th rounded up a few German prisoners in Eindhoven and sent them into captivity, but the clock was ticking and the enemy had succeeded in disrupting the timetable of Garden, the ground phase of the elaborate Allied plan. The revelry of the Dutch civilian population complicated the movement of Allied troops and armour as well. Finally, around 5 p.m., on September 18, the spearhead of XXX Corps rolled through Eindhoven – almost without stopping.

At Son, Canadian engineers had been working through the night to deploy a prefabricated Bailey bridge across the Wilhelmina Canal. It had taken quite some time for the bridging equipment to be brought forward from the XXX Corps column before the engineers could even begin the task. At last, though, around 6:45 a.m. on September 19, the tanks, personnel carriers, and halftracks of XXX Corps were rumbling over the waterway. Still, precious time had melted away. The ground force was 33 hours behind schedule in its race for Arnhem.

Just before midday on the 19th, XXX Corps was crossing the Willems Canal and the River Aa at Veghel and moving into the zone of operations of the 82nd Airborne Division. The troopers of the 101st Airborne were subsequently required to maintain their positions and hold the route of the ground advance open against German counterattacks. The enemy did attempt to cut the road on several occasions around Eindhoven, Veghel, St. Odenrode, and Son, but the Screaming Eagles held their ground. General Taylor later described the fighting as reminiscent of the bushwhacking cowboy and Indian duels of the old American West. The German attacks were relentless. Roads were sometimes cut temporarily, but the enemy was beaten back to its starting positions each time.

One particularly vicious assault struck Veghel on September 22, as German ground troops were supported by heavy artillery bombardment and aircraft. Private Daniel Kenyon Webster of Company E, 506th PIR remembered that the enemy onslaught was not repelled completely for two arduous days as artillery shells rained down on the town. "It was a very depressing atmosphere listening to the civilians moan, shriek, sing hymns and say their prayers," he noted. British tanks and rocket-firing Hawker Typhoon fighter bombers of the Royal Air Force were eventually called on to batter the Germans into retreat, and Webster remembered hiding in a foxhole with fellow trooper Private Don Wiseman. "Wiseman and I sat in our corners and cursed," he later wrote. "Every time we heard a shell come over, we closed our eyes and put our heads between our legs. Every time the shells went off, we looked up and grinned at each other."

Sergeant Don Burgett of the 1st Battalion, 506th PIR, witnessed the aftermath of a vicious firefight along Hell's Highway on September 24, when the Germans ambushed a British column at Koevering northeast of Eindhoven. "...Germans brought up some 40mm cannons and they had some self-propelled guns and they shot the British who were lined up on the side of the road and they were brewing tea in these five-gallon tins and the Germans just opened up on them. When we got down to Koevering, the trucks were still burning. We went into the attack immediately. I remember we killed two Germans in a haystack. Then we made an attack west across the road to a farmhouse. The farmhouse was set on fire. We went into the German side and we drove them back."

By the conclusion of Operation Market Garden, the troopers of the 101st Airborne

A tribute to the US 101st Airborne Division adorns a building in the Dutch town of Veghel where the Screaming Eagles fought in September 1944. *(Creative Commons Loek Tangel via Wikimedia Commons)*

Division had inflicted significant losses on the Germans, killing and wounding many while capturing more than 3,500. The 101st lost 2,110 casualties in the tough fighting. When the Allied offensive ended, though, the division was not immediately withdrawn. Days of difficult combat in The Netherlands still lay ahead. ∎

American airborne troops take cover as a convoy of Allied lorries comes under fire between Eindhoven and Son in The Netherlands, Operation Market Garden. *(Public Domain collections of the Imperial War Museums via Wikimedia Commons)*

A section of the Wilhelmina Canal courses through the landscape in the south of The Netherlands not far from Son. *(Creative Commons Ron Maijen via Wikimedia Commons)*

FIGHT AT SON BRIDGE

The 506th Parachute Infantry Regiment approached the bridge over the Wilhelmina Canal at Son from two directions, the 1st Battalion from the west and the 2nd and 3rd Battalions from the northwest. The 506th had already engaged German patrols that had ventured forward to fire at American glider troops disgorging from their air transport and fought for possession of several farmhouses in the open fields surrounding the landing zones.

Royal Engineers construct a Bailey bridge similar to the temporary span across the Wilhelmina Canal at Son. This construction project took place in Italy in 1943. *(Public Domain collections of the Imperial War Museums via Wikimedia Commons)*

Once the enemy patrols were pushed back, both airborne contingents chose routes that were concealed partially by wooded areas along the roads, and numerous houses closer to town were bypassed rather than cleared as the American officers chose to minimise the risk of observation by the Germans.

Nevertheless, when the Americans reached the vicinity of Son, an antiaircraft battery comprised of at least two 88mm flak guns, mortars, and machine guns opened fire, temporarily halting the advance. Apparently, Dutch Resistance operatives had warned the Allies of the battery's existence near the Son bridge, but word had failed to reach the 506th PIR prior to its movement.

Enemy fire was heavy, and shells struck with deadly accuracy. The town's sanatorium had been damaged, and a brisk firefight broke out in a municipal park directly behind the structure. The facility had not been evacuated, and patients witnessed the small-arms fire, hand grenade detonations, and sometimes close-quarter combat that ensued. When the fighting erupted, the 2nd Battalion did begin clearing German soldiers from houses along the direct route to the Son bridge while other paratroopers continued to engage the defenders.

Sergeant Don Burgett of the 1st Battalion, 506th PIR remembered the rapid assault of the airborne troops that finally silenced the deadly German artillery. "We organised, and we began to charge the guns," he commented. "The only way we were

going to survive was to knock out the 88s even though a lot of us were going to die trying to do it. As we were running toward them, they fired at us at point-blank range. We overran their positions. There were several 88s. They were sandbagged and dug in and used for antiaircraft. A trooper from D Company got in close enough and fired a bazooka and knocked out one of the guns."

Both contingents of the 506th, after sustaining significant casualties, continued toward the Son bridge. However, German engineers were watching and waiting. Seconds before the Americans reached the span, the Germans detonated pre-planted explosives, sending the structure

This German 88mm flak gun, similar to those that defended the approaches to the Son bridge in The Netherlands, resides in the Imperial War Museum. *(Creative Commons Richard Angman via Wikimedia Commons)*

Cheering crowds greet the 2nd Welsh Guards and their Cromwell tanks as XXX Corps pushes through Eindhoven toward Son, where the 506th PIR, 101st Airborne Division has reached the Wilhelmina Canal, September 19, 1944. *(Public Domain collections of the Imperial War Museums via Wikimedia Commons)*

This church tower in the town of Son remains a conspicuous landmark, identifiable for a considerable distance out of the town. *(Creative Commons Wammes Waggel via Wikimedia Commons)*

sky high and dousing the Americans closest to the canal with a cascade of water and debris.

Burgett recalled, "We overran the 88s, took the German gunners prisoner, and someone said, 'Let's take the bridge.' We started running toward the bridge. We were within yards of the bridge when the Germans blew it up. It went off with quite a force…We hit the ground. I rolled over on my back because everything got real quiet, and I saw the debris in the air. I remember seeing this tiny straw that was turning slowly way up in the air and as it hit its maximum trajectory and as it started to come down, it became larger and larger. About halfway down we realised the size of this thing. It was probably about two feet wide and forty feet long. There was no place to run. When it hit the ground, the ground shook like Jell-O."

Sloughing off the shock of seeing the Son bridge blown to pieces right in front of them, the troopers of the 506th were immediately confronted with the need to get some men across the Wilhelmina Canal to establish a defensive perimeter. While the German engineers who had blown the bridge ran for their lives, an officer, followed by several other troopers, jumped into the water and swam across the canal. They found a small rowboat and pressed it into service as a ferry to deliver a handful of paratroopers to the opposite bank of the canal for the establishment of a thin defensive line.

Troopers of the 326th Airborne Engineer Battalion began gathering materials that might be used to construct a temporary footbridge.

They discovered a cache of lumber and other building materials that had been hidden by the Dutch Resistance and local civilians near the canal's edge and set to work feverishly. While word was passed to the rear that a Bailey bridge, conceived prior to the outbreak of World War Two by British engineer Donald Bailey who worked in the War Office, would be needed to provide a sturdy structure for the tanks and armoured vehicles of XXX Corps to cross the Wilhelmina Canal en route to Eindhoven and then Arnhem, the American engineers put their footbridge together in a remarkably short time, allowing most of the 506th PIR to cross the canal with dry feet and head up the road toward Eindhoven.

By the morning of September 18, Canadian engineers were busily clearing the remains of the original Son bridge to make way for the component trusses of the Bailey bridge that would be assembled as soon as possible. When the trucks carrying the bridging equipment arrived that afternoon, the Canadian engineers began their hours-long overnight labour. The first tanks and trucks of XXX Corps, including those of the Household Cavalry and Irish Guards, roared across the bridge in the early morning of the 19th.

That evening, the Germans counterattacked the Son lodgement. As many as half a dozen PzKpfw. V Panther medium tanks of Panzer Brigade 107, a component of the LXXXVI Panzer Corps, 1st Parachute Army, and supporting infantry battered their way along a narrow axis of advance

adjacent to the Wilhelmina Canal and came within 60 yards of the Son bridge. Hurriedly, a towed 57mm anti-tank gun of the 81st Antiaircraft and Anti-tank Battalion was pulled forward by a Jeep. Moments after their weapon was offloaded from a glider, the anti-tank gunners fired an accurate round, setting the lead Panther aflame and forcing the others to retire out of range.

The Bailey bridge at Son was defended against further enemy probing attacks and continued to serve as a vital link through the remainder of Operation Market Garden. ∎

This monument to Allied airborne forces of Operation Market Garden is located in the Dutch town of Son. *(Creative Commons Wammes Waggel via Wikimedia Commons)*

THE ISLAND

A 17-pounder gun of the 21st Anti-Tank Regiment, Guards Armoured Division, is positioned to defend the Nijmegen bridge at a road embankment on 'the Island.' *(Public Domain collections of the Imperial War Museums via Wikimedia Commons)*

A fter the fighting at Son and along the 15-mile section of Hell's Highway under the control of the 101st Airborne Division had subsided, General Maxwell Taylor, the division commander, realised that the narrow corridor remained vulnerable to German counterattacks from both east and west. Despite the failure at Arnhem, if the Allied ground gains into The Netherlands were to be held, the 101st depended on relief from both the British VIII and XII Corps advancing on its flanks. Taylor, therefore, conducted limited offensive operations in late September to keep the Germans off balance, assess their strength, and to disrupt any enemy preparations for a counterattack.

While most of the tired troopers of the 101st Airborne contemplated withdrawal from the line at the end of September 1944, the division was placed under the control of the XII Corps on the 28th and trucked northward to an area of the front line between the Lower Rhine and the River Waal. This three-mile strip where the Screaming Eagles and elements of the 82nd Airborne Division would join the British to experience intense combat was known as "the Island," and the resulting battles that recovered ground lost to the Germans and to the retained the Allied Nijmegen salient tested their endurance. This was polder country, ground that was below sea level but kept dry by a series of dikes that were sometimes 20 feet high. Farms, fields, and orchards dotted the flat landscape, and here and there were drainage ditches and culverts, ideal spots for enemy soldiers to hide and set ambushes.

Since the British were in desperate need of troops after sustaining heavy casualties during Market Garden, they had prevailed on the Americans for infantry support. Soon enough, the American paratroopers were experiencing warfare similar to that in the trenches of World War One a generation earlier. Sharp clashes between opposing troops were punctuated by artillery duels between the British and German artillerymen.

On October 2, the 506th PIR loaded aboard lorries and passed over the battle-scarred bridge at Nijmegen to take up positions in the north. The next morning, the Americans relieved the British 43rd Wessex Division, which had taken serious casualties during the attempt to take the crossings on the Lower Rhine and the evacuation of remnants of the 1st Airborne Division from the vicinity of Arnhem. The 506th was the first substantial component of the 101st to move into the Island, and its first order of business was to clear the area of the German 363rd Volksgrenadier Division, which had suffered heavy losses during the fighting in Normandy but received replacements and approached combat strength once again.

Captain Richard Winters, who had received the Distinguished Service Cross for heroism in Normandy, remembered that the British troops look spent after two difficult weeks of fighting. And he fully appreciated the fact that his own Easy Company would be in the thick of it for the foreseeable future. Each company of the 506th's 2nd Battalion covered about a mile to a mile and one-half of the perimeter, and the five officers and 130 enlisted men of Easy Company were placed to the right with the 1st and 2nd Platoons in front, the 3rd Platoon in reserve.

Two days of relative quiet were shattered by a German infantry assault supported by heavy-machine gun and mortar fire on the morning of October 5. The enemy moved

On September 28, 1944, amphibious DUKW craft transport supplies across the River Waal at Nijmegen after German divers have destroyed the centre span of the railway bridge. *(Public Domain collections of the Imperial War Museums via Wikimedia Commons)*

During fighting at 'the Island' a British soldier crouches beside a destroyed German PzKpfw. III tank in Nijmegen on September 27, 1944. *(Public Domain collections of the Imperial War Museums via Wikimedia Commons)*

Knocked out by an anti-tank weapon, a German Sturmgeschütze III self-propelled assault gun lies abandoned at the railway bridge near the Dutch town of Driel. *(Creative Commons Universal Public Domain via Wikimedia Commons)*

forward at 4 a.m. and hit 3rd Battalion hard. The battalion commander was killed in the sharp exchange, and 20 minutes later a four-man patrol sent out by Winters returned with disturbing information. All four troopers had been wounded by enemy small-arms fire, and one of them reported a large concentration of German infantry at a crossroads just three-quarters of a mile from the Company E command post.

Winters set out to assess the situation for himself and subsequently led his company brilliantly. "As I got closer to the crossroads, I heard voices and then I observed seven enemy soldiers silhouetted against the night sky, standing on top of the dike by the machine gun," he later wrote. "They were wearing long winter overcoats and distinctive helmets. I crawled until I was about 25 yards behind them in the drainage ditch at the bottom of the dike...I halted the patrol and instructed Sergeant Dukeman and Corporal Christenson to set up our machine gun. I then went to

On October 17, 1944, British soldiers man a 6-pounder anti-tank gun along a road near the town of Nijmegen. *(Public Domain collections of the Imperial War Museums via Wikimedia Commons)*

each man and in a whisper assigned each a target on the German machine gun crew with instructions to fire on my command... The rifle fire was good, but our machine gun fired a bit high. Three Germans started running for the other side of the dike. I joined in with my M-1, as did everybody else. In short order we accounted for all seven enemy soldiers."

The fight, however, had just begun. Winters began to pull his squad back down the drainage ditch, but sporadic enemy rifle fire grew in intensity. He radioed for reinforcements, while troopers of Easy Company eliminated the immediate threat. He then advance alone about 50 yards into a field between his own squad-sized detachment and the expected enemy line, determining the Germans had the tactical advantage, both in numbers and in position to outflank his unit or even proceed down the road straight into his company command post. Rather than allow the Germans to take the initiative, Winters audaciously attacked.

As his reinforcements trickled in, Winters organised the assault and sprinted forward, reaching the roadway that approached the dike. Leading the rush, he found himself alone, confronted by a German sentry only a few yards away and observing a concentration of enemy infantry that had taken cover at the junction of the road and the dike. Winter shot the sentry and then opened fire on the mass of German infantrymen, probably restricted in movement because of the full packs and long coats they wore.

"The movements of the Germans seemed to be unreal to me," Winters remembered. "When they rose up it seemed to be so slow, when they turned to look over their shoulders at me, it was in slow motion, when they started to raise their rifles to fire at me, it was in slow, slow motion. I emptied the first clip [eight rounds] and, still standing in the middle of the road, put in a second clip and, still shooting from the hip, emptied that clip into the mass."

When the vicious, one-sided firefight was over, Easy Company, supported by a detachment from Company F, had shredded two companies of SS troops attempting to

infiltrate the American lines in support of the attack by the 363rd Volksgrenadier Division.

Winters described that particular engagement as the "highlight of all E Company actions for the entire war, even better than D-Day, because it demonstrated Easy's overall superiority in every phase of infantry tactics: patrol, defense, attack under a base of fire, withdrawal, and above all, superior marksmanship with rifles, machine gun, and mortar fire."

In late November, after 72 days in the front line and combat areas, the 101st Airborne Division was withdrawn from the Island to rest and refit at Camp Mourmelon, just outside the French village of Mourmelon-le-Grand. In addition to its losses during Operation Market Garden, the grinding battles at the Island had inflicted nearly 1,700 more casualties on the weary airborne division. ■

Wearing the rank of major, Richard Winters led the daring attack of October 5, 1944, during action at 'the Island.' *(Creative Commons https://i0.wp.com/farm3.static.flickr.com/2563/3768712594_6e7c823569.jpg via Wikimedia Commons)*

82ND AIRBORNE IN ACTION

Young but experienced, Brigadier General James M. Gavin, commander of the veteran US 82nd Airborne Division, evaluated the task laid before his paratroopers as Operation Market Garden took shape.

North of the lodgements of the 101st Airborne, the 82nd "All American" was to capture the bridge across the River Maas at the town of Grave. It was the longest in Europe at 1,960 feet. In addition, the 82nd was assigned the seizure of the at least one of four bridges across the Maas-Waal Canal, another span across the River Waal at Nijmegen, and the area encompassing the Dutch village of Groesbeek. If successful, the 82nd would pave the way along Hell's Highway for XXX Corps to speed along toward relief of the British 1st Airborne Division, holding the vital bridge at Arnhem.

It was a big "if." Gavin understood several aspects of the pending operation clearly. His troopers were to capture all of their objectives in a single day, September 17, 1944, and hold them until relieved by XXX Corps, presumably some time the following day. That meant

This artist's watercolor depicts a Dutch strongpoint at Nijmegen with the arches of the highway bridge in the background. *(Public Domain collections of the Imperial War Museums via Wikimedia Commons)*

the lightly-armed paratroopers were to take care of themselves for at least 36 hours. Intelligence reports indicated that only light German resistance would be encountered during the "Market," or airborne phase, of the offensive. In fact, General Frederick "Boy" Browning, deputy commander of the Allied First Airborne Army, had been said to have described the effort as a "Party."

Still, Gavin was troubled. He could see from available maps that the terrain surrounding the towns and bridges was dominated by a triangular ridgeline running from just southeast of Nijmegen past a resort hotel called the Berg en Dal and through the towns of Wyler, Groesbeek, and Riethorst along the banks of

The highway bridge spans the wide River Waal at Nijmegen. Note the damage to buildings in the town. *(Public Domain US Government via Wikimedia Commons)*

Paratroopers of the US 82nd Airborne Division descend on their drop zone near Grave in Operation Market Garden. *(Public Domain US Army via Wikimedia Commons)*

Cromwell tanks of the 2nd Welsh Guards cross the Nijmegen highway bridge during Operation Market Garden, September 21, 1944. *(Public Domain collections of the Imperial War Museums via Wikimedia Commons)*

Battalion reported later, "We could not have landed better under any circumstances."

The 505th PIR, under Colonel William Ekman, was the tip of the 82nd Airborne spear, the first combat troopers to exit their transports. General Gavin jumped with them and remembered, "As far as one could see, the sky was filled with planes and gliders, and as we neared the coast of Europe, we could see the fighter-bombers flying back and forth over the land beneath us, looking for antiaircraft guns and enemy weapons to knock out…Everything that I had memorised was coming into sight. The triangular patch of woods near where I was to jump appeared under us just as the jump light went on."

General Gavin ordered Colonel Roy Lundquist, commander of the 508th PIR, to send the single battalion hurriedly to perhaps grab the Nijmegen bridge while the rest of the regiment moved to secure six miles of the commanding ridgeline from Nijmegen south to Groesbeek. The 508th would also turn its attention to assisting with the seizure of the bridges across the Maas-Waal Canal at Hatert and Hininghutje, cut the roads approaching the canal from the north, and secure the glider landing zones south of Wyler for resupply and reinforcement.

British soldiers remove explosives planted by the Germans on the highway bridge at Nijmegen, September 1944. *(Public Domain collections of the Imperial War Museums via Wikimedia Commons)*

the Maas. The high ground was roughly eight miles long and rose to a substantial height of 300 feet, providing a virtually unobstructed view of the surrounding area and broad fields of fire for some distance before terminating along the Dutch-German frontier, disappearing into the nearly impenetrable depths of the Reichswald, Germany's national forest.

Gavin and Browning contemplated the role of the 82nd and agreed that priority should be given to taking the ridgeline and then all other objectives prior to the concerted movement against the bridge across the Waal at Nijmegen. Still, if the Nijmegen bridge could be taken swiftly so much the better. Gavin later determined that he could spare a single battalion for a run at the key bridge, hopefully before the surprised Germans could react in force.

The IX Troop Carrier Command supplied 480 C-47 transport aircraft along with 50 gliders and tow planes for the insertion on September 17. The pilots flew a course over the estuary of the River Scheldt and the River Maas, covering 80 miles above German-held territory. The 7,250 paratroopers of the 82nd Airborne were delivered by the 50th and 52nd Troop Carrier Wings to the drop zones near the Maas south of Nijmegen. The 315th Troop Carrier Group delivered 78 sticks of paratroopers within 1,500 yards of their designated beacons set by the Pathfinders of the 82nd Airborne under Lieutenant G.W. Jaubert, first to jump into the Netherlands at 12:47 p.m.

The entire 504th PIR, except Company E, 1st Battalion plummeted successfully within its designated drop zone. Company E had been given a separate drop zone on the west bank of the Maas just west of the city of Grave. From

that position it would support other companies of the 504th PIR in capturing the Maas bridge.

After C-47s of the 440th and 441st Troop Carrier Groups dropped the headquarters of the 508th PIR and two battalions just beyond the northern edge of their assigned drop zone, the 3rd Battalion descended within the eastern boundary. The 508th PIR was rapidly assembling, and in just over an hour and one-half, it was 90 percent consolidated. The commander of the 3rd

After fighting at Nijmegen has subsided, Dutch civilians wave to British tankers on the highway bridge. *(Public Domain United Kingdom Government via Wikimedia Commons)*

Dutch civilians ride atop an Allied Jeep during celebrations in Nijmegen on September 20, 1944. *(Public Domain United Kingdom Government via Wikimedia Commons)*

Eckman and the 505th were to take Groesbeek and occupy the ridgeline south of the town to Kiekberg, taking Hill 77.2 and holding a second glider landing zone. At the same time, Colonel Reuben Tucker's 504th PIR was to capture the big bridge over the Maas near Grave, take the bridges over the Maas-Waal Canal at Heumen and Malden, and then block the enemy from shuttling soldiers to the hotspots between the Maas and the Maas-Waal Canal.

Only light resistance was encountered in the drop zones, and the 82nd Airborne quickly went to work. One stroke of luck occurred when the Grave bridge was easily taken. Sixteen troopers of the 504th PIR under Lieutenant John S. Thompson aboard a lone C-47 had been delayed just a few seconds in jumping. Thompson was looking down, and when the green light was illuminated he noticed that the plane was directly above a cluster of buildings. He decided to delay his men for a moment, adjusting their destination to a nearby open field.

After Thompson's men parachuted, the commander of the stick was pleasantly surprised to find that they were only 700 yards from the southern end of the Grave bridge. Although the rest of the 504th PIR was more than a mile distant, Thompson displayed daring initiative. The handful of troopers disregarded sporadic rifle fire and crouched along shallow drainage ditches. A bazooka team rose up and blasted a 20mm flak gun with a pair of rockets. Wires to demolition charges were quickly cut, and the southern end of the bridge belonged to the 504th PIR in minutes.

The rest of Thompson's battalion surged toward the Grave bridge from the other side of the Maas. A single flak gun at the water's edge barked in an anti-infantry role but failed to deter the Americans. Within three hours one of the 82nd Airborne's principal objectives in Operation Market Garden was firmly in its control. Patrols sent into Grave to reconnoitre came back with reports that the Germans had pulled out of town. The citizenry had flooded into the streets and begun celebrating to the popular tune "Tipperary."

Major Willard E. Harrison, commanding the 3rd Battalion, 504th PIR, ordered single companies to take the Maas-Waal Canal bridges at Malden and Heumen. From an island in the canal at Heumen, German soldiers sprayed machine-gun and rifle fire at the attackers, but eight paratroopers stealthily moved forward to place covering fire on the enemy positions while two officers, a radio operator, and a corporal rushed the bridge. One trooper was shot in the attempt, but six more men rowed a small boat across the canal to support the three who survived the harrowing sprint. When darkness closed in, a reinforced patrol dashed over a footbridge to take on the Germans defending the island. In a few minutes the enemy guns were silent.

As Captain Thomas Helgeson led his company toward the bridge at Heumen, he expected to see it erupt as the German blew it to pieces. Demolition charges were spotted, but the Americans sent a team in to cut the wires. But just as a squad of paratroopers reached the edge of the canal at Malden, that bridge went up in a tremendous blast, showering debris for several hundred yards. Troopers of the 504th and 508th PIRs discovered the bridge over the Maas-Waal Canal at Hatert had also been destroyed. In the predawn hours of the next day, men of the 508th advanced toward the last bridge across the canal at Hononghutje. They found that the Germans had detonated explosives that failed to destroy the span but damaged it extensively enough that it could not be used for vehicle crossings. The bridge at Heumen would later become the primary northward route of XXX Corps.

The 82nd Airborne consolidated its hold in the central course of the XXX Corps advance. A battalion of the 508th PIR occupied the northern end of the ridgeline for three and one-half miles from the outskirts of Nijmegen to the resort of Berg en Dal. Only light resistance was encountered during the movement, and the next day the battalion cut the Kleve-Nijmegen highway when troopers occupied the village of Beek at the foot of the ridge. A second battalion set up roadblocks to deny the Germans any movement south on the highway between Mook and Nijmegen.

The Waal runs deep and formidably wide at Nijmegen, and Lieutenant Colonel Shields Warren, Jr., took the 1st Battalion, 508th ahead in the quick strike against the span. Gavin remembered his orders to Colonel Lundquist

A British tank passes a knocked out German PzKpfw. III tank along a road in The Netherlands. *(Public Domain collections of the Imperial War Museums via Wikimedia Commons)*

as instructing the battalion to move against the bridge "without delay after landing." Lundquist, however, may have misinterpreted this order and apparently relied on the original directive to secure other objectives before any concerted move was made against the highway bridge across the Waal.

With Warren on the move, Lundquist ordered him to set up defensive positions in De Ploeg, a suburb of Nijmegen, and establish communications with other paratrooper positions at the Berg en Dal. It took Warren more than three hours to get his troops forward to De Ploeg, and by the time the defensive positions were established per Lundquist's order it was 6:30 p.m. Dutch civilians had filtered into the airborne perimeter and informed the Americans that only 18 German soldiers were guarding the southern end of the big bridge. Warren sent a reinforced patrol, including a rifle company and his intelligence section, into Nijmegen to validate the reports, but a radio malfunction prevented any information from reaching the battalion commander until the next day.

Meanwhile, Gavin was growing uneasy. He sensed an opportunity and issued a sharp order to Lundquist that conveyed his disappointment with the progress thus far. It instructed Lundquist "...to delay not a

This Nijmegen hotel served as a headquarters during the liberation of the city in September 1944. *(Creative Commons Havang(nl) via Wikimedia Commons)*

After German frogmen have disabled the railway bridge at Nijmegen, British soldiers load an amphibious DUKW vehicles to transport supplies across the River Waal. *(Public Domain collections of the Imperial War Museums via Wikimedia Commons)*

American soldiers enter the city of Nijmegen following the street to street battle for the liberation of the city. *(Creative Commons Regional Archives Nijmegen via Wikimedia Commons)*

A German 50mm PAK 38 anti-tank gun remains in place long after the battle for Nijmegen. *(Creative Commons Roger Veringmeier via Wikimedia Commons)*

second longer and get the bridge as quickly as possible with Warren's battalion."

After seven long hours, the first real attempt to seize the Nijmegen bridge finally got underway. At first, a Dutch civilian offered to guide Warren's battalion directly into the town, but he chose to order Companies A and B to link up southeast of town at 7 p.m. before following the Dutchman into Nijmegen. More time slipped away. Company A reached the rendezvous point at the designated time, but Company B got lost during its march. After another hour lapsed, Warren decided he could wait no longer. Leaving a guide for Company B, he started off in the direction of the bridge with Company A. The streets were dark and shadowy as the troopers cleared houses on the edge of town. They encountered no opposition and crept forward to a traffic circle, the Keizer Karel Plein, in the centre of Nijmegen. The jig was suddenly up when German rifle and machine-gun fire halted their progress at 10 p.m.

General Wilhelm Bittrich, commander of the German II SS Panzer Corps, had sensed that the Allies were after the major bridges in the south of The Netherlands. He responded intuitively to the threat, and his insight was to prove costly as Operation Market Garden proceeded. While the American paratroopers took cover from the enemy small-arms fire, they heard the growing growl of engines, squeaking brakes, and soldiers jumping from trucks. The vanguard of the 10th SS Panzer Division Frundsberg was arriving in Nijmegen.

Either through miscommunication or lack of initiative, the Americans had squandered their opportunity to seize the big bridge across the Waal, and many a good man would die because of the grievous error. Hours earlier, only a few German soldiers of inferior combat efficiency had stood in their way, but these SS troops were battle-hardened veterans who knew their business. After Company A tried twice to rush the southern end of the bridge and was twice thrown back by SS counterattacks, the effort on September 17 came to an ignominious close. General Gavin ordered the troopers in Nijmegen to "withdraw from close proximity to the bridge and reorganize."

Just as operations were petering out during the night, a member of the Dutch Resistance had passed word to Captain Jonathan Adams, Jr., of the 1st Battalion, 508th PIR, that the detonation equipment for the explosives wired to the Nijmegen bridge was housed in the town's nearby post office. A 1941 graduate of the US Military Academy at West Point who had received a Silver Star Medal for valour in Normandy, Adams organised a patrol that shot its way past the guards at the post office door, burst inside

into the teeth of German rifle and machine-gun fire. The enemy fell back just as the expected gliders began to touch down. The Americans lost 11 casualties in the fight, killing 50 Germans and taking another 150 prisoner.

While the 82nd Airborne Division held the ground it had won, General Browning considered a night assault across the Waal to capture the Nijmegen bridge but then decided to wait for XXX Corps. Gavin agreed as rumours of German tanks being sighted in the Reichswald flitted through his headquarters. Within a few hours of crossing the Wilhelmina Canal at Son, the spearhead of XXX Corps arrived at Nijmegen. Both Gavin and General Brian Horrocks, commander of XXX Corps, realised that time was of the essence as the 1st Airborne clung to its lodgements in and around Arnhem.

Gavin told Horrocks about a plan to take the Nijmegen bridge. "There's only one way to take this bridge," he had said to his own staff. "We've got to take it simultaneously from both ends." The 82nd Airborne commander had decided to send paratroopers across the Waal in small boats downstream from the highway bridge and a railroad bridge that was identified as a secondary objective. Once these men had come ashore, they would outflank the German defenders at both bridges. Meanwhile, the remaining paratroopers would be joined by the infantry and tanks of XXX Corps to keep the Germans at the southern ends of the bridges busy. Swift execution could, though the plan was risky, win the day at Nijmegen.

Gavin was facing multiple obstacles, including the stubborn Germans in Nijmegen, the security of the glider landing zones, and shortages of troops to deal with both, not to mention the prospects of an enemy counterattack. After two days of fighting, Company A, 505th PIR was down to only 42 men and two officers, but efforts to clear Nijmegen and take the bridge continued on September 19 as plans for the river crossing and combined attack with XXX Corps were being drawn up.

On the afternoon of the 19th, Lieutenant Colonel B.H. Vandervoort led the 2nd Battalion, 505th PIR with the support of British infantry and tanks of the Guards Armoured Division against the southern end of the railroad bridge. Lieutenant Oliver B. Carr's Company D, 505th took fire from the rail marshalling yard about 1,000 yards from the southern end of the bridge. The company managed to move 500 yards closer but could make no further gains as the lead British tank was disabled by a direct hit from a German 88mm shell.

and quickly destroyed what they believed to be the detonation equipment. Seconds later, the Americans found themselves cut off and unable to return to their jump-off position near the traffic circle. Adams and his patrol held out until they were rescued three days later.

On the morning of September 18, the effort to take the bridge was renewed. Captain Frank Novak and Company G, 3rd Battalion, 508th PIR were called up from Hill 64 about a mile from the southern end of the bridge. Joyful townspeople greeted the troopers as Novak led them through back streets along the edge of Nijmegen, shielding them from the Germans' view. The Americans were pelted with flowers and handed fresh fruit, but as they drew closer to the bridge the crowd evaporated.

The Germans had been thoroughly surprised by the airborne offensive, but they responded quickly, working through the night to strengthen their defences. When the Americans came into view, they unleashed a torrent of small-arms, 20mm antiaircraft, and 88mm cannon fire. Novak's company reached within a block of the traffic circle before it was halted, but reinforcements could not be introduced in Nijmegen without seriously weakening the security of the glider landing zones, where aircraft were expected imminently. By 2 p.m., Company G had been pulled out of the town and returned to Hill 64.

German infiltrators had used the cover of darkness to threaten the thin American line. Creeping in from the Reichswald, they initiated pitched battles with the paratroopers. In one encounter, a company of the 508th PIR was temporarily surrounded, and in another the 505th PIR was late in securing a landing zone when it had to fight for the ground.

When Colonel Lundquist sent a company of the 508th on a sweep of the northern landing zone, the exhausted paratroopers completed a gruelling eight-mile forced march and then executed a Hollywood-style downhill charge

A Sherman tank of the 13th/18th Hussars, 8th Armoured Brigade maintains watch along the River Waal at Nijmegen, October 1944. *(Public Domain collections of the Imperial War Museums via Wikimedia Commons)*

King George VI reviews troops of the British 2nd Army along with XII Corps commander General Neil Ritchie near Nijmegen in October 1944. *(Public Domain collections of the Imperial War Museums via Wikimedia Commons)*

A combined attack also hit the southern end of the highway bridge, the attackers reaching within 300 yards of the traffic circle and then splitting into two groups. Suddenly, a German cross-fire erupted from houses surrounding the circle and enemy troops inside it. Company F, 505th continued forward, but its supporting tanks were stopped by a log barricade. Company E got within 100 yards of the circle, but an anti-tank round demolished the lead British tank, and three others were disabled in rapid succession.

As evening descended on September 19, the Allies had been denied four times. The highway and railroad bridges at Nijmegen remained firmly in German hands. During the night, Gavin ordered Colonel Tucker to detach two companies of the 504th to defend the bridges over the Maas and Maas-Waal Canal.

The rest of the 504th PIR was directed to execute Gavin's plan for the hazardous waterborne crossing of the River Waal on September 20. ∎

After the liberation of Nijmegen, students perform a satirical play regarding their former Nazi occupiers. *(Creative Commons Regional Archives Nijmegen via Wikimedia Commons)*

MAJOR COOK'S CROSSING

Troopers of the 504th Parachute Infantry Regiment crouch along a roadway in The Netherland during Operation Market Garden. *(Public Domain US Army via Wikimedia Commons)*

The paratroopers of the 3rd Battalion, 504th PIR, 82nd Airborne Division, had hardly ever thought about making a riverine crossing. After all, they descended from the sky.

On the morning of September 20, 1944, at the height of Operation Market Garden, all that changed. The highway and railroad bridges at Nijmegen were in German hands, and XXX Corps had to get across the wide River Waal. So, into its swift current, the American paratroopers would plunge, rowing small boats to the river's hostile north shore to take on the enemy and wrest control of the bridges from that side. Simultaneously, successful attacks against the Germans at the southern ends of the bridges would complete their seizure, according to the plan devised by General James M. Gavin, the division commander.

This photo of the 504th Parachute Infantry Regiment was taken during its service in Italy. *(Public Domain US Army via Wikimedia Commons)*

The first order of business for the 3rd Battalion was to scrounge enough small boats to make the crossing. When the paratroopers came up short, the British offered to bring 33 collapsible boats of the XXX Corps engineers forward. They could reach Nijmegen by mid-day and be assembled rapidly. The 3rd Battalion attack, originally set for 1 p.m., was delayed two hours while the boats were brought up through snarled traffic.

While the boats were in transit, the fighting at Nijmegen continued. Strong German counterattacks from the depths of the Reichswald forced the 1st Battalion, 505th PIR to give ground around the villages of Mook and Riethorst. Two platoons of infantry were sent to reinforce the defenders, but they were the battalion's last reserve. Tanks of the Coldstream Guards lurched ahead from XXX Corps in support, but by the time the Germans were pushed back, 1st Battalion had lost 20 killed, 54 wounded, and seven missing.

Further north, the two platoons of the 508th PIR holding the town of Wyler were forced out, and troopers at Beek were pushed back toward the resort at Berg en Dal. Tactically, the Germans failed to take advantage of an opportunity to skirt the Allied right flank and slip into Nijmegen with opposition. In the event, the 508th fought throughout September 21 to retake the lost towns.

Back in Nijmegen, Major Julian Cook, commander of the 3rd Battalion, 504th PIR, contemplated the looming mission that would become legend, one of the most stirring assaults of World War Two. As the 3 p.m. h-hour approached, Cook looked at the situation and did all he could to prepare his men for the coming trial. The British boats were flimsy, made of canvas and plywood. His troopers would

be obliged to paddle across the 400-yard breadth of the Waal, battling its swift current – estimated at eight to 10 miles per hour in some areas – all the while, and right under the noses of German defenders who could probably see their every move even before they went into the water.

The boats were 19 feet long, and when they arrived the troopers counted 26 of them rather than 33. They had to be assembled and carried to the riverbank near a power plant about a mile north of the railroad bridge. The boats arrived only 20 minutes before the attack was set to launch. Three engineers of XXX Corps would be in each of the craft, their task to keep the small, dangerously overloaded boats on course. More than one wave would be necessary to get the entire 3rd Battalion across the Waal, so these brave engineers would be required to paddle back across the river, pick up another load, and again run the gauntlet to the north bank.

In support of the daring 3rd Battalion crossing, a detail from another battalion of the 504th was assigned to the assault. Allied aircraft, including rocket-firing Hawker Typhoon fighter-bombers, were expected to roar overhead and pummel the German defences along the river. Roughly 100 artillery pieces and the main guns of some XXX Corps tanks were ordered to fire a 15-minute barrage in preparation for the landing, forcing the enemy soldiers to keep their heads low. Then, the Allied artillery would lay a heavy smokescreen, the planners hoping that winds would be favourable enough to keep the smoke close and obscure the vision of German gunners watching the 3rd Battalion row across the Waal like ducks in a shooting gallery, utterly but temporarily defenceless.

General Gavin noted that the terrain surrounding both sides of the river was open, flat ground. He realised that his original intent to have the boats load in a secluded area near the mouth of the Maas-Waal Canal was unworkable due to the swift river currents. The troopers would be required to board the rickety boats in

Major Julian Cook led the 3rd Battalion, 504th Parachute Infantry Regiment in the daring river crossing of the Waal at Nijmegen. *(Public Domain US War Department via Wikimedia Commons)*

Armoured vehicles and troops of XXX Corps are greeted by Dutch civilians in Grave en route to Nijmegen. *(Public Domain collections of the Imperial War Museums via Wikimedia Commons)*

make the return trip, and the heroic engineers eventually ran the gauntlet six times before their hazardous duty was over, delivering the balance of the 3rd Battalion and then the 1st Battalion, 504th to the far shore.

In the first wave, Major Cook paddled furiously. A devout Roman Catholic, he literally shouted the Hail Mary repeatedly as he went. Several paratroopers remember vividly his recitations amid the storm of enemy fire. Cook tried to organise the attack once he reached the north bank, but unit cohesion was impossible. The troopers fired their rifles at the closest Germans, and for a few minutes the exchange was reminiscent of a bar brawl. Small groups of paratroopers advanced, leaving 50 enemy dead along the riverbank. The first men sprinted across an open field devoid of cover, reaching a road bed lined with dikes roughly 800 yards from the river. They cleared the Germans to their front with grenades and the point of the bayonet as some engaged in hand-to-hand fighting.

Moving rapidly with some troopers under the command of unfamiliar officers due to the confusion, the Americans proceeded to scatter enemy defenders and silenced machine-gun nests. They happened across a strongpoint at Fort Hof van Holland, which they had been ordered to bypass. But they took it anyway.

Wrecked vehicles and debris litter the road approaching the highway bridge at Nijmegen after its capture during Operation Market Garden. *(Public Domain collections of the Imperial War Museums via Wikimedia Commons)*

the open. Early in the process, German gunners on the north bank began to train their weapons on the assembly area, and enemy soldiers perched among the steel girders of the railroad bridge squeezed off rifle rounds to harass the Americans while aware of their every move.

At the appointed time, the artillery boomed, the RAF fighter bombers swooped in, and the paratroopers began carrying the boats on their shoulders to the edge of the Waal, some of them slipping as they stepped into the muddy water and falling into the current. The Germans opened up with machine guns, rifles, and 20mm flak guns placed near the railroad bridge. Bullets hissed, some tearing gaping holes in the canvas of the boats as they ripped through.

The paratroopers climbed aboard while some men were mired in the muck of the shallows. Then they began paddling for their lives. Moments after the artillery had switched from high explosive to smoke shells, the wind shifted and much of the covering shroud was swept away.

Several boats were shredded by German fire as they struggled to maintain course against the river current. One boat was hit by a mortar shell and capsized just 20 yards from the north bank. When the boat rolled over, Private Joseph Jedlick immediately sank straight to the bottom of the Waal in eight feet of water. He did, however, have the presence of mind to hold his breath, keep a sturdy grip on his Browning Automatic Rifle (BAR), and walk toward the shoreline where all hell had broken loose. The chaotic scene of men leaping from boats, pitching over mortally wounded, or just simply disappearing into mist from a direct hit by a German shell was unnerving.

Almost miraculously, some paratroopers escaped injury amid the fusillade, took quick cover, and then began to move off the shoreline. Lieutenant Colonel J.O.E. Vandeleur,

commander of the 3rd Battalion, Irish Guards, was mesmerized as the drama of the moment unfolded. He later commented, "It was a horrible, horrible sight. Boats were literally blown out of the water. Huge geysers shot up as shells hit and small arms fire from the northern bank made the river look like a seething cauldron. I remember almost trying to will the Americans to go faster."

Half the boats in the first wave were lost, but the engineers turned the remaining 13 back toward the south bank of the Waal to pick up their second load. Eleven of them managed to

British armoured vehicles cross the River Waal on the highway bridge at Nijmegen a day after the heroic seizure of its north end by troopers of the US 3rd Battalion, 504th Parachute Infantry Regiment. *(Public Domain collections of the Imperial War Museums via Wikimedia Commons)*

This contemporary aerial view of the River Waal and highway bridge at Nijmegen reveals the distance covered by Major Julian Cook and the 3rd Battalion, 504th Parachute Infantry Regiment during the waterborne assault of September 20, 1944. *(Public Domain collections of the Imperial War Museums via Wikimedia Commons)*

Four British paratroopers, escaped from Nazi captivity, come ashore at Nijmegen after crossing the River Waal in a small boat. The highway bridge is shown in the background. *(Public Domain collections of the Imperial War Museums via Wikimedia Commons)*

Sergeant Leroy Richmond of Company H swam underwater across a moat that surrounded the fort. Rising up on the other side, he motioned to onlooking troopers to use a nearby causeway. Once across, the attackers took out machine guns and a troublesome 20mm flak gun that had been firing from the fort's towers. Moments later, troopers of Companies H and I reached the north ends of both the railroad and highway spans.

The Germans apparently never attempted to blow up either bridge, and at 4:20 p.m. their stubborn defences at the traffic circle began to falter. Troopers of the 505th PIR and British tanks and infantry at last chased the enemy from the south end of the highway bridge. When the British tankers saw an American flag fluttering from the railroad bridge, they mistakenly took it as a signal to cross the highway bridge, although the 3rd Battalion troopers were still some distance from that span at the time.

Nevertheless, four tanks of the Grenadier Guards led by Captain Peter Carrington, the future Lord Carrington, started across the highway bridge, even though they knew it might be blown up at any moment. Three of the tanks reached the north end. In the years since the great fight at Nijmegen, Lord Carrington has been erroneously criticized by some observers as reluctant to move forward to the immediate relief of the 1st Airborne Division at Arnhem after crossing the Waal. On the contrary, Lord Carrington displayed tremendous bravery during the battle and later received the Military Cross for heroism.

Officially, three privates of H and I Companies greeted the vanguard of XXX Corps at the highway bridge's north end at 7:10 p.m. German defenders streamed back toward the Waal from the railroad bridge and became trapped. Dozens of them were captured and 267 killed.

General Brian Horrocks, commander of XXX Corps, later called the 3rd Battalion crossing of the Waal "the most gallant attack ever

carried out" during World War Two. Major Cook survived to receive the Distinguished Service Cross, while the 3rd Battalion lost 28 killed, 78 wounded, and one man missing. At the traffic circle, the 505th PIR lost 200 men, and in all of Operation Market Garden the 82nd Airborne suffered 1,432 casualties.

Finally, the road to Arnhem and the beleaguered 1st Airborne Division lay open. Colonel Reuben Tucker, commanding the 504th PIR, was

justifiably proud but equally dumbfounded when the tanks of XXX Corps halted. "We had killed ourselves crossing the Waal to grab the north end of the bridge," he lamented. "We just stood there seething, as the British settled in for the night, failing to take advantage of the situation. We couldn't understand it. It simply wasn't the way we did things in the American Army – especially if it had been our men hanging by their fingernails 11 miles away."

Still, there was good reason for XXX Corps to pause. Much of its infantry was still engaged clearing buildings and rounding up prisoners in Nijmegen. Tanks proceeding alone up the road toward Arnhem might have been easy pickings for German anti-tank guns. The tankers were exhausted, and their armoured vehicles were low on fuel as the gloaming meant nightfall was upon them.

To this day, conjecture surrounds the disposition of XXX Corps on the evening of September 20, 1944. ∎

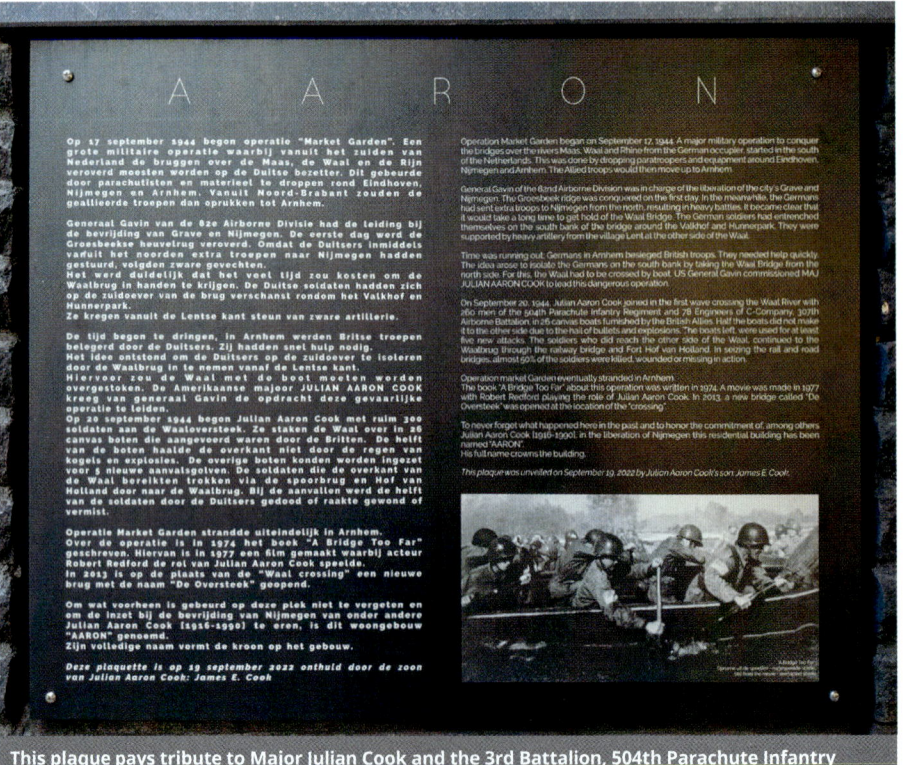

This plaque pays tribute to Major Julian Cook and the 3rd Battalion, 504th Parachute Infantry Regiment at an apartment building in Nijmegen named in honour of the heroic American officer. *(Creative Commons FakirNL via Wikimedia Commons)*

1ST AIRBORNE IN ACTION

O n the clear morning of September 17, 1944, the sky was filled with Allied aircraft. Such a show of aerial might amazed onlookers, civilian and military alike. Operation Market Garden was a massive air/ground undertaking, fraught with risk.

And the riskiest component of the offensive rested with the British 1st Airborne Division, the "Red Devils," under the command of Major General Roy Urquhart. Tasked with seizing the rail, pontoon, and highway bridges across the Lower Rhine at Arnhem, the Red Devils were the furthest north of the Allied airborne troops. Their success depended on holding the bridges, particularly the big highway bridge, until relieved by the spearheads of XXX Corps, hopefully within 48 to 72 hours.

Nearly 9,000 strong, and slated later to be reinforced by nearly 1,700 troopers of the Independent Polish 1st Airborne Brigade, the 1st Airborne Division included three brigades, the 1st Parachute Brigade, commanded by Brigadier Gerald Lathbury and comprised of the 1st, 2nd, and 3rd Battalions; the 4th Parachute

Inside their C-47 transport plane, British paratroopers exude optimism prior to the commencement of Operation Market Garden. *(Public Domain collections of the Imperial War Museums via Wikimedia Commons)*

Field Marshal Walter Model, commander of German Army Group B, confers with General Heinz Harmel, commander of the 10th SS Panzer Division Frundsberg during the response to Operation Market Garden. *(Creative Commons Bundesarchiv Bild via Wikimedia Commons)*

Brigade, under Brigadier John Hackett with the 10th, 11th, and 156th Parachute Battalions; and the 1st Airlanding Brigade, under Brigadier Philip Hicks fielding the 1st Border Regiment, 7th King's Own Scottish Borderers, and 2nd South Staffordshire Regiment. The pilots of the Glider Pilot Regiment, more than 1,300 of them, would also be fighting on the ground once their aircraft landed. By the time Market Garden was over, 229 men of the Glider Pilot Regiment were killed with nearly 500 wounded or captured.

Although the air armada was massive, the 1st Airborne Division faced an early challenge. It could not be inserted entirely in a single airlift. Subsequent waves would be necessary. At the same time, suitable drop and glider landing zones were as many as eight miles west of Arnhem. A

foot march, possibly against German resistance, would be required to reach the bridge objectives.

Urquhart proceeded, assigning the initial airborne insertion to the 21st Independent Parachute Company to mark drop zones and secure them for the follow-on 1st Parachute Brigade, 1st Airlanding Brigade and the division Reconnaissance Squadron under Major Freddie Gough. A total of 475 C-47 troop transports and 321 gliders were filled with paratroopers and equipment when the first plane scratched into the sky, its glider in tow, at 9:45 a.m. The 21st Parachute Company followed, overtaking the lumbering glider-towing aircraft. The remainder of the 1st Airlanding Brigade and the 4th Parachute Brigade were scheduled to arrive on September 18, D+1, and the Polish contingent

Infantrymen of the 50th Northumbrian Division, XXX Corps, move into positions for the Market Garden ground advance on September 16, 1944. A knocked-out German 88mm gun sits at left. *(Public Domain collections of the Imperial War Museums via Wikimedia Commons)*

German soldiers move along a trench line in the vicinity of Arnhem, September 1944. *(Creative Commons Bundesarchiv Bild via Wikimedia Commons)*

Hit by German fire on the ground, a British Horsa glider burns in a landing zone in The Netherlands. *(Creative Commons Bundesarchiv Bild via Wikimedia Commons)*

of Arnhem proper as the reconnaissance squadron raced ahead of everything else to hold the highway bridge in advance of airborne battalions – if all went according to plan.

Circumstances intervened, and the situation unfolded quite differently, however. From the outset there were obstacles for the 1st Airborne Division. Some of the reconnaissance squadron's Jeeps were destroyed in the glider landings, and the short range of the Type 22 radios rendered them virtually inoperable in the heavily wooded area. Worst of all, there was organised German resistance early in the advance. Not only were elements of the II SS Panzer Korps in the vicinity, but the 435-man 16th SS Panzergrenadier Depot and Reserve Battalion, led by Hauptsturmführer (Captain) Sepp Krafft, was also in the area for training, and coincidentally RAF bombing hours earlier had driven the unit into the woodlands in near perfect position for an unexpected interception.

Although some of his troops were raw recruits, Krafft's command posed an early threat. Even as the 3rd Battalion set off on the Utrecht road, the competent officer had established roadblocks there and on the railroad line.

The German response was swift elsewhere as well, and in much greater force than the Allies expected. Field Marshal Walter Model dispatched a battle group of the 10th SS Panzer Division toward Nijmegen, while the western edge of Arnhem was occupied by two panzergrenadier regiments and the artillery regiment of the 9th SS Panzer Division. By September 24, the tanks of the 506th Heavy Tank Battalion, massive Tiger II models with 88mm main weapons, were placed at Model's disposal. More than 60 Tiger IIs reached the combat zone, and 45 of them were allocated to the 10th SS Panzer Division.

After advancing only a mile and one-half, Gough's reconnaissance squadron and the 3rd Battalion were stalled by Krafft's troops, while the blocking line west of Arnhem under SS Obersturmbannführer (Lieutenant Colonel) Ludwig Spindler halted the 1st Battalion. Only Frost's 2nd Battalion, skirting the Lower Rhine, reached the river at Arnhem. When 2nd Battalion approached the city, joyous Dutch civilians greeted them, slowing their progress. Frost was informed that the pontoon bridge was no longer a viable objective since its centre section had been floated away. He dispatched Company C to capture the railroad bridge, but the troopers watched in dismay as it was blown sky high – and in short order they were taken prisoner by the Germans. The rest of 2 Para occupied buildings, courtyards, and streets along the north end of the highway bridge, but three attempts to seize the span were unsuccessful. The ordeal of 2 Para became epic, unfolding over several desperate days.

While the 1st Airborne Division deployed, the American 101st and 82nd Airborne Divisions proceeded toward their objectives at key locations further south at Son, Veghel, Grave, and Nijmegen.

With the Irish Guards Battle Group, under Lieutenant Colonel Joe Vandeleur, in the lead, General Brian Horrocks's XXX Corps initiated

SS troops ride bicycles forward as they establish defensive positions during Operation Market Garden. *(Creative Commons Bundesarchiv Bild via Wikimedia Commons)*

on D+2. The paratroopers and glider troops would be delivered by the aircraft of No. 38 and No. 46 Group, RAF Transport Command.

The combat paras jumped during early afternoon, coming down for two hours, while gliders skidded to a halt, some of them crashing into trees or other obstacles. Although there were casualties, the insertion was accomplished in good shape, a couple of hours required for units to organize and larger equipment, primarily Jeeps and anti-tank guns, to be offloaded. Three approaches to Arnhem were to be followed. Southernmost, 2nd Battalion, under Lieutenant Colonel John Frost was to capture the railroad and pontoon bridges following a route designated "Lion" along the Lower Rhine. The 3rd Battalion was to take the Utrecht road on the most direct route code named "Tiger," while the 1st Battalion, after following "Leopard" route, was to hold ground just north the ground advance up the narrow road from the area of the Meuse-Escaut Canal across the Belgian-Dutch frontier and on toward Arnhem. Behind the Irish Guards, the 43rd Wessex Division, commanded by General Ivo Thomas, and the 50th Northumbrian Division, under General Douglas Graham, both experienced infantry formations, followed. The 43rd Division had previously undergone special training in riverine operations while under combat conditions. In addition to the direct thrust of XXX Corps, the VIII and XII Corps would add power to the offensive with flank advances into The Netherlands.

The going was rough virtually from the outset. The war diary of the 3rd Battalion, Irish Guards recorded, "The Battalion Group crossed the Division start line behind a rolling barrage, but we had not gone far before the leading squadron was halted by enemy battle groups with 88mm guns and spandaus in the woods which flanked the roads. Progress was then slow, but the Typhoons (RAF Hawker fighter bombers) who made 200 sorties during the afternoon were able to overcome the enemy opposition, and after taking approximately 100 prisoners we crossed a small bridge just south of Valkenswaard in the evening and entered the town just as night fell. During the day Lt. Russell was wounded by an enemy sniper, and seven other ranks were killed and 18 wounded."

The XXX Corps advance covered just over 13 miles on the first day.

When the radio communications problems arose at General Urquhart's headquarters, he decided the best option was to set out in search of General Lathbury to develop a tactical approach to dislodging the opposition to the advance on Arnhem. Urquhart found Lathbury's brigade headquarters on the Lion

A Waffen SS officer pauses during Operation Market Garden. The response to the Allied air/ground offensive in the autumn of 1944 was swift. (Creative Commons Bundesarchiv Bild via Wikimedia Commons)

During the build-up of forces surrounding the Oosterbeek lodgement of the 1st Airborne Division, SS troops advance along a dirt road toward their assigned position. (Creative Commons Bundesarchiv Bild via Wikimedia Commons)

British paras guard four Waffen SS prisoners captured during fighting on September 18, 1944. (Public Domain collections of the Imperial War Museums via Wikimedia Commons)

Airspeed Horsa gliders lie where they skidded to a halt in drop zones some distance from Arnhem. (Public Domain United Kingdom Government via Wikimedia Commons)

route but learned that Lathbury was actually with the 3rd Battalion at the time. Urquhart located Lathbury, but in the confusion of the fighting the route of return to their respective headquarters was barred by German armour and infantry. These senior officers managed to evade capture, but they were holed up in the attic of one or more Dutch houses for 39 critical hours. Brigadier Hicks assumed command at division headquarters during that period.

Both stiff German resistance and bad weather contributed to the difficulties that persisted into the second day of Operation Market Garden. While Spindler's line received reinforcements and

thoroughly blocked the direct route into Arnhem, the second Allied airlift was postponed for several hours, arriving at 3 p.m. Alternate routes into Arnhem were reconnoitred, but neither 1st nor 3rd Battalion could make headway against German defences that had been extended to the banks of the Lower Rhine. While attempts by the glider-borne infantry to break through to 2 Para were thwarted with heavy losses, Frost's battalion bloodily repulsed an attempt by SS Hauptsturmführer Viktor Gräbner's 9th SS Reconnaissance Battalion to dislodge it from the north end of the highway bridge.

At the same time, XXX Corps got underway after a delay in the arrival of a battalion of 50th Division infantry that was to lead the advance. It was after 9 a.m. when the column moved out, and soon enough, according to the 3rd Battalion, Irish Guards war diary, "...we encountered a nest of anti-tank and machine gun posts in concrete emplacements supported by infantry. Unfortunately, owing to bad weather, we were unable to obtain air support but the gunners did good work and at 1700 (5 p.m.) the enemy decided to withdraw after destroying their weapons, and we were able to have a clear run through Eindhoven to the Wilhelmina Canal. Here we found troops of a U.S. airborne division who were guarding the canal where the Germans had blown the bridge. The battalion group accordingly harboured the night south of the canal, during which time an excellent bridge was constructed by the royal engineers."

On D+2, the British frustration mounted. Although 2 Para continued to resist, the situation grew more critical by the hour. Hicks ordered the 1st and 3rd Battalions to attack Spindler's line in the predawn hours with the added strength of the South Staffords and the 11th Battalion. Poor communications caused the attack to jump off late, and the 1st Battalion was caught in the open. Raked by enemy small-arms and artillery fire, it suffered such heavy casualties that its further use was in doubt. Both the South Staffords and the 11th Battalion suffered in similar fashion.

Urquhart managed to reach his headquarters later in the day, calling off further attacks, but not before the strength of all four involved battalions had been reduced to only 500 men capable of

Brigadier Philip Hicks commanded the 1st Airlanding Brigade and temporarily the entire 1st Airborne Division during Operation Market Garden. *(Public Domain collections of the Imperial War Museums via Wikimedia Commons)*

shouldering a rifle. Meanwhile, the scheduled parachute insertion of the Polish Brigade, under the command of General Stanislaw Sosabowski, was postponed. When the glider portion of the Polish deployment went forward anyway, the landing zone was under intense German fire. In fact, the British troops were struggling to prevent it from being overrun. Careening groundward in the midst of the firefight, the Poles took heavy casualties.

The advance of XXX Corps had been halted with the demolition of the Son bridge in the 101st Airborne sector, its tanks and armoured vehicles forced to sit idle while engineers threw the "excellently constructed" Bailey bridge across the Wilhelmina Canal. The vanguard rumbled on toward Nijmegen beginning at 6:45 a.m. on September 19. German flanking attacks and resistance along the road continued, forcing the XXX Corps column to halt, deploy infantry to reduce the defences forward, clear the roadway of destroyed or damaged vehicles, and move out once more. At times, the road was elevated distinctly above the surrounding polder country, and the high silhouettes of the Irish Guards' Sherman tanks made prime targets for German anti-tank guns.

At Nijmegen, the 82nd Airborne Division was heavily engaged with the 10th SS Panzer Division for control of the railway and massive highway bridges over the River Waal. Both remained in German hands at nightfall on the 19th, and the arrival of XXX Corps, deploying tanks and infantry to clear the town, was required to take the spans on the 20th in concert with an epic river crossing by the 3rd Battalion, 504th Parachute Infantry Regiment to help take both ends of the bridges at the same time. Nevertheless, the Market Garden timetable had been irretrievably disrupted.

The American paratroopers and XXX Corps fought feverishly to keep the stretch of road nicknamed "Hell's Highway" open, but time was slipping away for Frost and his embattled 2 Para at Arnhem. Compounding the problems for the Allies, several of their original drop zones had been overrun by the Germans, and poor communications had led to parachute resupply efforts that were largely unsuccessful. Everything from ammunition to chocolate bars fell into the hands of the Germans, and throughout Market Garden only an estimated 15 percent of the supplies, 21 of 390 tons, meant for Allied troops actually reached them.

Urquhart and Frost finally were able to communicate directly on September 20, and the two officers concluded that neither was in any shape to come to the relief of the other. Understandably, both were still under the impression that the arrival of XXX Corps was rather imminent. Urquhart had only about 3,600 troopers still able to fight, and eight of his nine battalions had been mauled. He pulled his available forces into a tight elliptical shaped enclave around his headquarters at the Hotel Hartenstein in Oosterbeek, a western suburb of Arnhem, hugging the Lower Rhine, solidifying a defensive perimeter as best he could, intending to await the clank of XXX Corps Shermans.

Frost was wounded, and Gough took active command in Arnhem. Forced into an ever-tightening perimeter, the paratroopers ran from house to house as German tanks and panzergrenadiers continued their relentless attacks. The number of wounded steadily

Soldiers of the 1st Battalion, Border Regiment are dug in just 100 yards away from German positions on the perimeter at Oosterbeek. *(Public Domain collections of the Imperial War Museums via Wikimedia Commons)*

increased, while ammunition, food, water and medicine were increasingly in short supply. Truces were called intermittently to allow the British to evacuate seriously wounded men that were to be treated in German field hospitals.

The end was in sight for the 2nd Parachute Battalion. Even as XXX Corps cleared Nijmegen, the fighting near the Arnhem road bridge was coming to a close. Resistance had essentially ceased there by the morning of September 21. However, the ordeal of the defenders in the pocket at Oosterbeek continued. Urquhart became aware that XXX Corps was approaching, but the armoured advance was halted roughly six miles from the highway bridge at Arnhem when a single German anti-tank gun barked and other defences grew formidable. Some support for the besieged was offered with the introduction of artillery fire from the 64th Medium Artillery Regiment, but the outlook remained bleak for the remnants of the 1st Airborne Division.

Meanwhile, the drop zone for the parachute component of the Polish Brigade had been switched to an area near the Dutch town of Driel, two miles south of Arnhem. Even then, about 30 percent of the paratroopers were returned to England. With those that made the airdrop, General Sosabowski looked for a local ferry that was to be used to move his command across the Lower Rhine. However, it had been untethered and drifted downstream. The Poles had come down at about 5 p.m. and immediately come under heavy German fire as they consolidated their position.

On September 22, XXX Corps had fought its way through the town of Elst, five miles north of Nijmegen, and a trio of armoured cars from the 2nd Household Cavalry sped down side roads to make contact with the Poles at Driel while elements of the 43 Wessex Division subsequently came up. Sosabowski received a message from Urquhart, delivered by an officer who had to swim the Lower Rhine to make the delivery, and it conveyed the urgency of the situation. Sosabowski tried to cross the river in the evening, but only 52 men, using rubber rafts, made it into the Oosterbeek perimeter to bolster Urquhart's beleaguered defenders. Another attempt the following night

Both weariness and defiance are reflected in the eyes of these British paras captured during the fight for Arnhem bridge. *(Creative Commons Bundesarchiv Bild via Wikimedia Commons)*

brought 153 Polish paras into Oosterbeek, and losses in the movement were again heavy.

By September 24, what remained of the 1st Airborne Division was hanging on by a thread. Urquhart radioed General Frederick "Boy" Browning, deputy commander of the 1st Allied Airborne Army and tactical airborne commander of Market Garden, "Must warn you unless physical contact is made with us early 25 September consider it unlikely we can hold long enough. All ranks now exhausted. Lack of rations, water, ammunition, and weapons with high officer casualty rate... Any movement at present in face of enemy is not possible. Have attempted our best and will do so as long as possible."

As the 24th drew to a close, XXX Corps had driven to the south bank of the Lower Rhine while some elements had actually crossed the German frontier southwest of Nijmegen. At Arnhem, a two-hour truce was arranged that afternoon and 450 seriously wounded British soldiers were transferred to the care of the Germans. General Horrocks arrived at Sosabowski's command post, and during a council of war that included General Thomas of the 43rd Division and General Browning it was decided to attempt a rescue of the trapped paras.

Placed under the command of Thomas, Sosabowski was told the Polish 1st Battalion would join the 4th Dorsetshire Regiment in crossing the river to reinforce the corridor of escape for the trapped 1st Airborne survivors. Sosabowski protested the mission that he believed was suicidal. When only enough boats were available to carry the Dorsets, the nocturnal crossing proceeded into dismal failure. Two hundred men were captured by the Germans. The Polish crossing was duly cancelled.

Captain James Ogilvie of the Glider Pilot Regiment, who has gone into battle wearing his kilt, stands with another soldier and a Dutch civilian during Operation Market Garden. *(Public Domain United Kingdom Government via Wikimedia Commons)*

The aftermath of the abortive escape attempt left Urquhart to devise his own course of action. He did so.

The battered shell of the 1st Airborne Division pulled out of Oosterbeek on the rainy night of September 25, eight days after its arrival in The Netherlands. Those wounded too seriously to move were left to the care of the enemy. Operation Market Garden ended in a noble sacrifice that had fallen short of its loftiest ambition. Urquhart went into the Arnhem offensive with more than 10,000 men. He came out with fewer than 2,500. ■

The former Hotel Hartenstein in Oosterbeek that served as General Urquhart's headquarters during Market Garden is now a museum. *(Public Domain Deben Dave via Wikimedia Commons)*

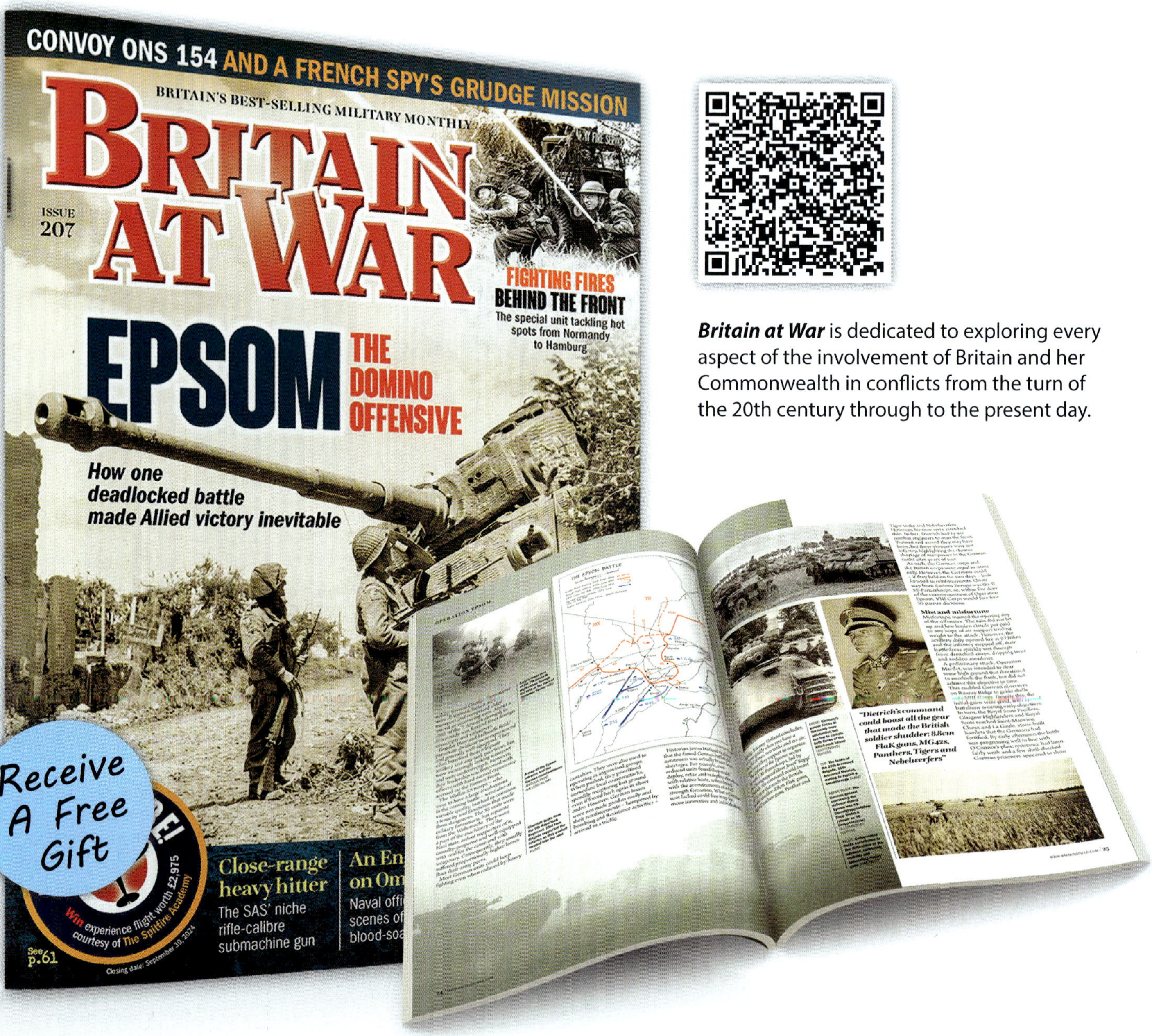

SUBSCRIBE TODAY!

Classic Military Vehicle is the best-selling publication in the UK dedicated to the coverage of all historic military vehicles.

2ND BATTALION AT ARNHEM

There was jubilation, but it was only temporary. Lieutenant Colonel John Frost, a veteran of Operation Biting, the famed Bruneval Raid of 1942, brought his elite 2nd Battalion, Parachute Regiment forward with alacrity.

Proceeding from jump and landing zones west of Arnhem, the 2nd Battalion moved as rapidly as possible along Route Lion toward its objectives, the railroad, pontoon, and most significantly, the highway bridge, across the Lower Rhine. Seizure of these key bridges until relieved by the tanks and troops of XXX Corps would facilitate the dagger stroke into the Ruhr, the industrial centre of the Third Reich.

Frost was well aware that there were Germans about, and in greater numbers than anyone had originally thought. But 2 Para pressed on. "The Dutch people rushed out of their houses, cheered us, shook hands, gave us drinks, apples and marigolds – and some of us were lucky enough to receive the odd kiss," remembered Private Sidney Elliott. "How could this be war? It was a question that would be answered very soon."

The troopers of the 2nd Battalion did enjoy their enthusiastic welcome, but the grim business at hand soon became all too real. The unit, which numbered fewer than 500 men when fully assembled, was charged with holding the bridges – probably for two days at the most –

A pair of British paratroopers, one of them wounded, display the effects of prolonged combat on their faces during Operation Market Garden. *(Creative Commons Nijmegen Regional Archives via Wikimedia Commons)*

until relieved. Of course, that was assuming that the rest of the 1st Airborne Division and in due course the might of XXX Corps came up as well to solidify the British grip on these spans. Therein lay much of the undoing of the great Market Garden plan and the inception of the ordeal that befell 2nd Battalion during more than four harrowing days at Arnhem.

The airdrop of September 17, 1944, had gone extremely well. Frost's command had formed up and set out on the route that followed the course of the Rhine. They tramped through the towns of Heveadorp and then Oosterbeek, just west of Arnhem. They felt the enthusiasm of the liberated civilians who spilled into the streets to welcome them and brushed aside the Germans to their front.

Lieutenant Peter Barry and his 9th Platoon, Company C, rushed toward the railroad bridge in Oosterbeek. The officer saw a German soldier crouching and assumed he was accomplishing the last step in preparing the bridge for demolition. He halted the run just as a tremendous explosion signalled the demise of the rail span.

"It was lucky that we stopped when we did," Barry remembered. "Otherwise we would have all been killed. No one was injured in the explosion. Immediately afterwards I felt

This aerial view shows the highway bridge over the Lower Rhine at Arnhem just days before Operation Market Garden. *(Public Domain Royal Air Force Government of the United Kingdom via Wikimedia Commons)*

something hit my leg. I asked if anyone had fired a shot, but they all shouted in unison that no. It must have been a German bullet. Then I felt a bullet sear through my right upper arm."

Daly was among the first of many casualties sustained by the 2nd Battalion at Arnhem. And to make matters worse, Lieutenant Colonel Frost was soon informed that the pontoon bridge was now useless as its centre span had apparently been removed and floated down the Rhine. The only viable objective left was the highway bridge.

Frost had originally intended to use the railroad bridge to take the highway bridge from both ends simultaneously. Now, the direct approach was the only available option. The bulk of 2nd Battalion pushed into Arnhem and occupied buildings, private residences, gardens, and walkways. Frost set up his command post on the upper floors of a home while the few available 6-pounder anti-tank guns were placed on the lawn of an office building. More paratroopers trickled in, including more than 100 of the 1st Parachute Battalion Headquarters.

Taking stock of his situation, Frost could count more than 700 men from various units that were filtering into the 2 Para positions. Around 8 p.m., he had received information from a Dutch constable that only about 25 Germans were guarding the 2,000-foot highway bridge, but a pillbox, silent for now, presented an obvious obstacle.

Within minutes, 16 paratroopers scrambled up an embankment adjacent to the road and headed across the bridge. A German machine gun opened fire from the pillbox, and an enemy armoured car came into view, its turret-mounted cannon shooting as well. The first attempt was pushed back. A second try at the bridge was undertaken a bit later as Lieutenant Jack Grayburn exhibited tremendous courage. Grayburn took a bullet in the shoulder, and seven other paras were wounded before this effort was called off.

A German counterattack materialized, the enemy soldiers running between the steel girders of the bridge. Although the assault was beaten back, these troops surprisingly

German soldiers service a 20mm flak gun during the fighting in Operation Market Garden. *(Creative Commons Bundesarchiv Bild via Wikimedia Commons)*

Exhausted British troopers of the 1st Airborne Division, having survived the ordeal of Operation Market Garden at Arnhem, await their time as prisoners of the Germans. *(Creative Commons Bundesarchiv Bild via Wikimedia Commons)*

appeared to be panzergrenadiers, the supporting infantry of an armoured formation. A second German probing attack, utilising soldiers driven into the fight aboard lorries, met a similar fate. The Germans were stopped cold, and several of the lorries were set on fire, their hulks littering the north end of the bridge.

The British next attempted to take the bridge around 10 p.m., when an anti-tank gun and flamethrower were brought forward to deal with the troublesome pillbox. At Frost's order, the 6-pounder fired on the pillbox – and missed – setting off a terrific explosion in a tool shed that was being used for ammunition storage. A streak from the flamethrower also missed its mark, and the result of this

failed attempt was to set the flammable paint covering the bridge structure alight. It burned through the night. In all the hubbub, the paratroopers bagged 17 German prisoners.

As they made these several attempts to take the bridge, the 2nd Battalion was also being cut off from the main force of the 1st Airborne Division. Significant resistance, primarily from an SS reserve battalion in the area for training, as well as elements of the 9th SS Panzer Division, halted the larger advance to the bridge in its tracks. Although he was unaware at the time, Frost and the 2nd Battalion were marooned. Communications with division headquarters was non-existent, but the battalion was still full of fight.

Over his shoulder, a British soldier carries a PIAT anti-tank weapon such as those used by the 2nd Battalion at Arnhem. *(Public Domain collections of the Imperial War Museums via Wikimedia Commons)*

Major Digby Tatham-Warter was conspicuous with his folded umbrella during the fighting at Arnhem. *(Public Domain United Kingdom Government via Wikimedia Commons)*

This photo was taken moments after the capture of these two British paratroopers in the rubble of Arnhem. *(Creative Commons Nijmegen Regional Archives via Wikimedia Commons)*

A helmet crowns the simple grave of an unknown British paratrooper killed and buried by the Germans at Arnhem. *(Public Domain collections of the Imperial War Museums via Wikimedia Commons)*

At dawn on September 18, German tanks and infantry counterattacked from the east but were driven off. "The gun spades were not into the pavement edge, nor firm against any strong barrier," wrote Lieutenant Arvian Lewellyn-Jones, who watched a 6-pounder in action targeting a German tank. "The gun was laid, the order to fire given, and when fired ran back 50 yards, injuring two of the crew. There was no visible damage to the tank. It remained hidden in part of the gloom of the underpass of the bridge. The gun was recovered with some difficulty. This time it was firmly wedged. The Battery Office clerk, who had never fired a gun in his life, was sent out to help man the gun. This time the tank under the bridge advanced into full view and looked to be deploying its gun straight at the 6-pounder. We fired first. The aim was true; the tank was hit and it slewed and blocked the road."

The Germans came on again, SS panzergrenadiers riding in lorries. They jumped from their transport, some of them taking terrific fire from the Bren guns and rifles of the paratroopers ensconced in windows and dug in along the road. An ambulance even came forward, packed with SS troops, rather than on a mission of mercy. The occupants were slain to a man when they emerged.

Frost watched the gruesome display and quipped, "I suppose they'll send a hearse next." Indeed, the Germans' collective nose was bloodied, and one panzergrenadier remembered, "This was a harder battle than any I had fought in Russia. It was constant, close range, hand-to-hand fighting. The English were everywhere. The streets for the most part were narrow, sometimes not more than 15 feet wide, and we fired at each other from only yards away. We fought to gain inches, cleaning out one room after another. It was absolute hell!"

After a brief respite in the early morning, the largest attack yet against the British toehold took place. Captain Viktor Gräbner and the Reconnaissance Battalion of the 9th SS Panzer Division stormed across the highway bridge and into the teeth of the determined defenders.

The paras lashed out with small-arms fire and spring-fired PIAT anti-tank weapons. A dozen German armoured vehicles were destroyed in the attempt, and Gräbner was among the 70 panzer troops who died.

They had held their own for a time, but it was becoming more apparent to the embattled men of 2nd Battalion that relief was not arriving in a timely manner. They clung to optimism that the rest of the 1st Airborne Division and XXX Corps itself would appear at any time, and they clung to that hope as tenaciously as they did the north end of the highway bridge.

One last German attack hit the eastern edge of the British defences late on the 18th. The paras knocked out the two tanks that accompanied infantry emerging from under the bridge access ramp. The Germans intermittently lobbed mortar shells into the British positions, and artillery fire gradually intensified. In the absence of 1st Brigade commander Brigadier Gerald Lathbury, Frost assumed command of the brigade assemblage while Major Digby Tatham-Warter, a colourful officer who was everywhere seen with his umbrella, wrapped and ready, stepped into the battalion command role.

During the night of September 19, engineers checked the underside of the highway bridge as far as they could for explosives and structural integrity. A house was set on fire to provide illumination in the otherwise quite darkened area. Oddly, a group of enemy soldiers made its way onto the bridge in the dead of night. Apparently unaware of the nearness of peril, they were ambushed. At least 20 were killed by small-arms fire and hand grenades, while a few astonished men scattered.

At noon on Tuesday, September 20, three German tanks assaulted the paratroopers from the east again, driving toward a house occupied by Company A near the ramp. The British were driven from the structure, but one of the tanks was immobilised by a PIAT round. There was no sign of relief or reinforcement, either from the rest of the 1st Airborne Division, XXX Corps, or the expected introduction of the 1st Polish Independent Parachute Brigade, whose insertion had been disrupted by inclement weather.

The Germans, meanwhile, realised that the situation of the 2nd Battalion was deteriorating by the hour as the number of wounded steadily

British prisoners await disposition after their capture during the fighting at Arnhem. *(Creative Commons Bundesarchiv Bild via Wikimedia Commons)*

A number of British officers had been wounded in nearly four days of fighting. Among them were Frost and Major D.E. Crawley, hit by fragments from a mortar shell on the afternoon of the 20th, Major Tatham-Warter who was struck twice, and the 2nd Battalion Catholic Priest Father Bernard Egan, wearing captain's rank. As many as 150 men had been wounded in a single day. With Frost out of action, Major Freddie Gough, commander of the 1st Division Reconnaissance Squadron, assumed command of what was left of a rapidly diminishing force.

Critical defensive strongpoints began to fall into German hands with alarming regularity, including the Van Liburg Stirum School building that dominated the eastern edge of the access ramp. Engineers pulled out of the structure under heavy fire, reluctantly leaving their wounded and a few men who were looking after them to be captured.

A coordinated British defence was rapidly coming apart. In a deadly game of cat and mouse, clusters of paras fought and dashed in and out of cover. The Germans wiped out isolated pockets. Private Kevin Heaney and six others were trapped by Germans just 50 yards distant. They attempted to surrender, and when

German self-propelled assault guns like this Sturmgeschütz III were used to destroy British defences at the Arnhem highway bridge. *(Creative Commons Propagandakompanie der Luftwaffe Dutch Ministry of Defence via Wikimedia Commons)*

increased and ammunition, medical supplies, food and water were ebbing to dangerously low levels. They offered a truce and sent a prisoner, Lance Sergeant Stan Halliwell of the Royal Engineers, back to Frost with an overture to arrange his command's surrender.

Halliwell was accompanied by a few Germans to the front line and then brought across. He spent 10 minutes running between houses trying to locate Frost. Finally, he delivered the enemy's message. The response from the tough lieutenant colonel commanding was terse. "Tell them to go to hell!" Although he had promised to return to the Germans, Halliwell thought better of delivering such a response and decided to remain with his comrades.

When it was apparent that the British would not surrender, the Germans intensified their bombardment of the lodgement at the north end of the bridge. They brought artillery fire to a crescendo, while self-propelled assault guns and mortars rained a terrific barrage with little pause. At some point, Field Marshal Walter Model, commander of German Army Group B, issued the ominous order to "Flatten Arnhem." By late afternoon, heavy Tiger II tanks with 88mm cannon were moving to the attack, blasting houses and buildings with defiant paras inside. Those who attempted to displace through the rubble strewn streets where chased by machine-gun bullets that stitched the cobblestones behind them. When night came, buildings and burning vehicles gave an eerie glow to the detritus of battle, and one paratrooper described the scene as a "...sea of flame."

The British defensive perimeter was shrinking, bit by bit. When dawn came on September 20, only 10 of the original 18 buildings they had occupied were still held. No word from XXX Corps sent a shiver of isolation through the officers of 1st Brigade. When the click-clack of tank treads was heard, there was a glimmer of hope that the Irish Guards had arrived. But it turned out that two German tanks had come up just to fire their guns. Meanwhile, Lieutenant Colonel Frost and Major General Roy Urquhart, commanding

the 1st Airborne Division, finally spoke by radio and decided that neither could come to the aid of the other. Both, then, would depend on the arrival of XXX Corps whenever it might appear.

The German panzergrenadiers picked through rubble, blasted their way into houses, and evicted the paratroopers in sharp clashes. The British fought back, one of their few remaining Gammon bomb hand grenades finding the open troop compartment of a Nazi halftrack. When the grenade detonated, bodies were shredded and blown into the air. Still, enemy infantry pushed ahead intent on seizing the area around the ramp to deny any advancing Allied relief the use of the bridge across the Lower Rhine. They tried to attach explosives along the ramp and its supporting arch that would block an advance, but a group of Royal Engineers got in their way. Lieutenant Grayburn, wounded on September 17, and again in the fighting of the 20th, gave his life in the action that day and received a posthumous Victoria Cross.

German SS panzergrenadiers inspect ground retaken from the British near Arnhem. A Sturmgeschütz III self-propelled gun is visible in the background. *(Creative Commons Jacobsen (Propagandakompanie der Luftwaffe) Dutch National Archives via Wikimedia Commons)*

A German halftrack sits in position near Arnhem during Operation Market Garden. Note the British parachute in the background. *(Creative Commons Bundesarchiv-Bild via Wikimedia Commons)*

British prisoners captured in the fighting at Arnhem are marched off into captivity in September 1944. *(Creative Commons Bundesarchiv Bild via Wikimedia Commons)*

The wreckage left in the wake of the battle for the highway bridge at Arnhem is shown after the fighting during Operation Market Garden subsided. *(Public Domain United Kingdom Government via Wikimedia Commons)*

the Germans called them out, the first four to emerge were mowed down by a machine gun.

Charitably, Heaney deduced that the enemy must have been under fire from elsewhere at the time. The wounded were pulled back to cover. "We were there for about two hours," he recalled. "I had my prayer book open and was saying the Prayer for the Dying. Later on, the Germans came in, rescuing the trapped men and taking them prisoner, and this great big German came and took the two of us also."

Two Tiger tanks advanced directly across the big bridge, shunting aside the wreckage of Captain Gräbner's attack. They methodically blasted any structure within range, while the strength of two German battle groups detailed to eliminate the paratroopers went

about their deadly business. Here and there, exhausted paratroopers, pummelled by tanks and heavy artillery, famished and thirsty, low on ammunition, many walking wounded, began to surrender, having come to the realisation that no relief was in sight. There was no dishonour in avoiding further loss of life. The 2nd Battalion and other British soldiers in Arnhem had earned the grudging respect of their enemies while exacting a toll of their own.

One German tanker took out his personal camera and recorded poignant scenes of the scarred streetscape. Another said of the paras that stumbled into captivity, "They came in most cases quite peacefully. Poor blokes, they were rather tired and exhausted from their continuous time in action."

The modern John Frost Bridge, named for the commander of the 2nd Battalion, Parachute Regiment, spans the Lower Rhine today. *(Creative Commons michiel1972 via Wikimedia Commons)*

Those British who continued to fight were resigned to their fate, but they remained defiant. Nineteen-year-old SS panzergrenadier machine gunner Rudolf Trapp remembered his halftrack confronting one of the last operational British 6-pounder anti-tank guns while under orders to wipe out resistance. "Bernd Schultze-Bernd was our driver, a farmer's son from Sendenhorst in Muensterland. He was one of three old company veterans...there were tears in his eyes. He told our company commander that this was not going to work. But an order is an order...We raced past the crossroads and got hit on the left, near Bernd's driver's seat. The vehicle came to a halt. Bernd was dead, a direct hit from the shell."

While the combined efforts of the US 82nd Airborne Division and XXX Corps secured the road and rail bridges over the River Waal at Nijmegen, the Germans used the Arnhem highway bridge to bring all the strength available to mop up in Arnhem, September 20-21. As the rest of the 1st Airborne Division remained besieged at Oosterbeek, a truce was declared for the wounded in Arnhem to be removed to German medical facilities.

During the two-hour cease-fire, Major Gough told a gathering of troopers near a building where Frost and other wounded were lying to try their best to escape the Germans and make their way back to their own lines. He wished them well and said cheerfully as he could, "...And just remember that you belong to the finest division in the British Army."

Gough, the nearly 300 wounded in the building, and those who chose to remain behind as small clutches of paratroopers struck out on their own, became prisoners of the Germans. Seventy-one of the gallant British defenders at the bridge, nearly 10 percent of their number, were dead on the doorstep of the Rhine.

Lieutenant Colonel Frost, foggy from the morphine he had been administered, was taken captive. He remembered, "Both sides laboured together to get the wounded out, and I saw the Germans were driving off with Jeeps full of bandaged men. The SS men were very polite, but the bitterness I felt was unassuaged. No living enemy had beaten us. The battalion was unbeaten yet, but they could not have much chance with no ammunition, no rest, and with no positions from which to fight. No body of men could have fought more courageously and tenaciously than the officers and men of the 1st Parachute Brigade at Arnhem."

The valiant Frost's assessment was accurate. His command had etched its name in glory amid the shortfall of an epic offensive, and its example of sacrifice endures. ■

CAPTAIN GRÄBNER'S ATTACK

Captain Gräbner rode into battle in Arnhem in a captured British Humber armoured car similar to this example. *(Creative Commons Dutch Ministry of Defence via Wikimedia Commons)*

This aerial view of the road bridge at Arnhem was taken on September 19, 1944, and shows the wreckage of German vehicles destroyed during the fighting. *(Public Domain collections of the Imperial War Museums via Wikimedia Commons)*

After the first night of Operation Market Garden, with its sporadic firefights and general confusion, the German response to the British airborne presence at the north end of the Arnhem bridge across the Lower Rhine was rapid.

There were probing attacks to assess the strength of the British perimeter, where the 2nd Battalion, Parachute Regiment had occupied some buildings and surrounding courtyards and streets of Arnhem. At daybreak on September 18, tanks, PzKpfw. III and IV types, rolled forward from the east only to be driven back by rounds from the few anti-tank guns and shoulder-fired PIAT weapons available, although the fighting was bitter and close-quarter at times before petering out.

Lieutenant Colonel John Frost, commanding 2 Para and the assortment of other men who had managed to find their way into Arnhem, including more than 100 from the 1st Parachute Brigade headquarters, recalled the lull that followed the early fighting as "a time when I felt everything was according to plan, with no serious opposition and everything under control."

Frost's perspective was soon to change. On the afternoon of the 17th, Hauptsturmführer (Captain) Viktor Gräbner had led the 9th SS Panzer Division's reconnaissance battalion on a

Troopers of the 2nd Battalion, South Staffordshire Regiment, 1st Airlanding Brigade, advance toward Arnhem on September 18, 1944, along with a 6-pounder anti-tank gun. *(Public Domain collections of the Imperial War Museums via Wikimedia Commons)*

southward sweep along the highway between Arnhem and Nijmegen in response to reports of an Allied airborne insertion. The route was determined clear of enemy forces, but Gräbner received another report noting that British paratroopers had captured the north end of the

Arnhem bridge. Gräbner left some of his troops and vehicles at the town of Elst and proceeded northward during the night. He arrived in Arnhem around 9:30 on the morning of the 18th with 22 of his original complement of 40 vehicles, including armoured cars, halftracks, motorcycles, and trucks carrying Waffen SS combat troops.

Gräbner was determined to retake the north end of the bridge and eliminate the British incursion. By mid-morning, Frost and his paratroopers could hear the rumbling of engines.

An experienced officer, Gräbner had received the Knight's Cross for heroism in Normandy in August during ceremonies just a day earlier. Thirty years old, he had joined the German Army in 1937, participated in combat on the Eastern Front during Operation Barbarossa, the invasion of the Soviet Union, and received rapid promotion. In the spring of 1942, he was awarded the German Cross in Gold. Transferring to the Waffen SS in January 1943, he received the Close Combat Clasp for action in Normandy.

Described as "an impressive soldier, the right man for the job," whatever that might be, Gräbner was well liked by his men, cutting a dashing figure in either the black dress or mottled camouflage SS combat smock, although he was dark and slight of build. He had earned a reputation for leading from the front and was not afraid to expose himself to enemy fire.

Gräbner's plan was straightforward – his vehicles would make a quick dash across the Arnhem bridge, straight at the British defenders. With armoured cars leading the way, followed by halftracks and then trucks carrying the SS troops, they would rush down the two-lane highway reaching speeds up to 25 miles per hour, cover more than 600 yards up a ramp and across the bridge itself, and then rapidly subdue the British resistance.

As the sun climbed in the morning sky, exhaust fumes billowed from the SS vehicles. Gräbner mounted his captured British Humber armoured car a signalled his command forward with two stiff motions of his arm. All the while, the troopers of 2 Para were watching. They could see the massing assault.

On came the SS, machine guns and light cannon opening fire as they reached the edge of the bridge. According to some eyewitnesses, the action opened so swiftly that the first five armoured cars, their drivers deftly avoiding mines the British had laid and the wreckage of earlier actions, made it across the span intact. Others offer that

Men of the 2nd Battalion, Parachute Regiment are shown in Tunisia in 1942. During Operation Market Garden, many of the troopers of 2 Para were combat veterans. *(Public Domain collections of the Imperial War Museums via Wikimedia Commons)*

the British merely waited for the right time to open fire and allowed these vehicles to cross.

Regardless, within seconds, the paras began blazing away with anti-tank guns, shoulder-fired PIAT anti-tank weapons, Bren light machine guns, and Lee-Enfield rifles. Sergeant Cyril Robson and a gun crew fired into the flank of the German advance, their initial shells cracking an opening in the wall adjacent to the bridge to permit their continuing fire to strike effectively. One armoured car struck a mine that blew a wheel off and caused the vehicle to career out of control.

An SS corporal who survived the melee remembered, "Suddenly, all hell broke loose ahead of us. All around my vehicle there were explosions and noise, and I was right in the middle of this chaos."

Paratroopers flipped grenades into the open troop compartments of halftracks, and wounded men spilled out into the road. Major Freddie Gough, commander of a British reconnaissance squadron, blazed away with a Jeep-mounted Vickers machine gun, and it is believed that one of his rounds struck and killed Captain Gräbner moments into the fight.

Some SS soldiers managed to exit their vehicles and formed squad-size groups to take on the paratroopers. Sharp staccato reports echoed off the buildings of Arnhem as machine-gun and rifle bullets ricocheted.

"I had a German Schmeisser and had a lot of fun with it," recalled Corporal Geoff Cockayne. "I shot at any Jerry that moved. Several of their vehicles – six or seven – started burning. We didn't stay in the room we were in but came out to fire, keeping moving, taking cover and firing from different positions. The Germans had got out of their troop carriers – what was left of them – and it became a proper infantry action. I shot off nearly all my ammunition. To start with, I had been letting rip, but then I became more careful; I knew there would be no more. I wasn't firing at any German in particular, just firing at where I knew they were."

The Germans were taken aback by the ferocity of the British defence, and the bridge became littered with riddled and blackened vehicles, their drivers and many occupants dead within. Other vehicles were run off the slope of the nearby embankment, while many SS soldiers were trapped aboard their halftracks, pinned down by the galling fire. German bodies were strewn across the road and among nearby

buildings and alleys. One halftrack driver tried to back out of the maelstrom and rammed the vehicle to his rear. The two became hopelessly entangled and were shot up by the British. Another vehicle sat motionless, its jammed horn wailing mournfully. Artillery fire from the 1st Airborne Division positions several miles away added to the devastation.

The battle raged for two hours, and virtually every British soldier on the scene had fired at the enemy with the exception of Lieutenant Colonel Frost, who commented after the fighting subsided, "A commander ought not to be firing a weapon in the middle of an action. His best weapon is a pair of binoculars."

Frost witnessed the total defeat of the confident 9th SS Division reconnaissance battalion. More than 70 Germans, including Gräbner, were dead, and many were wounded. Twelve of the 22 German vehicles engaged were destroyed. By noon, the remnants of the German column had begun falling back to Elst to play no further role in Operation Market Garden. The British lost 19 men.

Captain Gräbner's assault on the north end of Arnhem bridge had taken place rather early in the ordeal of the 2nd Battalion. Though it was a defeat for the Germans and the paras shouted their war cry, "Whoa Mohammed!" in celebration, the result caused the commander of the 9th SS Panzer Division, Standartenführer (Colonel) Walter Harzer, to bring heavier strength to bear against the stubborn paratroopers, which ultimately led to their heroic sacrifice. ■

British paratroopers pick their way through Oosterbeek, a suburb of Arnhem, during the opening hours of Operation Market Garden. *(Public Domain collections of the Imperial War Museums via Wikimedia Commons)*

Now a museum piece, this Schwerer Panzerspähwagen, or heavy armoured reconnaissance vehicle, is similar to those employed by Gräbner's battalion at Arnhem. *(Creative Commons Klaus Nahr via Wikimedia Commons)*

OPERATION
BERLIN – ARNHEM EVACUATION

The tanks and troops of XXX Corps were hardly a mile away, but they were separated from the exhausted remnant of the heroic 1st Airborne Division, hemmed in at Oosterbeek, by the expanse of the River Rhine.

There was no alternative, and Major General Roy Urquhart, the commander of the Red Devils, was battling despondency when he contemplated the failure of the offensive that had been undertaken with such ambitious objectives. Urquhart had fewer than 2,500 men still alive under his command, and many of them were wounded. Operation Market Garden was in its eighth day by the evening of September 25, 1944, and an attempted rescue operation involving the 4th Dorsets and the 1st Battalion of the 1st Independent Polish Parachute Brigade the previous night had come to naught.

Now, it was up to Urquhart, and he employed his knowledge of British Army history to help put an evacuation plan together. He remembered the withdrawal from Gallipoli in 1916, when the British and ANZAC forces had lost their venture into the Dardanelles during the Great War.

"I planned the withdrawal like the collapse of a paper bag," Urquhart explained later. "I wanted small parties stationed at strategic places to give the impression we were still there, all the while pulling downward and along each flank."

Operation Berlin – as the retrograde movement was dubbed – would have to take place under cover of darkness. As a thin line of paras kept up a distracting fire, artillery would continue its shelling as well. Normal radio traffic would be kept up as long as possible, and the guards holding German prisoners at the Hotel Hartenstein tennis court complex would be the very last to pull out. The ruse might buy precious time.

Urquhart conferred with Major General Ivor Thomas, commander of the 43rd Wessex Division, to coordinate the evacuation effort and held a meeting with the handful of senior officers who remained unwounded or had not been killed in action. He went over the details of the plan, and Colonel Graeme Warrack, the 1st Airborne Division's chief medical officer appeared despondent. He later related that he was "downcast and unhappy," according to author Cornelius Ryan's seminal narrative from the book *A Bridge Too Far*, "not because I had to stay – I had an obligation to the wounded – but because up to this moment I had expected the division to be relieved in a very short time."

A group of surviving paratroopers extracted from the Arnhem area manage smiles after reaching Nijmegen. *(Public Domain collections of the Imperial War Museums via Wikimedia Commons)*

The words were difficult to utter, but Urquhart told the gathered officers, "We're getting out tonight." It was critical that every man keep moving, he emphasised. Clogging the escape routes or bunching up could easily give the evacuation away and produce a massacre. "While they should take evasive action if fired upon, they should only fire back if it was a matter of life or death," he warned.

In the movement, Urquhart would depend on glider pilots acting as guides to help the evacuees along the single escape path down each side of the ever-shrinking perimeter. Some areas of the routes were marked with white tape to

British infantrymen are shown aboard a universal carrier and an amphibious DUKW craft such as those used in Operation Berlin. This photo was taken in The Netherlands on September 18, 1944. *(Public Domain collections of the Imperial War Museums via Wikimedia Commons)*

The Old Church at Oosterbeek served as a landmark for the evacuating British paratroopers during Operation Berlin. *(Creative Commons Kuile, E.H. ter (Fotograaf) via Wikimedia Commons)*

help the exhausted paras to navigate in the darkness. The evacuating paras were to use the venerable Old Church in the floodplain of the Lower Rhine as a landmark while they reached for the river's edge. Once there, they would load aboard 14 engine-powered assault boats along

with a hodgepodge of other small watercraft, including some of wood and canvas, as well as the marvellously versatile amphibious DUKW. In the event, some anxious troopers decided to swim the 400-yard breadth of the great river.

No one really knew how many boats there were, but four field engineer companies, the Royal Engineer 260th and 553rd and the Royal Canadian 20th and 23rd, were there to manage the transit. Some of the boats could carry up to 14 people, others not so many. No matter. They would have to do.

Although the weather was foul, rainy with clouds, mist, and poor visibility, it may well have helped keep Operation Berlin under cover. The engineers found their departure points hours ahead of the scheduled start of the evacuation, 10 p.m. on the night of September 25. They had come to the south bank of the Lower Rhine, maintaining stealth and secrecy, under the noses of the Germans

When the procession toward the shoreline began, it became an effort to maximise efficiency

German Fallschirmjäger parachute troops hold a position outside Oosterbeek during Operaiton Market Garden. *(Creative Commons Bundesarchiv Bild via Wikimedia Commons)*

while minimising interference. The paras wrapped their boots in strips of cloth to muffle the sound of rustling leaves and branches as they trudged along. As Operation Berlin progressed, the boats were shuttled back and forth as quickly as possible amid the chatter of enemy small-arms fire and frequent mortar and artillery rounds detonating uncomfortably close. While XXX Corps would be firing as furiously as possible to cover the movement, there was still the broad concern of a German attack and breakthrough to the base of the collapsing bag, and that base was only 650 yards wide.

In the midst of the desperate effort to escape, the officers of the 1st Airborne Division were determined to keep their military bearing and to hold their troopers to the same standard. More than one para was advised to shape up a bit and even to get himself clean shaven. An officer barked to a harried man, "You get yourself a dry shave. Hurry up. We're crossing the river and by God we're going back looking like British soldiers."

The withdrawal took hours to accomplish.

Poignant vignettes played out before and during the movement. Author Ryan related that Sergeant Ron Kent and his platoon of pathfinders gathered in a cabbage patch to rendezvous with the remaining men of the 21st Independent Parachute Company filtering in. With little initial information to go on, the assemblage stepped ahead. "Although we knew the Rhine lay due south, we didn't know what point they were evacuating us from," recalled Kent. When red tracer bullets were spotted zipping across the river from the south bank, the men took that as a directional indication. They found the white tape and the helpful glider pilots working feverishly in the dark shadows.

As Sergeant Kent neared the boats, he heard the staccato of a machine gun and the explosion of a hand grenade. Another group of paras had encountered a German patrol and were fighting for their lives. When the brief but sharp skirmish ended, two troopers had been killed, so tragically close to sanctuary.

By 5 a.m., the Germans were finally fully aware of what was going on and opened a heavy fire on the evacuation area, bringing Operation Berlin to a close. More than 2,100 men reached safety during the hazardous movement. Some had drowned. Others had been lost even as their boats neared relative safety only to be riddled with enemy fire.

Although it had been far from triumphant, there was at least some solace in the fact that anyone had made it out of the cauldron of Oosterbeek. The 1st Airborne Division had fought bravely, but it is doubtful that the thin perimeter could have held even a few more hours. ◾

German soldiers advance on the perimeter at Oosterbeek during the last hours of Operation Market Garden. *(Creative Commons Bundesarchiv Bild via Wikimedia Commons)*

A memorial commemorating Operation Berlin stands along the south bank of the Lower Rhine today. *(Creative Commons Vu Do Quynh via Wikimedia Commons)*

VICTORIA CROSS IN MARKET GARDEN

During Operation Market Garden, five courageous individuals earned the Victoria Cross, the highest award of Great Britain and the Commonwealth for valour in the face of the enemy. Four of these were later presented posthumously, and while bravery against overwhelming odds was common during those desperate days, their stories of heroism stand apart

At 21 years of age, Lance Sergeant John Baskeyfield of the South Staffordshire Regiment, 1st Airlanding Brigade, was already a veteran of 1st Airborne Division operations in Sicily and Italy. When Operation Market Garden commenced, the bulk of the brigade reached landing zones in the vicinity of Arnhem on September 17, 1944, with the remaining troops to follow the next day.

Baskeyfield was a member of the anti-tank platoon, 2nd Battalion, which serviced the heaviest weapon available against German tanks that was organic to the South Staffordshire Regiment, the 6-pounder gun, which fired an effective 57mm shell capable of penetrating substantial thickness of armour plating. As the situation around the northernmost of Allied airborne insertions during Market Garden became more desperate, the South Staffordshire Regiment was committed in the effort to reach the beleaguered 2nd Battalion, Parachute Regiment at the crucial road bridge over the Lower Rhine.

The South Staffordshires moved forward on the second day of Market Garden to support the continuing effort to link up with 2nd Battalion, and early on September 19 a concerted attack was launched in the narrow confines between a local railroad line and the riverbank. That attack was turned back with significant losses. Rapidly roles were reversed, and it was the 1st Airborne Division that was forced onto the defensive. A perimeter was built to hold off German

Major Robert Cain led a desperate defence during the German onslaught at Arnhem, earning the Victoria Cross. *(Public Domain collections of the Imperial War Museums via Wikimedia Commons)*

counterattacks, and Lieutenant Colonel Sheriff Thompson, commander of the 1st Airlanding Brigade artillery, ordered Major Robert Cain to take charge and stiffen the line with 75mm pack howitzers and the 6-pounders, two of which were directed by Lance Sergeant Baskeyfield.

Major Richard Lonsdale went forward to take command of the defenders that later became known as "Lonsdale Force." Shortly after sunrise on September 20, German tanks and infantry rolled forward, hitting the airborne line hard. Baskeyfield's 6-pounder section was positioned to cover a road junction at the southernmost portion of the line connecting Arnhem and its western suburb of Oosterbeek. Paratroopers of the 11th Battalion, taking up positions in houses and nearby buildings, opened a withering fire on the exposed German infantry, and two enemy

This monument at Etruria, Stoke-on-Trent, commemorates the valour of John Baskeyfield at Arnhem. *(Creative Commons Steve Birks via Wikimedia Commons)*

tanks and a self-propelled gun came clanking down the road into the range of Baskeyfield's guns. Ordering his crews to hold their fire until the enemy vehicles were fewer than 100 yards distant, Baskeyfield gave the word when results were assured. The 6-pounders barked, and all three enemy armoured vehicles were disabled.

Although devastating return fire took out one of the gun crews and Baskeyfield was badly wounded as well, the lance sergeant remained

Two British soldiers demonstrate the firing of a PIAT anti-tank weapon. *(Public Domain Library and Archives Canada via Wikimedia Commons)*

Captain John Grayburn died while fighting the Germans, cut down by machine-gun fire at Arnhem bridge. *(Public Domain United Kingdom Government via Wikimedia Commons)*

A German self-propelled gun lumbers down a street in Arnhem during Operation Market Garden. *(Creative Commons Bundesarchiv Bild via Wikimedia Commons)*

at his post, turning away entreaties to move to the rear. The enemy continued to advance, and Baskeyfield found himself alone, operating one 6-pounder until it was put out of action and then repeating the act with the other. Baskeyfield loaded the second gun, took aim, and fired two shells that destroyed another self-propelled gun. Seconds later, however, his position was overwhelmed, and he was killed in a hail of fire from yet another German armoured vehicle.

In giving his life, Lance Sergeant Baskeyfield demonstrated selfless courage and played a significant role in beating back the enemy attack. From that point until the withdrawal across the Lower Rhine on September 25, the South Staffordshire Regiment and Lonsdale Force held the line, safeguarding the perimeter against repeated attacks. Baskeyfield's citation read in part: "The superb gallantry of this N.C.O. is beyond praise. During the remaining days at Arnhem stories of his valour were a constant inspiration to all ranks...."

Baskeyfield's heroism came a day after Major Cain had begun to demonstrate tremendous courage under fire that was also worthy of the Victoria Cross. The 2nd Battalion, South Staffordshire Regiment became the only battalion of the British Army to receive two of its nation's highest awards for the same engagement during World War Two. During the September 19 attack toward Arnhem bridge and the 2nd Battalion, Parachute Regiment's precarious lodgement, Cain and his B Company advanced toward a small topographical depression near the town only to be confronted by German tanks and armoured vehicles.

Cain, who had served with his regiment during the Sicily campaign, ordered his men to deploy with their heaviest weapons, the springloaded 83mm PIAT spigot mortar anti-tank weapon and the 2-inch (51mm) mortar. During the spirited exchange of fire, no enemy tanks were damaged, but all PIAT ammunition was expended. The German tanks were virtually unstoppable – at least for a time. The British had entered the fight with four companies, but most of the

troopers were killed or wounded. Cain fell back with the survivors of Company B while the 11th Battalion supplied some covering fire.

Seeing an officer of the 11th Battalion, Cain yelled, "The tanks are coming; give me a PIAT." However, there were no such weapons available. Company B and other defenders held their ground momentarily but were then compelled to retire hastily to Oosterbeek. When Lieutenant Colonel Thompson ordered Cain to stabilise the defensive line, he rushed to the task. From an observation point in the garden of a laundry facility, Cain directed paratroopers to defensive positions, encouraged them, and warned them to be wary of snipers.

On the afternoon of September 21, the situation was critical all along the small, thumb-shaped 1st Airborne Division perimeter. German tanks and self-propelled guns were again hurled forward. As one armoured vehicle advanced, Cain waited in a trench for an opportune moment to strike, but the Germans fired first, a 75mm shell shattering a nearby building and killing a soldier just a few feet from the officer while showering him with shards of brick and masonry. Stunned, Cain regained his composure and fired several PIAT rounds, eventually disabling the enemy armoured vehicle. When another self-propelled gun came into view, he readied his

PIAT again only to have the charge explode before he could fire. Cain was temporarily blinded.

Pulled to a safe position, Cain waited a half hour. His sight returned, and he went back to the desperate fight. His eardrums burst due to the heavy din, but he persevered. On September 24, the officer rushed to assist as a 6-pounder gun disabled a heavy Tiger tank, and a day later he turned a mortar on the enemy, firing in the near-horizontal plane at onrushing German infantrymen. Standing his ground, Cain inspired others around him to hold on. By the time the 2nd Battalion was withdrawn across the Lower Rhine, he was known as a tank killer, personally responsible for the destruction or disabling of at least six tanks and several self-propelled guns.

Major Cain received the Victoria Cross for indomitable courage during those perilous days at Arnhem. King George VI presented the medal at Buckingham Palace on December 6, 1944. Cain survived the war and died of cancer at age 65 in 1974.

Captain John H. Grayburn earned a posthumous Victoria Cross commanding Company A, 2nd Platoon, 2nd Battalion, Parachute Regiment during the harrowing fight at Arnhem bridge. As 2nd Platoon led the battalion into the heart of Arnhem on September 17, Grayburn covered the ramp leading onto the span. An early attempt to

A German photographer took this image during a British resupply mission by parachute in Operation Market Garden. *(Creative Commons Bundesarchiv Bild via Wikimedia Commons)*

take the bridge was repulsed, and Grayburn took a bullet in the shoulder. He refused to leave the line, and during the ensuing hours as casualties mounted, he was wounded a second time. As his men ventured from cover to remove fuses from explosives underneath the bridge, Grayburn saw a German tank bearing down on them. He stood tall, in clear view of the enemy, to shout orders, and the German tank's machine gun cut him down. His Victoria Cross was awarded based on the eyewitness accounts of other officers and men.

Flight Lieutenant David Lord was well aware that the situation around Arnhem was deteriorating. Taking off on a resupply mission on September 19, he had already earned the Distinguished Flying Cross in the Mediterranean. His Douglas Dakota of No. 271 Squadron RAF took heavy flak, sustaining serious damage as one engine was set ablaze. The pilot knew that the plane's wing might disintegrate at any moment but continued his mission, dropping badly needed supplies to the troops below.

When the run was completed, Lord was informed that two canisters remained aboard. Realising that he probably would not survive a second run to the drop zone, Lord turned the Dakota around anyway. The two canisters were jettisoned, and the pilot ordered the crew to bail out. He was last seen holding the aircraft as steady as possible to assist in their exit. One crewman survived and returned from captivity to tell the story of Lord's bravery. His parents accepted the posthumous Victoria Cross at Buckingham Palace in December 1945.

Captain Lionel Queripel was a graduate of the Royal Military College, Sandhurst, and served in the 10th Battalion, 4th Parachute Brigade during Operation Market Garden. On the afternoon of September 19, he commanded a composite unit of paras from three different battalions. As

Captain Lionel Queripel covered the withdrawal of his troops and lost his life in Operation Market Garden. *(Public Domain collections of the Imperial War Museums via Wikimedia Commons)*

Future Victoria Cross recipient Lionel Queripel is shown with comrades during the 1930s. *(Public Domain United Kingdom Government via Wikimedia Commons)*

his troopers attempted to reach 2nd Battalion at Arnhem, heavy German machine-gun fire opened along their route. Captain Queripel crossed a road repeatedly while under continuous enemy fire to deploy his men effectively.

While assisting a badly wounded sergeant to safety, Queripel was wounded in the face. Undeterred, he gathered a few men and set out to silence enemy machine-gun positions. He was successful in killing the machine-gun crews and retaking a captured anti-tank

gun that had been turned on his men by the Germans. Orders were then received to occupy a wooded area northwest of Arnhem bridge.

The position was nearly untenable, continually raked by enemy small-arms and mortar fire. Queripel was wound at least two more times, and at one point leaped to toss back at the Germans a hand grenade that had fallen into the midst of a cluster of paratroopers. The small contingent was in jeopardy of being cut off, and Captain Queripel ordered his remaining men to withdraw while he provided covering fire. He was last seen alive resisting the enemy onslaught. The award of his posthumous Victoria Cross was announced publicly in February 1945. ∎

Flight Lieutenant David Lord flew a Douglas Dakota transport like this on his last resupply mission during Operation Market Garden. *(Public Domain collections of the Imperial War Museums via Wikimedia Commons)*

MEDAL OF HONOR IN MARKET GARDEN

The fighting for the bridges at Best, a small town in The Netherlands, was fierce during the opening hours of Operation Market Garden. Although the bridges there across the Wilhelmina Canal were not primary objectives of the US 101st Airborne Division on September 17, 1944, General Maxwell Taylor, the division commander, realised that they might be of value should the main route of the XXX Corps advance toward Arnhem through the town of Son become blocked. At the same time, securing one of the road and rail bridges there would provide additional security to his thin defensive perimeter.

When intelligence reports indicated that only a handful of German troops were guarding the road and rail bridges at Best, just four miles west of the main Allied ground advance route, Taylor seized the moment and ordered Captain Robert E. Jones to take Company H, 502nd Parachute Infantry Regiment (PIR) to exploit the apparent opportunity. Captain Jones ordered his men to move out, expecting

The Joe Mann monument stands adjacent to a theatre named in memory of the Medal of Honor recipient in the town of Best, Netherlands. *(Creative Commons Wammes Waggel via Wikimedia Commons)*

This memorial, placed where Private Joe Mann died near the town of Best, commemorates his sacrifice during Operation Market Garden. *(Creative Wammes Waggel via Wikimedia Commons)*

to encounter light resistance along the way to secure a 100-foot-long road bridge.

Moments after stepping off, the company ran into heavy German defensive fire, and Captain Jones sent a platoon-sized patrol under Lieutenant Edwin L. Wierzbowski ahead to reconnoitre. This small clutch of troopers approached the road bridge and appeared to have the span in its grasp. Then, just a mere few feet away, the enemy erupted with small-arms and mortar fire. There was no choice but to dig in as the platoon's numbers were rapidly reduced to just three officers and 15 troopers.

Contrary to the early expectation, the fighting for the canal crossings at Best would rage for two more days, continuing even after the Germans, defending in much greater strength than previously indicated, blew the road bridge to pieces on September 18. After the battle, it was estimated that as many as 1,000 German soldiers and 13 large-calibre guns defended the Best bridges.

With his isolated patrol in jeopardy, Captain Jones tried to reach the surrounded men.

However, amid the confusion, no one was sure of the platoon's exact location, and the same was true for reinforcements sent to assist Company H.

One thing, though, was certain. There was no doubt that Company H was fighting for its life. Heroes were numerous, but one stood out among them. Private First Class Joe E. Mann was 22 years old, a native of the small town of Reardon, Washington, who had moved to the big city of Seattle after high school graduation in 1941 seeking work. Instead, he joined the US Army in August 1942, requesting flight training only to be denied because of a previous injury sustained while playing football. He was accepted for airborne service, completed training, and was assigned to Company H.

When Lieutenant Wierzbowski's platoon was ordered to take the road bridge at Best on the first

A portrait of Private John R. Towle is carried by Dutch citizens during ceremonies to honor the fallen soldier held in 2019. (Creative Commons Oldironnow via Wikimedia Commons)

day of Operation Market Garden, Mann served as a scout. After the Nazis blew the road bridge, Mann crept forward with a bazooka to assess the situation and came across an active 88mm flak gun being used as field artillery and pounding away at the surrounded patrol. He destroyed the German gun and an adjacent ammunition stockpile with a bazooka rocket and then killed several enemy soldiers with his M-1 rifle. During the exchange of fire, he was wounded four times.

After returning to his unit, Mann insisted on taking his assigned turn of guard duty during the night. The following morning, the Germans launched a heavy attack on the isolated platoon, and an enemy hand grenade landed in the midst of several paratroopers. Mann's hands were bandaged to his body at the time, and he was unable to raise his arms. He shouted, "Grenade!" and then fell upon the explosive, absorbing the blast and protecting the surrounding men from it. A lieutenant rushed to the side of the mortally wounded soldier. Mann looked up and whispered, "My back is gone," and then he died.

Mann's posthumous Medal of Honor was presented to his father in August 1945. His citation reads in part: "...Completely disregarding the great danger involved, he remained in his exposed position, and with his M1 rifle, killed the enemy one by one..." and continues, "...Unable to raise his arms, which were bandaged to his body, he yelled "Grenade" and threw his body over the grenade, and as it exploded, died..."

Private John R. Towle of Cleveland, Ohio, joined the US Army in March 1943, shortly after turning age 18, and volunteered for the airborne service. During training, he wrote a letter home to his parents commenting, "Well, the first jump is over, and I landed like a feather. You have no sensation of falling at all. I've seen some beautiful things in this world, but, oh brother, nothing can compare with that big, white, silk, beautiful chute."

Towle was assigned to the 504th PIR, 82nd Airborne Division, and by the autumn of 1944, he had served in the Mediterranean theatre, although his only combat jump of the war occurred during Operation Market Garden. On

Lieutenant Colonel Robert Cole's grave, noting his Medal of Honor, is located in Netherlands American Cemetery and Memorial in Margraten, Netherlands. (Creative Commons Wammes Waggel via Wikimedia Commons)

September 21, 1944, his unit occupied defensive positions in the Dutch town of Oosterhout, on the western edge of the road and rail bridges across the River Waal near Nijmegen.

The Germans mounted a heavy counterattack with 100 infantrymen supported by halftracks and a pair of tanks. Without orders, Towle advanced with his bazooka to an advantageous firing position approximately 200 years beyond the tenuous American bridge defence. He went into action alone.

"With full knowledge of the disastrous consequences resulting not only to his company but to the entire bridgehead by an enemy breakthrough, Pvt. Towle immediately and without orders left his foxhole... in the face of intense small-arms fire to a position on an expose dike roadbed," his citation reads. "From

Private John R. Towle, who earned a posthumous Medal of Honor during Operation Market Garden, sat for this portrait in 1943. (Public Domain US Army via Wikimedia Commons)

Lieutenant Colonel Robert Cole was killed by a sniper during Operation Market Garden before he could receive his Medal of Honor earned in Normandy. (Public Domain United States Government via Wikimedia Commons)

First Sergeant Leonard Funk survived the war and exhibited incredible heroism during Operation Market Garden and other engagements. *(Public Domain US Army via Wikimedia Commons)*

this precarious position Pvt. Towle fired his rock launcher at and hit both tanks to his immediate front. Armored skirting on both tanks prevented penetration by the projectiles, but both vehicles withdrew slightly damaged. Still under intense fire and fully exposed to the enemy, Pvt. Towle then engaged a nearby house which nine Germans had entered and were using as a strongpoint, and with one round killed all nine…"

Towle was not finished. He found more ammunition and then rushed another 125 yards amid heavy fire to another exposed position, engaging an enemy halftrack with his bazooka. Just as he took aim, a German mortar shell exploded nearby, and he was mortally wounded. The posthumous Medal of Honor was presented to his family six months later, on March 25, 1945, and Towle was the first trooper of the 82nd Airborne Division to receive his nation's highest honour for courage in combat during World War Two.

Towle's citation concluded, "By his heroic tenacity, at the price of his life, Pvt. Towle saved the lives of many of his comrades and was directly instrumental in breaking up the enemy counterattack." At the time of his death, Private Towle was only 19 years old.

Colonel Robert Cole, commander of the 3rd Battalion, 502nd PIR, 101st Airborne Division, had earned the Medal of Honor in Normandy while leading a bayonet charge in the fight for tactically important causeways crossing from Utah Beach toward the town of Carentan, France. Cole, however, was shot and killed by a German sniper on September 18, and the posthumous medal was presented to his mother at Fort Sam Houston, Texas, a month after his death.

Although First Sergeant Leonard A. Funk, Jr., was destined to receive the Medal of Honor for heroism during the Battle of the Bulge in January 1945, his display of mettle during Operation Market Garden was indicative of his conduct in combat throughout his extraordinary wartime service. He received the Distinguished Service Cross (DSC) for gallantry while serving with the

508th PIR, 82nd Airborne Division, on September 18, 1944, near the Dutch town of Voxhill.

Watching gliders as they approached a landing zone under German fire, Funk and three other paratroopers located the source of the persistent enemy interference, a battery of three 20mm flak guns, and took action.

The DSC citation reads that the guns were "…firing on American gliders then circling to land. He drove off all enemy security around the guns and led an assault which killed approximately twenty members of the crews and inflicted other casualties. The flak guns were silenced before effective fire could be placed upon the aircraft due to the courageous and heroic actions of Sergeant Funk. The courageous action of Sergeant Funk contributed in large part to the prompt seizure of his company objective and assistance in driving the enemy from the landing zone. His initiative, outstanding bravery, and strong personal leadership, despite overwhelming enemy superiority in both numbers and firepower, enabled him to render a distinguished service in the destruction of the enemy…"

At the time of the Market Garden action, Sergeant Funk was 28 years old. He had enlisted in the Army in Braddock Township, Pennsylvania, in 1941. During the D-Day parachute operations three months earlier, his company had come to earth 40 miles from the French coastline, and several days of fighting and evasion were necessary to locate and rejoin their regiment. Funk was also decorated for the action in Normandy. After the war, he returned home, married, and became the father of two daughters. He worked for the Veterans Administration in the Pittsburgh, Pennsylvania, area and died at age 76 on November 20, 1992.

This stone located at Camp Blanding, Florida, commemorates the courage of First Sergeant Leonard Funk during World War Two. *(Creative Commons FLJuJitsu via Wikimedia Commons)*

Sergeant Funk's story is noteworthy not only because of his heroism during Operation Market Garden, but also due to his repeated acts of courage during two combat jumps and subsequent ground operations. When his military career was completed, he had received each of his country's highest awards for bravery in combat, the Medal of Honor, Distinguished Service Cross, Silver Star, Bronze Star, and for wounds in battle the Purple Heart with two oak leaf clusters. ∎

This memorial to Lieutenant Colonel Robert Cole is located in Best, Netherlands. *(Creative Commons Wammes Waggel via Wikiedia Commons)*

MARKET GARDEN IN FILM AND TELEVISION

Actors portraying German soldiers congregate around their vehicles during filming of *A Bridge Too Far*, May 1976. *(Creative Commons Dutch National Archives via Wikimedia Commons)*

A compelling real-life drama, and one of the great war stories of the 20th century, Operation Market Garden has been the subject of numerous film, television, and documentary accounts since the end of World War Two. Each of these has told and retold the series of events that led to the failure of the ambitious offensive in the autumn of 1944.

The landmark feature film *A Bridge Too Far*, released in June 1977, stands out among the efforts to bring the epic story to the big screen for several reasons. Just four minutes shy of three hours, its running time tests the interest level of the viewer who may not find military history a favourite topic. Its budget of $25 million was substantial for its time, more than twice that of the blockbuster *Star Wars*, which

made its debut in the same year. *A Bridge Too Far* featured an all-star cast, carrying more box office power than any other film of the period.

Based on the book of the same name by historian and author Cornelius Ryan, *A Bridge Too Far* was produced by Joseph E. Levine and Richard Levine and directed by Richard Attenborough with a screenplay by William Goldman. Composer John Addison, a veteran of XXX Corps and the actual Operation Market Garden as a soldier of the 23rd Hussars, penned the memorable musical score that garnered a BAFTA (British Academy of Film and Television Arts) Award. Popular with theatre audience, the film earned nearly $51 million at the box office. During production, a number of British M4 Sherman medium tanks are shown along with other armoured vehicles, and some

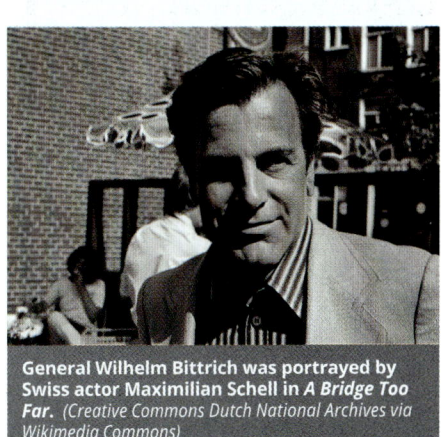

General Wilhelm Bittrich was portrayed by Swiss actor Maximilian Schell in *A Bridge Too Far.* *(Creative Commons Dutch National Archives via Wikimedia Commons)*

Actor Sean Connery, who played General Roy Urquhart in *A Bridge Too Far*, is shown in Amsterdam in 1976. *(Creative Commons Dutch National Archives via Wikimedia Commons)*

of these are wooden dummies placed atop the chassis of Land Rover automobiles. Eleven C-47 transport aircraft were used, and 1,000 parachutists were dropped. These planes were also featured in the film's airdrop supply missions.

The cast includes a who's who in motion pictures of the period. Dirk Bogarde portrayed General Frederick "Boy" Browning. Bogarde had served in the British Army as an air photograph interpreter during Market Garden with the rank of captain. Sean Connery plays General Roy Urquhart of the 1st Airborne Division; Edward Fox is General Brian Horrocks of XXX Corps; Michael Caine is Lieutenant Colonel Joe Vandeleur of the Irish Guards; Anthony Hopkins is Lieutenant Colonel John Frost of the 2nd Battalion, Parachute Regiment; and Ryan O'Neal is Brigadier General James Gavin of the 82nd Airborne Division.

Among other well-known stars, Robert Redford is Major Julian Cook; Elliott Gould is the Colonel Robert Stout (based on Colonel Robert Sink of the US 101st Airborne Division); Arthur Hill portrays a US Army surgeon; James Caan is Staff Sergeant Eddie Dohun; Gene Hackman is General Stanislaw Sosabowski; Maximilian Schell is General Wilhelm Bittrich of the German II SS Panzer Korps; Hardy Krüger is General Karl Ludwig (based on General Heinz Harmel of the 10th SS Panzer Division); Lawrence Olivier is Dr. Jan Spaander; and Liv Ullman is Kate ter Horst. A number of veterans, including General Urquhart and Horrocks, served as military advisors to enhance the historical and technical accuracy of the film, while Fox and Horrocks had become personal friends earlier. Fox reportedly went to great lengths to deliver an accurate portrayal of Horrocks.

The sixth most popular film of 1977, *A Bridge Too Far* was well received by audiences, although critics were sometimes strained in their patience with its length and detail. Charles Champin of the *Los Angeles Times* wrote, "In strictly cinematic terms, the appeal of *A Bridge Too Far* is easy to state: it is spectacular in size and range of its effects, earnestly well-acted by a starry and able cast, well-paced and swift despite its length,

and marked by an evident attempt to give the balanced truth of a tragic episode from history."

However, Roger Ebert whined that the film was "...such an exercise in wretched excess, such a mindless series of routine scenes, such a boringly violent indulgence in all the blood and guts and moans they could find, that by the end we're prepared to speculate that maybe Levine went two or even three bridges too far. The movie's big and expensive and filled with stars, but it's not an epic. It's the longest B-grade war movie ever made."

Interestingly, Attenborough chose not to include an actual portrayal of General Bernard Montgomery, the father of the ill-fated Market Garden adventure. While the name of Montgomery is frequently mentioned, the figure of the 21st Army Group commander is never seen. Perhaps the director's decision was out of respect for the single most towering British military figure of World War Two, particularly because of the historical analysis and evaluation of it that remained emotionally charged even 33 years after the event.

Ullman's character, Kate ter Horst, tended approximately 250 wounded British paras during the fight as her home was occupied as a regimental aid station. She wrote of her experiences in her subsequent book titled *Cloud Over Arnhem* and narrated the opening moments of the film. In addition, Sir Laurence Olivier delivers a memorable portrayal as Dr. Spaander, a local physician who works with Brigadier Graeme Warrack, senior medical officer of the 1st Airborne Division, to tend the wounded and to prevail upon ter Horst to allow her home to be used as a refuge.

Washington Post critic Gary Arnold called *A Bridge Too Far* "an unusually conscientious and impressive war epic" and offered that such an effort justified the sizable budget. *A Bridge Too Far* was Ryan's second book to reach the big screen, following *The Longest Day* in 1962, which also had featured a cadre of notable film stars. Perhaps the most disappointing appraisal of the film was that of Colonel Frederick Gough, MP and once colonel commanding the 1st Airborne Reconnaissance Regiment at Arnhem. Taken prisoner as the fighting at Arnhem ended, he escaped in 1945. Gough assessed the film as

Actors rest during the 1946 filming of *Theirs is the Glory*, detailing the story of the fight at Arnhem two years earlier. *(Creative Commons Dutch National Archives via Wikimedia Commons)*

Kate ter Horst was a Dutch civilian caught in the midst of the fighting near Arnhem. *(Creative Commons Dutch National Archives via Wikimedia Commons)*

Richard Attenborough directed to epic film A Bridge Too Far, released in 1977. *(Creative Commons Dutch National Archives via Wikimedia Commons)*

Actor James Caan is shown during the filming of A Bridge Too Far in 1976. *(Creative Commons Dutch National Archives via Wikimedia Commons)*

a game of "ducks and drakes with historical facts in order to dish up an extravaganza for the American massed cinema market."

Given the gravitas of those retired senior officers who consulted with the production, it seems the perception of the accuracy of *A Bridge Too Far* lies well within the subjective realm. While the film delivers in its apparent mission to highlight the heroism of the individual soldier, it also casts responsibility for the debacle on several senior commanders. One of these was General Browning, commander of the I Airborne Corps. Browning died in 1965, and his widow, famed author Daphne du Maurier, took exception to his portrayal in the film. She wrote to Lord Louis Mountbatten, a senior Allied command figure during World War Two, asking that he boycott the film's premiere. Mountbatten attended and wrote back to du Maurier that he believed the portrayal of Browning to be accurate. Market Garden, he reasoned, had been a terrible defeat, and Browning had to share in the blame along with others. He confirmed that Browning's reputation remained intact despite the film's perspective.

Released in August 1946, the 82-minute film *Theirs Is The Glory*, directed by Brian Desmond Hurst, tells the story of the ordeal of the 1st Airborne Division during Market Garden. The screenplay was written by Louis Golding and Terence Young, a veteran of the Irish Guards. More than 200 veterans of the fighting, Frost and Gough among them, portrayed themselves in the film, as did Kate ter Horst, while the actual locations of the fighting were often included.

The acclaimed 2001 Home Box Office miniseries *Band of Brothers*, based on the 1992 book by Stephen Ambrose, includes an account of the 506th Parachute Infantry Regiment, 101st Airborne Division's air drop into The Netherlands, the liberation of Eindhoven, and later fighting at "the Island" in episode 4 titled "Replacements." Episode 5 titled "Crossroads" relates the 506th participation in Operation Pegasus, the October

1944 evacuation of nearly 150 men trapped in The Netherlands in the wake of Market Garden.

In 2021, the film *The Forgotten Battle* made its debut. A Dutch production directed by Matthijs van Heijningen, Jr., the film follows a female resistance fighter, a Dutch soldier in service with the Germans, and a British glider pilot whose aircraft crashes during Market Garden. Running 123 minutes, the fictional account finished third among the most commercially successful films of 2021 in The Netherlands and was the highest rated Dutch film that year.

Numerous documentaries exploring Market Garden have been released through the decades, and many are regularly aired on television or remain available through subscription services. Each of these presents Market Garden from a somewhat different perspective. The narratives range from that of harsh criticism of Montgomery and his strategy to simple stark presentations of the course of events as they unfolded. One 2019 release by documentary

Sir Laurence Olivier played the role of Dr. Jan Spaander in the 1977 film A Bridge Too Far. *(Creative Commons Allan warren via Wikimedia Commons)*

Joseph E. Levine, producer of the film A Bridge Too Far, and Cathy Ryan, widow of author Cornelius Ryan, attend a media event promoting the film based on Cornelius Ryan's book. Cornelius Ryan died in 1974, the year of the release of the book A Bridge Too Far. *(Creative Commons Dutch National Archives via Wikimedia Commons)*

filmmaker Sandra Parry titled *Arnhem For Ever: A Pilgrimage*, commemorates the 75th anniversary of Operation Market Garden, the annual Bridge to Liberation observance, and remembrances of veterans who were there.

The acclaimed documentary series *The Twentieth Century*, hosted by eminent news correspondent Walter Cronkite, includes a half hour of history and analysis of the Market Garden offensive. Titled "Air Drop At Arnhem," the episode premiered on network television in the United States for the first time in January 1963. ■

MARKET GARDEN ASSESSMENT

In the wake of Operation Market Garden, few would argue that the offensive into the southern Netherlands to seize a bridgehead over the Lower Rhine failed to achieve its primary objective. Allied casualties in killed, wounded, and captured totalled a staggering 17,000. The virtual destruction of the 1st Airborne Division at Arnhem and Oosterbeek was a bitter defeat tinged with incredible heroism in the face of long odds. But it was still a defeat.

One British para remembered his first moments of captivity. "A German officer entered and a Scot near me grabbed his Sten gun to shoot him. Luckily, he was overpowered. The German officer rapped out some orders and the cellar filled with Germans who commenced to evacuate us... The Germans seemed as interested in us as we were in them. They all spoke English and gave us coffee, sausage, and sour black bread. They were pleased to have won, and the atmosphere was rather like that of a football match that has just finished..."

General Dwight D. Eisenhower, Supreme Commander of Allied Forces in Europe, approved Operation Market Garden. *(Public Domain US Army via Wikimedia Commons)*

General Bernard Montgomery remained a staunch advocate of Operation Market Garden throughout his life. *(Public Domain collections of the Imperial War Museums via Wikimedia Commons)*

Perhaps so, but the stakes had been infinitely higher and the risk commensurate with the possible return. Had Operation Market Garden been successful as General Bernard Montgomery envisioned, the Allied 21st Army Group might have succeeded in occupying the Ruhr and then roaring ahead more than 300 miles to take the Nazi capital of Berlin. Some analysts, however, see Market Garden as more than simply a "bridge too far." More likely, they assert, it was a far-fetched scheme that was likely to fail from the beginning.

Few would dispute that the common soldiers of the 1st, 82nd, and 101st Airborne Divisions, XXX Corps, and all Allied units involved did everything that bravery and devotion to duty could do. In the end, though, Market Garden was simply too much. Several factors taken as a whole crippled the offensive even as it began.

Airborne divisions were lightly armed for swift movement and efficient insertion into

Members of the Dutch Resistance brief paratroopers of the 101st Airborne Division on the locations of German troops during Operation Market Garden. *(Public Domain Central Intelligence Agency via Wikimedia Commons)*

hostile areas. They were never intended to hold forward objectives for extended periods. When the last angry shot was fired at the north end of the Arnhem road bridge, Lieutenant Colonel John Frost and 2 Para had been in a constant state of siege for roughly four days.

Intelligence reports that indicated the Germans had stopped running, turned, and prepared to defend themselves in The Netherlands were discounted amid a euphoria – a victory disease – that has contributed to the undoing of armies swept up in the tide of apparent triumph on many occasions throughout history. Other reports that warned and then seemed to confirm the presence of significant German armour and battle-hardened SS troops in the Arnhem area were brushed off. Considering that these warnings emerged from multiple sources, including the Dutch Resistance, photo reconnaissance, and ULTRA decrypts of enemy radio traffic seems astonishing at first.

But then, it must be considered that Allied leaders were more than ready to finish the dirty business of war by the autumn of 1944. From the highest echelon to the lowliest private, the Allies were willing to take great risk in the hope that World War Two in Europe might be ended by Christmas 1944. Therefore, reports of stiffening German resistance were brushed off. At the same time the critical shortage of airlift capability, which meant that the already lightly armed airborne divisions would have to be inserted over three days, was discounted even with the

Paratroopers of the US 82nd Airborne Division plummet earthward near the Dutch town of Grave in Operation Market Garden. *(Public Domain US Department of Defense via Wikimedia Commons)*

Luftwaffe gunners man their 20mm antiaircraft gun and scan the sky above Arnhem. *(Creative Commons Bundesarchiv Bild via Wikimedia Commons)*

German soldiers drive a capture American Jeep while towing an anti-tank gun in the vicinity of Arnhem. *(Creative Commons Bundesarchiv Bild via Wikimedia Commons)*

knowledge that they would be required to fight the Germans, seize assigned objectives, and hold vital landing and drop zones for lengthy periods.

In addition to the known presence of the II SS Panzer Korps and the logistical airlift challenge, critics point to other flaws in the conception and execution of Operation Market Garden. Montgomery was adamant that his quick thrust would win the war, covering the British Army, 21st Army Group, and himself with glory. Besides, he regularly deemed General Dwight Eisenhower, Supreme Commander of Allied Forces in Europe, as incompetent. Montgomery once said of Eisenhower, "His ignorance as to how to run the war is absolute and complete."

Consider these facts. General Frederick "Boy" Browning, deputy commander of the Allied First Airborne Army and head of I Airborne Corps, was given command of the airborne operation, although he lacked the experience of American General Matthew Ridgway, commander of the XVIII Airborne Corps. Whether Browning fully appreciated the implications of the airlift shortage comes to light in the general's appropriation of more than 30 gliders for the transport of his headquarters entourage into the combat area. Further, Browning most vigorously dismissed the aforementioned ominous intelligence reports.

Browning gave little credence to the concerns of other officers, among them Eisenhower's chief of staff General Walter Bedell Smith and

General Stanislaw Sosabowski of the Polish 1st Independent Parachute Brigade who warned, "The British are not only grossly underestimating German strength in the Arnhem area, but they seem ignorant of the significance Arnhem has for the Fatherland." Indeed, Arnhem was only a few miles from the German frontier, and the enemy was bound to mount a ferocious defence there.

It must be remembered that the First Airborne Army, under General Lewis Brereton, constituted the bulk of the Allied strategic reserve in Western Europe, and senior officers were itching to put it to the test before the end of the war. Eisenhower approved Market Garden, and though he told Montgomery it was an extension of the broad front strategy and not a deviation from it, the supreme commander later stated, "I not only approved Market Garden, I insisted upon it."

In doing so, Eisenhower also approved the allocation of vital resources, manpower,

weapons, equipment, fuel, and more, to the enterprise. At the same time, he condoned the postponement of operations to clear the estuary of the River Scheldt and open the major port of Antwerp to Allied logistics, easing an already contentious shortage of supplies. Ever the diplomat and consensus builder, Eisenhower was eager to establish the Rhine bridgehead even in the context of supply and manpower constraints. When Market Garden failed, he blamed the weather as the primary cause. However, one must concede that the Germans had something to do with the outcome.

Weather did play a significant role in Market Garden, causing delays in follow-on troop airlifts, particularly that of the Polish brigade, and restricting resupply by air and tactical air support for the advance of XXX Corps. And then there was the single road, Highway 69 that coursed through the southern Netherlands, across six waterways, and on to Arnhem. And XXX Corps was obliged to take that single narrow route through polder country, terrain that was below sea level and unsuitable for armoured manoeuvre. The road was often elevated and vulnerable to enemy roadblocks that inflicted casualties and required time to clear.

Meanwhile, some criticism has been levelled at the performance of the American airborne divisions. In the case of the 101st, there was little that could have been done to prevent the Germans from blowing the Son bridge to pieces. Aware that a major airborne operation was afoot, the defenders did the logical thing and destroyed the vital bridge, slowing XXX Corps by several hours as a Bailey bridge was brought forward and constructed by engineers.

As for the 82nd Airborne Division, General James Gavin understood the importance of the big bridge across the River Waal and the necessity that it should be seized quickly. However, the 82nd was handed several tactical missions, including securing the high ground around its drop and landing zones and the capture of other

Soldiers pass an ambulance destroyed during the fighting in Operation Market Garden. *(Creative Commons Bundesarchiv Bild via Wikimedia Commons)*

Dutch Commandos who have taken part in Operation Market Garden pause for a photograph. *(Creative Commons Dutch Ministry of Defence via Wikimedia Commons)*

objectives. If these were not accomplished, then possession of the Nijmegen bridge would shrink to irrelevance. Besides, the division was simply too few in number to effectively deal with every assigned task in the timeliest manner. Still, the Germans did build up their Nijmegen defences during the two days that followed the insertion of the 82nd Airborne and the tanks and troops of XXX Corps were required to clear Nijmegen and gain control of the bridge.

In the case of the 1st Airborne Division, General Roy Urquhart accepted the best of available options when landing and drop zones were selected. When his paras commenced their ground operations, six to eight miles from Arnhem bridge, two of the fundamental elements of airborne deployment – speed and surprise – were thoroughly negated. The rush for the bridge was thwarted by stiff German resistance, and only 2 Para reached its north end, too weak to take control of the entire span. In the event, radio communications were spotty at best while Urquhart was isolated from his command for an extended period, dodging German patrols and hiding in houses around Oosterbeek.

Compounding the difficulties for the Allies, a copy of the Market Garden operations plan was found aboard a wrecked glider and delivered to senior German commanders, a talented group of experienced leaders, including Field Marshal Walter Model, commander of Army Group B, General Wilhelm Bittrich, commander of the II SS Panzer Korps, and General Kurt Student, newly-appointed to lead the embryonic First Parachute Army. Once the scope of the Allied offensive was realized these officers responded to the threat vigorously and effectively. They identified the bridges as primary objectives and moved to destroy or defend them, but estimates of German casualties run as high as 13,000 men killed, wounded, or taken prisoner.

When Operation Market Garden ended, the Allies had gained a finger-like salient into The Netherlands, ground that was defended for days against determined German counterattacks.

Some analysts aver that the ground was of no use in subsequent Allied operations, while others state that it served as a springboard for operations that did, after weeks of fighting, lead to the encirclement of the Ruhr.

During the evaluation, or post-mortem, of Operation Market Garden, Prime Minister Winston Churchill commented, "The battle was a decided victory… I have not been afflicted by any feelings of disappointment over this and am glad our commanders are capable of running this kind of risk."

Field Marshal Montgomery famously coloured the outcome of Market Garden as a substantial achievement, an operation that was 90 percent successful. He admitted to some difficulties but remained steadfast, writing in his 1958 memoir, "It was a bad mistake on my part – I underestimated the difficulties of opening up the approaches to Antwerp… I reckoned the Canadian Army could do it while we were going for the Ruhr. I was wrong… In my – prejudiced – view, if the operation had been properly backed from its inception, and given the aircraft, ground forces, and administrative resources necessary for the job, it would have succeeded *in spite of* my mistakes, or the adverse weather, or the presence of the 2nd SS Panzer Corps in the Arnhem area. I remain Market Garden's unrepentant advocate."

If, when Crown Prince Bernhard, chief of the Dutch armed forces, heard Montgomery's pronouncement, he responded coolly, "My country can never again afford the luxury of another Montgomery success."

Perhaps General Brian Horrocks, speaking from his XXX Corps perspective, best exemplified the mindset of the Allied command on the eve of Market Garden. "I knew that it would be a very tough battle; especially so, owing to the nature of the country, with its numerous water obstacles and the single main road available for thousands of vehicles; but failure never even entered my mind."

In the end, World War Two in Europe dragged on to its inevitable conclusion in May 1945. War is inherently risky business. Had Market Garden resulted in complete victory, the generals – responsible for what their troops do or fail to do – would have received the accolades. In defeat, acknowledged outright or characterized in any other way, they collectively bear responsibility. ∎

Dutch children place flowers on the graves of Commonwealth dead at the Airborne Cemetery in Oosterbeek. *(Creative Commons Dutch National Archives via Wikimedia Commons)*

REMEMBERING MARKET GARDEN

Parachute troops from around the world participate in a commemorative jump during the observances of the 70th anniversary of Operation Market Garden. *(Public Domain US Army via Wikimedia Commons)*

They are places of honour, quiet dignity, and great beauty. Eighty years after so many fought and died to liberate Western Europe from Nazi tyranny, the dead, known and unknown, lie in solemn repose.

The Commonwealth War Graves Commission maintains the Arnhem Oosterbeek War Cemetery, commonly known as the Airborne Cemetery, where 1,684 Commonwealth soldiers along with 79 Poles and three Dutch casualties of World War Two are either buried or remembered, 243 of them unknown. These final resting places are located in Oosterbeek, just west of Arnhem, and close to the locations where these men died, many of them during Operation Market Garden.

At Margraten, the American Battle Monuments Commission established the Netherlands American Cemetery, where 8,288 US military dead are interred and 1,722 names are engraved on the Tablets of the Missing. Many of these men died during Market Garden as well, others during the fighting that followed in late 1944 and early 1945.

Along with those of their grateful nations, the Dutch people remember these men who made the ultimate sacrifice in the name of freedom. Many of the graves have been adopted by local residents, who bring fresh flowers and regularly pay their respects while researching the lives of their fallen soldiers and coming to know them on a more personal level.

Elsewhere, along the roads, beside the bridges, near the waterways, and in the fields of the southern Netherlands and Belgium, monuments and memorials

Crosses stretch in graceful arcs at the Netherlands American Cemetery, where many of those killed in Operation Market Garden are interred. *(Creative Commons Norrin strange via Wikimedia Commons)*

have been erected to commemorate the valour the men of Market Garden.

At the Belgian town of Lommel, a simple marker identifies a bridge across the Meuse-Escaut Canal as Joe's Bridge. Captured prior to Operation Market Garden, the crossing served as a jump-off point for the ground phase of the great offensive. Its inscription notes: "Joe's Bridge/ In honour of the Irish Guards Group/ commanded by/ Lieutenant Colonel J.O.E. Vandeleur DSO/ which captured and held this bridge/ on 10th September 1944/ Quis Separabit".

Inside the Eusebius Church at Arnhem, 19 bronze parachutists are suspended from the ceiling in tribute. An adjacent plaque reads: "In remembrance of Market Garden 1944/ Parachutists on their way to Arnhem/ a creation by Simona Vergani/ presented by the 'Poorters van Arnhem'/ september 1994".

Nearby, the John Frost Bridge, named in honour of the heroic officer who led 2nd Battalion, Parachute Regiment in its gallant hour at the edge of the Lower Rhine, spans the waterway, its visual appeal quite similar to the one that was destroyed by Allied bombers just days after Market Garden ended. Also in the city, the Airborne Monument stands as a mute sentinel. Constructed of a damaged pillar from the former Palace of Justice placed atop a pedestal, its inscription reads simply: "17 September 1944". Two reliefs are adjacent to the monument, one of them depicting the Greek Hero Bellerophon riding the winged horse Pegasus as in the famous shoulder flash of the British airborne, and the other emblazoned with the slogan "Battle of Arnhem 44, Bridge to the Future 94".

In Oosterbeek, the former Hotel Hartenstein stands today as the Airborne Museum, housing an extensive collection of artifacts and memorabilia relating to Operation Market Garden and the heroism of the 1st Airborne Division. During the battle, the hotel served as the headquarters of General Roy Urquhart, commander of the 1st Airborne Division, and its presentations include the award-winning Airborne Experience exhibit, a series of dioramas depicting events during the fighting in the area of Oosterbeek and Arnhem.

At Nijmegen, the Commonwealth War Graves Commission maintains the Jonkerbos Cemetery, where 1,629 soldiers are buried, 99 of them unknown, and 13 of other nationalities. The cemetery is located on the original site of a temporary place of interment

The final resting places of many Commonwealth soldiers who fell during Operation Market Garden are located in the Airborne Cemetery, Oosterbeek, The Netherlands. *(Public Domain Ranger Steve via Wikimedia Commons)*

begun by personnel of a casualty clearing station that functioned during the fighting. At the road bridge across the River Waal stone monuments honour the bravery of the American paratroopers of the 3d Battalion, 504th Parachute Infantry Regiment, 82nd Airborne Division, who crossed the wide river under heavy enemy fire on September 20, 1944, to seize the crossing. The name of each of the 48 soldiers who perished in that memorable struggle is engraved there.

Not far away, a memorial to the Dutch Resistance during World War Two depicts fighter Jan van Hoof, who helped Allied forces during Market Garden, leading his comrades forward while carrying a defiant banner. A bronze relief by sculptor Charles Hammes was placed above the door of the Hotel Sionshoff in 1954. During the fighting around Nijmegen, the hotel served as a command post for the Dutch Resistance and the 82nd Airborne Division.

In the vicinity of Eindhoven, several memorials honour the valour of the paratroopers of the 101st Airborne Division. The Memorial to the Parachutist Son en Breugel depicts an airborne trooper advancing with determination. The inscription reads in part: "Liberated on the 17th of September 1944, by the 506th Parachute Infantry and elements of the 326th Airborne Engineers. This town was the command post of the 101st Airborne Division during the first three days of the Holland Campaign. The 506th Parachute Field Artillery, and the 81st Airborne AA Battalion, successfully repulsed all attacks on this position from D-Day to D Plus 3, thereby enabling division headquarters to establish the command function so necessary to the success of the overall mission...."

Annual observances, remembrances, and ceremonies keep the memory of Operation Market Garden alive, and at times more than 1,000 parachute troops from numerous NATO (North Atlantic Treaty Organization) countries have attended the proceedings, paying homage

At the Airborne Museum in Oosterbeek, a diorama of the 'Airborne Experience' exhibit brings Operation Market Garden to life. In 1944, the museum was the Hotel Hartenstein, headquarters of the British 1st Airborne Division. *(Creative Commons Airborne Museum 'Hartenstein' via Wikimedia Commons)*

to their airborne heritage. The commemoration of the 80th anniversary of Market Garden was held in September 2024 and involved military personnel, civilian dignitaries, government officials, honoured veterans, and their families.

Five Victoria Crosses and two Medals of Honor were presented for valour during Operation Market Garden, and one of these was earned by Major Robert Cain of the South Staffordshire Regiment. Some years ago, acorns were brought from the Arnhem area

to Dhoon Arboretum on the Isle of Man. A sturdy oak tree sprang up, and it was named the Arnhem Oak in commemoration of Major Cain's bravery. An inscribed base lies beneath.

These are but a few of the many memorials that will always serve as milestones of modern military history, remembrances of the great Operation Market Garden, begun with great expectations in the autumn of 1944 and ended with the lasting legacy of dedication unsurpassed. ∎

The Son en Greugel Airborne Forces Monument honours the paratroopers of the US 101st Airborne Division. *(Creative Commons Wammes Waggel via Wikimedia Commons)*

This wall painting was completed in Nijmegen in 2023 to honour the participants in Operation Market Garden. *(Creative Commons FakirNL via Wikimedia Commons)*